NEPAL
Nation-state in the Wilderness

NEPAL
Nation-state in the Wilderness

Managing State, Democracy,
and Geopolitics

Lok Raj Baral

SAGE www.sagepublications.com
Los Angeles • London • New Delhi • Singapore • Washington DC

First published in 2012 by

 SAGE Publications India Pvt Ltd
B1/I-1 Mohan Cooperative Industrial Area
Mathura Road, New Delhi 110 044, India
www.sagepub.in

SAGE Publications Inc
2455 Teller Road
Thousand Oaks, California 91320, USA

SAGE Publications Ltd
1 Oliver's Yard
55 City Road
London EC1Y 1SP, United Kingdom

SAGE Publications Asia-Pacific Pte Ltd
33 Pekin Street
#02-01 Far East Square
Singapore 048763

Published by Vivek Mehra for SAGE Publications India Pvt Ltd, typeset in 10/13 Berkeley by Star Compugraphics Private Limited, Delhi and printed at Chaman Enterprises, New Delhi.

Library of Congress Cataloging-in-Publication Data

Baral, Lok Raj, 1941–

Nepal—Nation-state in the Wilderness: Managing State, Democracy, and Geoploitics/ Lok Raj Baral.

p. cm

Includes bibliographical references and index.

1. Nepal—Politics and government—1990– 2. Democracy—Nepal. 3. Geopolitics—Nepal. I. Title.

JQ628.A58B36   320.95496—dc23   2012   2012001604

ISBN: 978-81-321-0875-7 (HB)

The SAGE Team: Gayeti Singh, Shreya Chakraborti, Nand Kumar Jha and Rajender Kaur

To Ganga, my late wife

Thank you for choosing a SAGE product! If you have any comment, observation or feedback, I would like to personally hear from you. Please write to me at <u>contactceo@sagepub.in</u>

—Vivek Mehra, Managing Director and CEO,
SAGE Publications India Pvt Ltd, New Delhi

Bulk Sales

SAGE India offers special discounts for purchase of books in bulk. We also make available special imprints and excerpts from our books on demand.

For orders and enquiries, write to us at

Marketing Department
SAGE Publications India Pvt Ltd
B1/I-1, Mohan Cooperative Industrial Area
Mathura Road, Post Bag 7
New Delhi 110044, India
E-mail us at <u>marketing@sagepub.in</u>

Get to know more about SAGE, be invited to SAGE events, get on our mailing list. Write today to <u>marketing@sagepub.in</u>

This book is also available as an e-book.

CONTENTS

LIST OF TABLES

LIST OF ABBREVIATIONS

APF	Armed Police Force
ASEAN	Association of Southeast Asian Nations
CA	Constituent Assembly
COAS	Chief of the Army Staff
CPA	Comprehensive Peace Accord
CPN (M)	Communist Party of Nepal (Marxist)
CPN (Maoist)	Communist Party of Nepal (Maoist)
CPN (ML)	Communist Party of Nepal (Marxist Leninist)
CPN–UML	Communist Party of Nepal–Unified Marxist Leninist
CPN (Unified)	Communist Party of Nepal (Unified)
CPN (United)	Communist Party of Nepal (United)
EPA	Eight Party Alliance
EU	European Union
GDP	Gross Domestic Product
GNI	Gross National Income
GoI	Government of India
INGO	International Nongovernmental Organizations
ISI	Inter Service Intelligence
MJF	Madhese Janaadhikar Forum
MIR	Monitoring, Integration, and Rehabilitation
ML	Marxist Leninist
MRP	Machine Readable Passport
NA	Nepal Army

NC	Nepali Congress
NC (D)	Nepali Congress (Democratic)
NCP	Communist Party of Nepal
NCCS	Nepal Centre for Contemporary Studies
NGO	Nongovernmental Organization
NSP	Nepal Sadbhawana Party
PR	Proportional Representation
RJP	Rashtriya Janasakti Party
RNA	Royal Nepal Army
RPP	Rashtriya Prajatantra Party
RPP–N	Rashtriya Prajatantra Party–Nepal
SAARC	South Asian Association for Regional Cooperation
SPA	Seven Party Alliance
T–MLP	Tarai–Madhesh Loktantrik Party
UCPN (Maoist)	Unified Communist Party of Nepal (Maoist)
ULF	United Left Front
UMC	Unified Military Command
UML	United Marxist Leninist
UN	United Nations
UNMIN	United Nations Mission in Nepal
YCL	Youth Communist League

PREFACE

The present book is the product of my long observation and study of Nepali state, politics, political elites, and their orientations. Stretching the narrative to the beginning of modern Nepali state (1768–1769), it dwells on the motivation of power elites to wage wars, conclude peace, and fix the boundary of the state. Despite occasional setbacks suffered at the hands of adversaries, the Nepali rulers have invariably tried to preserve the territorial integrity of the state. It could be called the expansionist ambition of rulers, but it was known as patriotic adventures essential for adding symbol and substance to the state. The Treaty of Sugauli (1815–1816), however, put a brake on the expansionist priority of rulers resulting in the shrinkage of Nepali territory. Yet, Jang Bahadur, the first Rana prime minister, could bring back some of the lost territories due to his overtly pro-British policy as well as his own style of handling foreign policy. Since then, the boundary of state has remained undisturbed, although the limitations on foreign policy were imposed on the rulers by the various treaties and understandings reached between Nepal and its southern neighbor, India. In addition, the geopolitical pulls and pressures did create impacts on Nepal's desire to be as much independent as possible. When such limitations are taken for granted with the new assertions against such compulsions, fissures in relations have been observed.

I have tried to make a unified theme by knitting together the origin, growth, and limitations of the modern Nepali state, people's role that came by way of their desire for democracy and the active geopolitics. Until recently, the traditional ethos of the state dominated national life as if the state was monarchy personified. Even the end of the 104-year-old Rana oligarchy did not introduce democratic substance in politics, despite many new changes introduced in various fields. On the contrary, the core value of some sort of a "patrimonial state" became pervasive in the post-1950 change. Yet, the monarchs who succeeded the Ranas in 1951 had to make compromises with the popular forces represented by political parties. Eventually, when monarchy failed to understand the significance of people's power, the same people or subject (*praja*) declared the end of monarchy in 2006.

Now the question that has arisen in Nepal is how could the people's power fritter away when political leaders who come from a variety of ideological backgrounds allow themselves to be irresponsive to the wishes of the people. The transition to federal republic is increasingly becoming painful due to the repetition of the same old games of intra- and inter-party bickering. All parties suffer from internal conflicts reminiscent of the 1950s and 1990s. Obsessed with a sense of triumphalism, the Maoist party is not only a prisoner of its own shifting decisions, its lack of ideological clarity has often harmed its own popularity that it had been able to achieve in the past. Its emergence as a first party in the Constituent Assembly (CA) did provide legal and popular legitimacy. But how can such gains be preserved if the party leaders quarrel for whether or not the party should be fully involved in multiparty pluralistic politics? A small section of the party still wants to retain its revolutionary identity that it had projected during the 10-year-long armed insurgency that aimed at destroying both monarchy and parliamentary democracy. However, it can be said that the Nepali communists cannot afford to ignore the reality that the people of Nepal are basically oriented to liberal democracy with all ingredients of social justice and inclusiveness.

The present book has grasped this vital subject with utmost frankness, suggesting that parliamentary democracy à la British and Indian models would not be practicable in the given political context of Nepal. Since stability is the primary condition for peace and order, democracy without governmental efficacy is a misnomer. If this aspect is ignored by showing penchant for the parliamentary model without guaranteeing governmental stability and efficiency, Nepal will continue to reel under anarchy.

Nepal has experienced various types of regimes in the past, but all of them failed to improve the conditions of ordinary people. A tiny new middle class has emerged but it can hardly become crucial for preserving democratic values. Its orientation to new consumerist culture and tendency to be greedy and selfish or what we call in Nepali, *subidha bhogi*, does not help promote democratic values. Sacrifice and hardships would no more guide politics as was observed during the long democratic struggle. All parties suffer from such trends.

The new political environment created by the multiplicity of factors and trends have given rise to serious questions regarding the sustainability of democracy itself. Moreover, the capacity of state is also on the decline due to rampant corruption, lack of political direction, and partisan spirit in all areas of public life. The governments headed by prime ministers are hamstrung by the chains put on them by their own parties as well as the coalition partners. Such pervasive pathetic conditions have reduced the credibility of effective governance.

The chapter 'Nepal and the World: Managing Geopolitics' tries to reflect on the emerging trends in global politics and their short-, medium-, and long-term impacts on Nepal. The triangular relations between Nepal, China, and India along with the larger interests of other powers also need to be dealt with to situate Nepal in such multiple dimensions. It is particularly important in the present context when Nepal's own internal upheavals are not settled. Whatever goodwill and sympathy Nepal has earned by serving the peacekeeping operations of the United Nations and by developing friendly relations with as many countries of the world as possible is also becoming controversial. Bilateral relations with neighbors that used to reap benefits in the competitive sense are also suspect. Monarchy that had provided a semblance of stability has been abolished but no alternative forces that fill up the vacuum have yet emerged despite the existence of political parties of all hues and orientations. Since most of them are in ferment and follow divergent approaches to vital issues confronting the country, they lack direction and confidence. The post-CA election scenario of Nepali politics suggests that both internally and externally Nepal's image has shrunk a great deal, and the principal reason for this is the loss of credibility of political leaders who now have come to the center stage but have failed to comprehend the emerging complexity of national, regional, and global politics.

The present book is the sum and substance of my long academic career as well as short diplomatic role as ambassador to India. Although Nepal–India relation is a vast ocean that cannot be easily fathomed, political leaders in general fail to develop an objective approach to Nepal–India relations. It is also extensive, touching all aspects of our lives. Since Nepal belongs to the core Indian heartland—the Gangetic plains—India becomes hypersensitive to its security environment in this geographical reason. China is no less sensitive on the issue of Tibet. An active geopolitics is also attributed to the emerging trends of global politics where new power configuration is taking shape, though it is not fully polarized along ideological lines. And economic globalization has made all big players central to each other.

I have developed the introductory outlines of the book at the Nepal Centre for Contemporary Studies (NCCS) in 2009–2010. Many of the theoretical and conceptual innovations were made during my lectures or seminars conducted by NCCS or by other institutions. My conclusion about the types of governments—parliamentary, presidential, or mixed—came on the basis of my deep study of Nepali politics. I have reached a conclusion that no model would be sustainable if parties lack strong democratic commitment to the process or act in accord with the set norms of the system. In the given Nepali context, all parties are fractured and conflict-torn. Some are national parties; others are regional and personal, thus, making the parliament a conglomeration of strange persons, groups, or parties. Assuming that there is very little scope for improvement soon, I have preferred the presidential system for maintaining political stability. Though debatable, it needs to be put on trial for making Nepal democratic and stable.

To be honest, the present work does not provide any definite clue to the future of Nepali state and democracy. Yet, it gives a perspective on the unfolding scenarios and their consequences. The timing of the book would also be significant as Nepal is in ferment in many respects.

Economic stagnation continues due to lack of strong policy decisions and their execution; politically Nepal is volatile, and internationally it is increasingly being isolated.

Few individuals and institutions have made this work possible. The NCCS staff especially deserve thanks for their administrative help during the preparation of the book. I would like to thank SAGE Publications India Pvt. Ltd. for promptly accepting as well as publishing the book. I have dedicated this book to my wife, Ganga, who died without seeing it in the present form.

Lok Raj Baral

I

Introduction

Parameters of Nepali Politics

Theorizing Nepali politics is a daunting task. Politics ordained by constraints of tradition and history, political culture embedded in past traditions, societal construct, and primordial loyalties with a modern mix have made it imponderable. So it is also full of enigmas and paradoxes that provide us with deceptive political scenarios. Students of Nepali politics are now required to unlearn many previously established beliefs for finding new contours of change. Are such changes and explosions of myth superficial for heralding a substantive change as wished by the people? Are they not fundamental and penetrating with which the new Nepal envisaged by the change agents and general people is likely to fall apart? To make an inquiry into some of these crucial aspects, Nepali politics can be conceptualized within certain parameters that have influenced the overall patterns of Nepal's development. To comprehend the sources of strengths and weaknesses of the Nepali state as well as the factors that have impeded democracy to strike institutional roots, a comprehensive approach to it is necessary.

Against such backdrop, Nepali history and political development need to be examined in order to establish a link between the past and the dynamics of the present. Historical narrative is easy but political development, as we have understood in political science theorization, seems to be problematic. However, given the trajectory of Nepali history, culture, economy, and societal construct, albeit in the traditional mold, it would accordingly be dealt with the thematic construct of this book. It cannot also be claimed that such theoretical postulation would not be at all influenced by concepts and theories of Western social sciences or by other scholars from the South Asian region, but much of present analyses and reflections are entirely shaped by the turn of events that have been taking place in Nepal since 1950, though the great influence of the Shah and Rana regimes cannot be underestimated.

The history of modern Nepal and its ups and downs, fault lines, and challenges would naturally cover various aspects of culture, religion, society, political economy, administration, and elites. But democracy today becomes difficult to comprehend without contextualizing it to the emerging trends that encompass social, economic, regional, and international dynamics. Driven sometimes by the wind of democracy and freedom and becoming emotionally involved or exposed to liberal democracy in the post-1950s and also attracted by personalities whom the Nepalis considered as messiahs for Nepal's radical transformation, democracy as was generally understood then did not go beyond the classical approaches.

Till today, democracy has no alternative despite its hostile environment in many countries of the world. Although becoming a bit emotional in arguing this theme, Fukuyama went to the extent of telling the world that there can be no further development of history because of the triumph of democracy in the world.[1] Compared to other systems—communism and authoritarian regimes or some other forms of archaic rule which are still prevalent in some parts of the world—democracy's attractiveness remains perennially the same. Nonetheless, it is ironic that such democratic acceptability—democratic culture that ensures both institutional behavior and political stability and progress—is still far off in Nepal. For political parties and other sections of society, monarchy was considered both a symbol and substance of political stability in the country. Yet, such a monarchical order also did not fail to swear

[1] See Francis Fukuyama, *The End of History and the Last Man* (New York: Free Press, 1992).

2

by democracy time and again and went on modifying the regime when the pressure developed for more democracy. Ironically, the same uncertainty about democracy prevails today despite the radical changes made through the unified people's movement. What the contradictions are and why democracy continues to be fraught with dangers require an objective analysis. The nature of the state and its core values that dominated political developments need to be brought into discourse. This section will therefore try to identify some of the crucial elements of Nepal's political trajectory.

Predominant Liberal Values

Nepali political history can be broadly divided into two distinct phases—the Shah–Rana and the post-1950 periods. The former was more or less archaic in nature and orientation with the Shah rulers, their courtiers, and the Rana family members occupying politics with the exclusion of their *praja* (subject) and the latter with the Palace and political parties together during the first spell of party politics in the 1950s. Such interaction was snapped following the December 1960 coup that dismantled the established semi-parliamentary experiment. Again the multiparty politics was revived as a consequence of 1990 mass movement, though the second experiment with party politics, in constitutional sense, was also short-lived. However, Jan Andolan II (2006) not only restored multiparty system but also ended the 238-year-old monarchy in the country and assigned the task of constitution making to the CA elected by the Nepali people.

Although Nepalis have suffered a lot due to unlimited lust of power of the kings and leaders of political parties, the spirit of liberal democracy and values continued to become a dominating force in all types of regimes practiced in the post-1950 period, so much so that even the communists parties of all hues have come to embrace liberal democracy despite their rhetorical declarations that they would like to aim at what the Unified Communist Party of Nepal (UCPN [Maoist]) today calls "People's Republic." Other communist parties such as the Communist

Party of Nepal–Unified Marxist Leninist (CPN–UML) did pass through various stages of political incarnation. CPN–UML, like the Maoist, first resorted to Naxalite method used in the name of "liquidation of class enemies" by killing people whom they thought as exploiters or informers, but later changed into a parliamentary party and became the second largest party in three parliaments in the 1990s. In the 2006 CA election, the Communist Party of Nepal (Maoist) (CPN [Maoist]) not only displaced it (CPN–UML) from the second position but also made the Nepali Congress (NC) the second party by attaining the first position. Today the CPN–UML and the UCPN (Maoist) are competing to outsmart the other, making the United Marxist Leninist (UML) come closer to the NC in order to checkmate its communist rival.

The Maoist transformation is now underway after it decided to join multiparty politics by signing the 12-point understanding with the Seven Party Alliance (SPA) in 2005.[2] It may be recalled that the SPA was formed following the state of emergency declared by King Gyanendra in February 2005 as well as by the ambition of the king to revive the absolute monarchical rule reminiscent of his father, Mahendra, and his brother, Birendra. The partyless regime, which was tailored to the ambition of King Mahendra, had been imposed after the 1960 coup promising stability, peace, democracy, and development. His search for legitimacy was anchored to the dismal failure of party politics or *parliamentary democracy as it was divisive and conflict-prone.*

Nevertheless, even within the partyless regime, liberal democracy and human rights haunted the king and his members of the entourage producing systemic idiosyncrasies and contradictions. Since the king had a guilty conscience because of his antidemocratic action, his regime could

---

[2] The 12-point understanding finalized by the SPA leaders, most notably G. P. Koirala and the CPN–UML leaders, was formed against the absolute monarchical regime on November 22, 2005, in New Delhi. Its major points include: end of autocratic monarchical rule, restoration of parliament, positive solution to the armed conflict, competitive multiparty system and other civil and fundamental liberties, return of displaced people and return of property confiscated by the Maoist during the insurgency, protection of independence, sovereignty, territorial integrity and national unity, and peaceful settlements of all disputes.

not fully berate the spirit of democracy.[3] During the entire partyless decades (1960–1990), liberal democratic ideology remained indispensable to the opposition forces as well as to the disgruntled royalists who wanted to establish themselves as democrats within the system. Such ideological dilemma of the King could spur his critics to be ambitious. The continuity of parliamentary features, without touching the core center of political power, which was an exclusive domain of the monarch, also helped a lot to impress on the people that liberal democracy was not likely to be fully berated as the King had wished in the early 1960s.

One of the pertinent aspects of the democratic development was that political parties continued struggling for democracy when in opposition but failed to build institutions while they were in power. After they became successful and occupied power and other positions, they soon forgot their mission. As movements alone do not sustain democracy, political forces involved in such movements should have minimum culture that can be manifested in institutions. In Nepal, however, neither procedural nor substantive aspects of democracy-building project are underway. Inclusiveness with empowerment of all segments of society makes democracy perfect. Freedom means the emancipation of ethnics, Dalits, gender, regions, and all other oppressed and suppressed strata of society. It has to be inclusive in nature and treatment, and therefore, needs to be more dynamic and effective.

One significant aspect of modern liberal democracy is related to the existence and recognition of the opposition. In Nepal, the oppositional politics works in a variety of forms and styles depending on the context and time. However, the traditional authoritarian background and oscillating strategies and tactics of both old and new parties have invariably overshadowed the institutional development in the country.

The origins and development of parties are also country specific as, unlike in Western democratic traditions, parties are not the creatures of parliament. They were created for opposing either the archaic rule of the Shah and the Rana varieties or for establishing democracy. Subsequently,

---

[3] For a full account of the post-1960 political dynamics, see Lok Raj Baral, *Oppositional Politics in Nepal* (Delhi: Abhinav Publications, 1977).

they changed from revolutionary parties into systemic parties. When the circumstances dictated them to be violent, they changed their strategies. The NC's shifting strategies in particular had such swings (from violence to nonviolence). During its 60-year-long history, the NC took up arms against the Rana and Shah regimes in 1950, 1961, and again in 1970–1975.

The other communist party—Communist Party of Nepal (Marxist Leninist), which later became CPN–UML following the merger of the Communist Party of Nepal (Marxist) (CPN [M]) in 1991, i.e., on the eve of the general election held in May 1991—had also strategic and ideological shifts from time to time. In 1990, this party supported the NC-initiated mass movement and later formally declared *Janatako Bahudaliya Janbad* or multiparty people's democracy.[4] Such a change paid rich dividends when it became the second largest party in the 1991 parliamentary elections by winning 69 out of 205 seats. To the surprise of its own leaders, the CPN–UML could come to power in 1994 following the defeat of the NC in the midterm election held in 1994. Although the UML failed to wrest absolute majority in parliament, it headed a minority government for nine months until it was dislodged by the combined three-party opposition led by the NC.

Some communist parties, including the UCPN (Maoist), first came as a revolutionary party by waging a 10-year-long armed insurgency against the Nepali state. Its mission was to establish a people's republic through the CA route. Now some of its demands such as holding of CA election, declaration of a republic, and restructuring of the state along federal lines have been accepted. Yet, the party seems to be struggling for transforming it into a "systemic party" as other parliamentary parties. It had an impressive show in the CA election in April 2008 when it displaced the two principal parties—the NC and the CPN–UML from their first and second positions—and won as many as 220-plus seats in a House of 601. It was a major gain for the party as the established parties were no

[4] For more details, see Krishna Hachhethu, *Party Building in Nepal: Organization, Leadership and People* (Kathmandu: Mandala Book Point, 2002) and Lok Raj Baral, "Political Parties in South Asia" in V. A. Paipanandiker, ed., *Problems of Governance in South Asia* (Delhi: Konark, 1999), pp.155–198.

more sole benefactors of the electoral politics. Such a gain was expected to encourage the Maoists to be within the system. As a result, the Maoist-led coalition government was formed by virtue of being the first party in the CA that also works as parliament.

It seems that Nepali political development has been able to crystallize liberal democratic ideology of all, despite the rhetorical statements of some Left parties that they are not necessarily the proponents of "bourgeoisie" democracy as is prevalent across the world. It is also mind-boggling for conservative liberal democrats or for those who fear to take progressive measures for transforming Nepal into a progressive democratic state. Yet, all parties, including the NC, have no option but to embrace the agendas of the restructuring of state in which power would be suitably distributed between the center and federal units so that people of all regions could be empowered.

It is also a truism that liberal democracy is likely to encounter a lot of difficulties due to the shallow democratic orientation of parties' elites. The dominance of capitalist trends of consumption, constraints of tradition and history that have had been ingrained in the Nepali society, flourishing antidemocratic political culture, and criminalization of politics are likely to be serious threats to democracy. Moreover, the crises of governance creating disorder and the failure of parties in uniting to grapple with such emergent crises have further endangered the liberal process to be set in institutional forms after the making of a new constitution. The culture of populism, self-aggrandizement, fragmentary trends seen in political parties, and extreme opportunistic alliances formed between parties and individuals would subordinate the vital agendas of both democracy and state and nation building. Even those parties which claim to be democratic have miserably failed to abide by the minimum values of democracy.

Two contradictory changes are simultaneously underway in Nepali politics. One is the acceptance of liberal democratic values by all the political forces including the Maoists, the other one is the rapid decline of political institutions, both formal and informal. When institutions erode due to the myopic roles of political leaders, the gains of the movement are also subordinated to parochial interests concerning particular groups, regions, religion, and castes. Thus, from ideological point of view, neither the liberal democracy has taken roots nor can other ideologies challenge liberal values in the country.

Nepali politicians have, in comparison with other countries' leaders, failed to build institutions commensurate with their role of waging movements for change. So they should not miss understanding the twined relationship between committed leadership and democratic institutions, without which neither the foundation of democracy can be laid nor can the much-needed performance legitimacy be possible. If elections held occasionally fail to promote democratic culture, then people become disenchanted with their own representatives. Above all, performance legitimacy of the new order would also determine the protection of democratic values and norms. Nepali politicians, however, soon forget this mutuality of values and norms and institution building. This results in people's frantic bid for joining the new movement, hoping to get effective governance to redressing their hardships.

Thus, the liberal constitutional state characterized by planned economy has become the hallmark of the Nepali state. Efforts for transforming the archaic monarchical rule into a liberal constitutional had been the dominant theme of the struggles carried out from within the monarchical authoritarianism as well as from outside. The commingling of various religious and cultural streams helped develop the moderate culture throughout history. Today, Nepalis are not fundamentalist by nature and have been maintaining social harmony despite the emerging trends of regionalization and ethnicization of politics. Politically, liberalism developed as a result of exposure to the British tradition, which came via India. If India would have experienced the antiliberal regime, Nepal's development would have also been shaped accordingly. Moreover, the liberal values internalized by the Indian leaders, both in government and outside, seemed to have been reflected in the 1950 Delhi compromise in which the idea of popular sovereignty found space. All elements of the compromise are committed to liberalism, including the making of a constitution through the popularly elected CA. It was a "new imaginary of sovereignty" or what we understand today as "popular sovereignty."

Since this idea was soon given up by all the stakeholders in the wake of the rapid rise of absolute monarchy, it could theoretically be revived only in the 1990 Constitution. In fact, this Constitution was also a bundle of contradictions as it, at the same time, mentioned sovereignty of people with the King as one of the participants in the compromise made between him and the two parties—the NC and the United Left Front (ULF)—a conglomeration of various communist groups. It was neither a parliamentary system with full popular sovereignty nor a full-fledged absolutist state as in the pre-1990 period. But such a dubious nature of the regime soon changed into absolute system with King Gyanendra resurrecting old panchayat spirit in the garb of party politics.

The theory and practice of popular sovereignty resurfaced when the Nepali people brought down the monarchical rule with a mission for turning it into a republic. It was an unprecedented moment in Nepal's history as, for the first time, people of all hues and regions, regardless of their political predilections, made it successful. All the political parties, regardless of their past records, decided to hold CA election with a presupposition that it would, after election, declare Nepal a republic.

Now the question that has arisen is, can the new republic survive at a time when there has been a trend of democratic erosion in the developed world, for instance, in Europe? It is said that general belief in democracy in Europe continues to "dwindle." Describing this situation full of "boredom, frustration and disillusion," Colin has coined the term "post-democracy,"[5] showing the gradual erosion of faith of common people in the democratic process itself. The latest election trends in Europe have also pointed to the fact that democracy as a principle and practice needs to be reinvigorated. In the given context, Nepali people have also reached a stage from where they can see the bright prospects of democratic future, despite the absence of other alternatives to which they could accept.

---

[5] Colin Crouch, *Postdemocratie* (Berlin: Suhrkamp,Verlag, 2009). As cited in Jan Niklas Engels/Gero Maass, "The New Promise of Happiness: Current State of Discussion on the Future of European Social Democracy," *International Politics and Society*, 4: 2010, p. 50.

Ambiguity and Change

Traditional authoritarianism, which was a mixture of the old and new values, had perennially played an obstructionist role in the post-1950 politics of Nepal. The old monarchical and feudal or semifeudal political culture continued to determine political course. Such values are deeply rooted in Nepali politics and continue to dominate the political culture of new elites who take their turn in power in the name of democracy. Until 2008, it was monarchy that continued to produce such mixture of traditional authoritarianism and liberal democracy, and now with the monarchy gone, the personalized parochialism seems to show its influence in a new form. Nevertheless, it too is being challenged within parties despite a long way to go for a minimum standard for conducting the affairs of the state. If analyzed from a perspective of transformation, many spectacular changes have taken place. The economists would see them through the prism of quantification of data or records of developmental projects and infrastructure building, etc. They go by numbers rather than by quality change in different sectors such as education, services, maintenance of roads, utilization of resources, and distribution sector reforms. However, data also tell the truth but not the whole truth.

In the political sector, much chaotic conditions prevail because of the declining ideological commitment to the political processes, including procedural aspects of change. Political parties are in ideological disarray notwithstanding their commitment to competitive party system, political pluralism, and establishment of a just society. Countercultural base is being searched for foiling the new agendas of republican order with supremacy of people.

It can be conveniently said that in the post-1950 Nepali society and polity, the end of the Rana rule could not end the Rana political culture. It was revived by the archaic monarchical dominance from the 1950 to the present. Many spectacular events, including the end of monarchy and the advent of Maoist party after its 10-year-long insurgency, could not make a dent in the entrenched culture. Nor could the prodemocratic outpourings of the other major parties such as the NC and the CPN–UML show any significant departure with the past. All routes of patronage continued uninterrupted together with the meteoric rise of the politics of inclusiveness. Various ethnic, gender, Dalit, Tarai, and hill groups are included in the CA through the route of mixed electoral system (first-past-the-post [42 percent] and proportional representation [58 percent]). Yet, such inclusion has not made any dent in political behavior and culture.

In this context, the "predicament of Left parties" can also be brought in view of their "makeshift" ideologies and the inherent contradictions they generate. Although the Left–Right divide seems to be a misnomer in the Nepali context, yet, for our convenience, this term here is used interchangeably for communist parties. Occasional ideological shift, using it more as tactics for coming to power or for not being sidelined in the mainstream liberal politics, the major Left groups add more confusion which, in turn, gives rise to fear and suspicion to non-Left parties. So, such mutual suspicion and trepidation have weakened the vital agendas of socioeconomic and political transformation as expected by the people. Nevertheless, such political gimmicks or even small ideological gaps are not of serious nature in view of the total background of Left politics. In essence, all have, since the very foundation of the CPN in 1949, veered around liberal tradition. It must, however, be added that the Maoist insurgency and its consequences have forced other parties to be more sensitive to social and economic agendas within the liberal democratic framework in order to reduce the disparity gaps in class and caste sense. So the raison d'être of the previous "extreme Left party" (Maoist) is no longer revolution but a quest for being different from other Left groups by offering more unconventional agendas that were otherwise unacceptable to other parties who did not gather courage to hug radical social policies for the general people. The Maoist agenda of the CA and republican system had not been accepted by other parties unless the Maoist advanced it as a major demand for joining the mainstream democratic politics.

It seems that all parties—Left and Right—suffer from internal crises due to their penchant to be more compromising when they run the government or sit in the opposition. The role of the "radical Left" is more circumscribed by the emergent trend of coalition politics that demands some sort of a compromise with bizarre parties in parliament or outside.

11

The UCPN (Maoist)–led government formed with the support of seven parties collapsed in nine months following the lack of support of other coalition partners to sack the army chief, a bête noire for the Maoist. The 18 parties, including the coalition partners, went to the president to stall the dismissal of the chief of the army staff (COAS or commander-in-chief) who, according to the Maoist leaders, defied the order of the government. Obliging the 18 parties and some other external powers who allegedly did not like to disturb the army, the president, by violating the spirit of the Interim Constitution, sent a direct letter to the army chief to continue in office despite the move of the government. Then the government headed by Maoist leader Prachanda resigned blaming the president and other parties for violating the very spirit of democracy, i.e., civilian control over the army. Although too much radical posturing and populism put any party in a "quandary" after they fall from power or fail to deliver anything to the people, same was applied to the Maoist party after its government fell from power. "The Maoists, it seems, are uncertain about the road ahead."[6] Other parties, too, are not dissimilar as they become expedient to garner their immediate gains.

Notwithstanding such developments, all parties, including the Maoist, have common stake for consolidating the political process started during and after the 2006 movement. The post-2006 politics has dictated all political parties to be inclusive and innovative, though the gradualists think that "radicalization" of society would only set in unsettling trends in the country. The emergence of a middle class or of nouveau riche has also not put up any resistance to the new change as they also think that all parties in Nepal are more or less moderate when they transform to be systemic.

What is more puzzling is that even after the end of monarchy, which was considered to be the main source of authoritarian culture and practices, leaders of political parties and their so-called Bhatri Sanstha (fraternal organizations) like youth, labor, peasant, teachers, etc., seem to have an increasing penchant for creating disorder, spreading trends of criminalization in politics, and showing utter intolerance. The police and

---

[6] See the editorial, The Kathmandu Post, August 5, 2009.

the home minister have come out openly that such criminal gangs and wrongdoers get patronage from their leaders and, hence, the failure of the concerned authorities to maintain law and order. All institutions— schools, universities, bureaucracy, police, and army—are affected by "politicization," which is in fact party-ization. For transfer, promotion, and other favors, all run after the influential leaders of parties. Leaders whose parties are a part of the coalition government exercise their authority as extra-power centers due to the helplessness of the prime minister whose survival is contingent upon the support of these leaders.[7]

Political Disjuncture

Nepali political history is not sequential and coherent and, therefore, defies many commonly held generalizations of such developments. Sometimes, it is both a long and a high jump, and sometimes it shows that changes made within the regime or the system are so new that to an extent these regimes could be suitably suited to the exigencies of time, context, and situation, both national and international. Probing deeply into the post-unification (1768–1769) period of history, actors seemed to have changed the regime as well because of the very narrow basis of power structure. After the death of Prithvi Narayan Shah, his successors were either short-lived or failed to leave behind any lasting impacts on the stability and progress of the country. Nonetheless, Nepal's expansionist adventures had been able to stretch its territories in the east and west, but these territorial gains were shrunk during the Treaty of Sugauli in

[7] The frequent shuffling of bureaucrats with a view to putting their own favorites in important places is the routine of any new government. Many papers and individual columnists have criticized such practices that are handed down to us from the past traditional authoritarian regimes. It has been said: "The helpless civil servants were also found knocking on the doors of politicians to curry favour." Discarding "meritocracy in bureaucracy," leaders of parties have continued the old system of *pajani*, *chakari*, and other forms of personalized behavior for encouraging their favorites and hangers-on. See the editorial, *Republica*, August 5, 2009.

13

1815–1816. Meanwhile, bouts of instabilities, plots and counterplots, and murder of courtiers and relatives led to the rise of Janga Bahadur as the first Rana prime minister, which led to the advent of the 104-year Rana rule in Nepal. Thus, Shah politics ended until it was restored by the 1950 anti-Rana movement. However, the end of the Rana rule and ushering in a multiparty system in the country in the 1950s was accomplished within a short time because of the crisis of legitimacy of the oligarchy as well as due to the pressure of India to introduce timely reforms so that the disgruntled King and the movement party, NC, could be accommodated in the new order.

Though called as anti-Rana movement (1950) and narrated only in the context of importing liberal political values as were understood in the post–World War II period or against the background of anticolonial movements across the world, particularly in South and Southeast Asia and Africa, it was indeed a historical watershed for opening up Nepal before the world. It was the opening up of a floodgate that brought within it a number of contradictory elements that only sowed the seeds of what Joshi and Rose describe as "democratic innovations."[8] In the same vein but more vividly, Kamal P. Malla, a Nepali scholar, has probed into the intellectual (elite) perspective of the post-1950 period:

> The post-1950 decade in Nepal is characterized, in the first place, by a sense of release and emancipation of the intellect from a century-old political and priestly yoke, and in the place, by an unprecedented expansion of intellectual and cultural opportunities. The decade can aptly be called a decade of extroversion. For it was a decade of explosion of all manner of ideas, activities and organized efforts. It was a decade when the pre-existing narrow stratum of the intelligentsia was frantically active and vocal—socially, culturally and most important of all politically. It thoroughly exposed the social attitude and political immaturity of the Nepalese intelligentsia, and the fluctuation—till the end of the decade—seemed to be more and more to the left.[9]

[8] Bhuwan L. Joshi and Leo E. Rose, *Democratic Innovations in Nepal: A Study in Political Acculturation* (Berkeley: University of California Press, 1966).

[9] Kamal P. Malla, "The Intellectual in Nepalese Society" in Pashupati Shsumshere Rana and Kamal P. Malla, eds, *Nepal in Perspective* (Kathmandu: Centre for Economic Development and Administration, 1973), p. 277.

In my opinion, the 1950 movement was not mass-based as witnessed later in the 1990s and during the 2006 Jan Andolan as its nature was totally different from India's movement of independence led by Gandhi. In stark contrast to it, it was an armed insurrection hurriedly carried out for taking the maximum political advantage against the Ranas following the flight of King Tribhuvan and his family members from the Royal Palace in November 1950. Being a dummy figure, the King was not happy with the Rana rulers and, hence, the connivance with the anti-Rana forces, who were then mobilizing resources for overthrowing the regime. The royalties were then flown to New Delhi to be the guests of the Government of India (GoI). It was due to this reason that the GoI, especially Prime Minister Jawaharlal Nehru, played a pivotal role for striking a deal between the Ranas, the King, and the NC.

The characteristic of the post-Rana political behaviors of people was closer to what Emile Durkheim has said "anomie," which is as Greenfeld has formulated as "a condition of acute inconsistency between different values, norms, and cognitions, including the perception of reality, which, as a result of this inconsistency, neutralize each other and lose their authority."[10] New changes introduced in the political structures were also characterized by both change and continuity. Changes were visible in government, administrative structure, and other agencies of the state but in the context of structure of power or empowerment of people, they turned out to be a sham. Pushed to the background by the 104-year-old Rana rulers (1846–1950), monarchy resurrected its role along with the old political culture that demanded obeisance, *chakari* (flattery), and such other traditional norms and traits. Thus, the prodemocratic change turned out to be more traumatic and uncertain, leading to the unraveling of a bout of political movements and instability. Nepalis have paid a heavy price for the democratic modernity, which ironically remains still elusive. The following paragraph, though used in a wider context of change, also tries to encapsulate such trends:

[10] Jonathan R. Eastwood, "A Student's Introduction" in Liah Greenfeld, ed., *Nationalism and the Mind: Essays on the Modern Culture* (Noida: Brijbasi Art Press, 2007, Indian edn), p. x.

The advantages of modernity come with a heavy price-tag. The greater is the choice one is given in forming one's destiny, the heavier is the burden of responsibility for making the right choice. The more opportunities one is offered to "find oneself", the harder it is to decide where to look. Life has never been so exciting and so frustrating; we have never been so empowered and so helpless. Modern societies, produced by nationalism, because of their very secularism, openness, and the elevation of the individual, are necessarily *anomic*.[11]

It seems that three types of political culture—traditional authoritarian, feudalistic, and a mixture of liberal and Left-oriented political culture—were in interplay during the era of party politics (1951–1960).[12] Monarchy could use the traditional culture for its own consolidation. The second was a continuation of the past and worked in tandem with the first. The beneficiaries of the Rana regime, especially the landlords, *chakaridars*, sycophants, etc., who were soon disillusioned with the working of political parties, became handy for a political backlash. Such regrouping of traditional forces against democratization provided grounds for political uncertainty.

Thus, the jump theory soon worked to dismantle the gains of the 1950 political arrangement that had revolutionary elements who espoused the agenda of the CA election to be held soon, permission for multiparty system, and all other freedoms that were granted in any liberal democratic countries of the world. Impatient and power seekers they were, both the kings were quick to exploit the troubled political situation created by the interparty and intraparty conflicts and personal quarrels among politicians. However, the Rana–Congress coalition with the king as the head of the state, expecting to be a constitutional monarch in the future, soon crumbled following B. P. Koirala's resignation. As Koirala was the principal actor for launching the armed insurrection and for mobilizing other support for it, his exit could naturally create negative impact on the unraveling political scenarios. Thereafter, both King Tribhuvan and his successor, King Mahendra, became active in giving monarchial rather

[11] Ibid., p. xxiii.

[12] For more details, see R. S. Chauhan, *Political Development in Nepal: Conflict between Tradition and Modernity* (New Delhi: Associated Publications, 1971).

16

democratic shape to the unraveling politics. Within a short period of two years, King Tribhuvan, the acclaimed "father of the nation," took all powers into his hand and said:

> The inherent sovereignty of the monarch and his special prerogatives over the executive, legislative and judicial wings as the supreme head have been handed over to us by the tradition and custom of the country ... the supreme authority in all affairs now rests on us.[13]

Consequently, leaders of political parties went on losing all battles, including B. P. Koirala's attempt where he went to the Supreme Court for reviving the agenda of the CA as promised by King Tribhuvan in accord with the Delhi compromise. Mahendra, instead, decided to give a constitution prepared by a five-member committee in which the representatives of the NC, the Rashtravadi Gorkha Parishad (Nationalist Gorkha Council), and independents were picked up as members. Thus, it was a major ideological climbdown on the part of a party like the NC, under whose leadership the 1950 armed movement had been successful.[14] When the source of popular sovereignty was compromised, succumbing to the rapid rise of monarchy, the constitutional experiment started under the 1959 Constitution also hung on to the discretion of the ambitious monarch. After 18 months of the elected government formed under the Constitution awarded by the King, Mahendra staged a coup against it by using the army and by dismantling the whole edifice of multiparty democracy along with the arrest of leaders of parties, including the members of the cabinet headed by B. P. Koirala. As Joshi and Rose remark:

> Historically, the nearest parallel to King Mahendra's action was the arrest of Prime Minister Bhimsen Thapa in 1836 by King Rajendra on specious charges, later recanted by the King himself, of disloyalty to the royal family. Those were the days of conspiratorial politics, and vicissitudes in political fortunes were

[13] *Nepal Gazette*, Vol. 4, Magh 25, 2011 VS, pp. 123–126. See also Anirudha Gupta, *Politics in Nepal* (Bombay: Allied Publishers, 1964).

[14] In detail, see Gupta, ibid. Also, Lok Raj Baral, *Oppositional Politics in Nepal* (Delhi: Abhinav Publications, 1977).

sometimes expressed through poisonings, hired assassins, bloody massacres, and dark dungeons. In 1960 the participants were different, and the political methods and vocabulary were modern, but the basic spirit and idiom of Nepali politics remained unchanged.[15]

Now another major jump came with the beginning of full-fledged absolute monarchy under which political parties were outlawed and freedom drastically curtailed. A new era of the so-called partyless regime was introduced with the king as "active and supreme leader." It has been said that the post-Rana politics in general and the post-1960 coup in particular had the mixtures of "two kinds of rule"—the patrimonial and feudal. "Monarchical societies presuppose rank or hierarchies which can be changed by the rulers to 'suit his purpose,'" writes Rishikesh Shaha, who had worked as an agent of the regime until he fell from the grace of the King. Burrowing Reinhard Bendix's formulation, Shaha writes:

> ... the patrimonial principle visualizes the king and his servants in the royal household with the implication that the king rules, through peremptory commands because he is master in his own house. The feudal principle presupposes the association between the king and nobles whose families also possess their own standing of various degrees of importance in the community on the basis of lineage, wealth and legitimate authority accompanying these attributes.[16]

Peremptory command means government by the will of the ruler, which suffers no limitation in theory but allows for much exercises of grace or indulgence in practice. Bendix has thus described the attributes of a patrimonial state where "the King's position will be most secure when it is upheld by those whose positions depend on the king in the situation where ranking is not static but remains fluid." In such a monarchical rule, "personal and governmental authority is indistinguishable and so are personal services to the ruler and service in an official capacity.

[15] Bhuwan L. Joshi and Leo E. Rose, *Democratic Innovations in Nepal: A Case Study of Political Acculturation* (Berkeley: University of California Press, 1966), p. 392.

[16] See Rishikesh Shaha, *Politics in Nepal 1980–1990* (Kathmandu: Ratna Pustak Bhandar, 1990), pp. 1–2.

Such rule approximates what the ancients called tyranny, or unlimited government, by an individual ruler."[17]

Feudalism is used here as a broad category for conveying the nature of the royal rule based on the landholding systems which Mahesh Regmi classifies in these categories—*Raikar, Jagir, Birta, Guthi,* and *Kipat.*[18] In political sense, it was *hukumi shashan* (rule by order) and other traditional methods of conducting the affairs of the state but with conspicuous salient features of the Nepali state. Connected to the medieval features of the "fief," the continuity of some of such features is "lumped together under the term feudalism, which comes from the Medieval Latin *feodum,* itself from the old German *fee,* meaning cattle or property."[19]

Although King Mahendra appeared to be reformist in the immediate post-1960 period by introducing legal and land reforms in order to demonstrate that his measures were more progressive and people-oriented than those of the steps taken by the previous Koirala government (1959–1960), his land reform policy could fragment landholding pattern but failed to improve the productivity of lands. Nevertheless, landless peasants, though not all, could become conscious among the peasantry in addition to getting land tiller certificate from the government. As a result, the landowners could not easily remove the tillers without compensation.

[17] Reinhard Bendix, *Kings or People: Power and the Mandate to Rule* (University of California, Berkeley, 1978), chap. VII.

[18] *Raikar* is tax-payable land, which is listed in the official records.

Land given to government servants as emoluments. Land given to private individuals is called *Birta. Guthi* land is assigned for the use of charitable, religious, or philanthropic institutions. *Kipat* is land given to certain ethnic communities, particularly the Limbus of the Eastern Nepal in return for committing the loyalty of the communities to the government. (Regmi 1978)

See in detail, Mahesh Chandra Regmi, *Land Tenure And Taxation in Nepal* (Kathmandu: Ratna Pustak Bhandar, 1978), pp. 21–29.

[19] Joseph R. Strayer, *Feudalism* as mentioned in Walter C. Opello, Jr. and Stephen J. Rosow, *The Nation-State and Global Order* (Delhi: Viva Books, 2005, Indian edn), p. 41.

Surprisingly, the royal regime always seemed to be paranoid with oppositional overtones that sometimes reverberated in different forms and symbols. Since it had no legitimacy, the king sought to introduce his own model of regime led by him. But it too was vulnerable to the oppositional politics then being conducted from across the border (India) and from within the country.

It is also interesting to know how the jump theory worked even in a regime whose stability was guaranteed by the involvement of the king. While amending the Constitution in 1967, 1975, and 1981, losing all his confidence, both King Mahendra and his son, King Birendra, went out of the way in compromising his proclaimed fundamentals in order to pacify the oppositional forces that operated from various declared and undeclared sites of opposition. Intellectuals, students, members of his regime, etc., mounted opposition when the opportunity arose. In 1975, the partyless Constitution was almost rewritten in the name of Second Amendment as the regime hard-liners were motivated to be expedient by the state of emergency imposed by Indira Gandhi in India. Inspired by it, they came to the conclusion that the days of parliamentary democracy were gone as India, in their opinion, the bastion of liberal democracy in the Third World, could not also retain it in the wake of the J. P. movement. Taking swift action, Indira Gandhi had taken several draconian measures for curtailing freedom of the press and individuals and had arrested top-ranking political leaders, including Jaya Prakash Narayan, the veteran Gandhian leader and freedom fighter.

Although the Constitution was amended to strictly reinforce the partyless spirit so that anti-regime opposition within and outside the regime could be nipped in the bud, it could not last long after the lifting of emergency in India. All those who were imprisoned by Indira Gandhi became heroes following the announcement of elections by her for a fresh parliament. The strong anti-emergency wave catapulted all her opponents into the center of power. Suddenly, the new liberal forces changed the context showing that Indian democracy could not be derailed despite occasional setbacks suffered by it from time to time. Later developments have also supported this hypothesis because the same Indira Gandhi swept the poll after the Janata experiment fell apart.

In Nepal too, the impact of India was once again felt when a minor student agitation was launched on the slight pretext of the death sentence handed to the former Pakistani Prime Minister Zulfikar Ali Bhutto. Moreover, the Khomeini revolution in Iran was no less significant for making the king jittery in 1979. So in the wake of the student agitation, which was spreading across the country, the king wanted to save the rule by throwing the card of holding referendum with two choices: panchayat system with reform or multiparty system.

But, using all the state resources and contriving divisions within the political parties for and against the preconditions to be put before the king, the Royal Government was eventually successful to ensure the "technical" victory of the "partyless regime."[20] The Constitution amended subsequently (Third Amendment); however, it departed from its past proclaimed electoral system by incorporating the election on the basis of universal adult franchise and the provisions for accountability of the prime minister to the legislature. The prime minister was supposed to be recommended by the legislature, which was composed on individual basis and not on organizational basis as in party system. Critics had pointed it out as yet another shift in the nature of polity, which continued to confirm the partyless nature of the system to change into direct election, based on adult franchise to be contested on an individual basis. It was indeed a kind of hybridization of electoral system that could trigger off partisan spirit within the regime.

As anticipated by political observers, this experiment was short-lived with both the regime supporters and opposition forces (legally outlawed but practically operational parties) mounting opposition. In 1990, the anti-regime opposition took momentum when the NC once again decided to launch a mass movement, demanding the revival of multiparty system. Other Left forces also joined it in order to give a big push for the overthrow of the regime, if not monarchy. It was supported by all

[20] For a detailed analysis of the politics of referendum, see Lok Raj Baral, *Nepal's Politics of Referendum: A Study of Groups, Personalities and Trends* (Delhi: Vikas Publishing House, 1983); and Urmila Phadnis, "Nepal: The Politics of Referendum," *Pacific Affairs*, 5, 3, Autumn: 1981, pp. 455–484.

the Indian political parties, international human rights groups, and Western governments including the US. Eventually on April 8, 1990, King Birendra decided to yield to the oppositional pressure and invited representative parties to declare the restoration of multiparty system in the country.

The Jan Andolan I and the Constitution prepared by the Interim Government—which consisted of the NC, the ULF, and the royalists—were the beginning of coalition politics in the country. First, the NC and the ULF that was made up of some Left parties launched the movement against the partyless regime demanding a multiparty system; and second, after the successful movement that forced King Birendra to give in, it prepared the ground to forge a compromise between the king and the movement parties, thus, resulting in a constitution based on the understanding of three forces—the king, the NC, and the ULF. According to the Constitution of the Kingdom of Nepal of 1990, four principles were declared unalterable: the monarchy, the multiparty system, the sovereignty of the people, and the basic rights of people. Even the Parliament, which was to be duly elected by the "sovereign people," could not alter any one of them.

Although the Constitution mentioned the sovereignty of people, in actual practice, political parties and leaders continued to look upon the Palace as the source of their power. So with the passage of time, when the parties started picking up quarrels on lame excuses or on personal grounds, the king as usual started asserting his own role and considerably circumscribed the power of the prime minister. Frequent changes of government, intraparty conflict, and interparty animosity led the king to be more aggressive. Consequently, the so-called elected prime ministers invariably felt their limitations to act independently of the Palace as the king tried to impede the decisions of the prime minister. Prime Minister G. P. Koirala, the first elected prime minister under the 1990 Constitution, had to confront the assertive monarchs during the Maoist insurgency (People's War), which started in 1996. Both King Birendra, who was assassinated in the bloody Palace massacre in 2001, and his brother, Gyanendra, who succeeded Birendra, did not allow the prime ministers to use the Royal Nepal Army (RNA) against the Maoists, nor were the elected governments allowed to negotiate with the Maoists on the issue of holding a CA election as demanded by the insurgents.

Thus, in course of time, the elected governments became a facade because of the continued domination of the king. The leaders of the government also did not assert their position vis-à-vis the king thinking that the latter had the backing of the army against the government, despite the prime minister's constitutional position as the chairman of the Defense Council with the power to appoint the commander-in-chief of the RNA.

The politics of disruption or jump was more vividly seen during 2002–2005 when King Gyanendra repeated the drama of his father, Mahendra, by hiring and firing prime ministers at his discretion. He not only abused the Constitution by using Article 127 that entailed the provision for removing inconveniences while implementing the Constitution but also dismantled the political process restoring the tradition of absolute monarchy. So, even the system produced by the movement (1990) could not be sustained due to lack of commitment to own it. It was believed that King Birendra himself was bent on taking some extreme action in order to find a suitable political space. He was not happy with the spirit of "constitutional monarchy," though it was a misnomer in the given context of politics of compromise among the king, NC, and the ULF, and hence, the king, time and again, had started putting obstructions in the working of the government. Yet, it was not only the fault of the king as the leaders of parties, including the prime ministers, invariably preferred not to annoy him.

Another disjuncture or break with the tradition was in 2006. Its antecedents or precipitating factors could be attributed to the decade-long Maoist insurgency (1996–2005), alienation of political parties from the regime after the rapid rise of monarchical absolutism, and the aspiration of the Nepali people for peace, stability, democracy, and progress. Trapped between the atrocities of the regime and Maoist insurgents, the people wanted to end the conflict soon, hoping for a respite where they could be resettled, secured, and be at peace.

The 2006 Movement as a Long Jump

The imposition of the state of emergency in February 2005 was the culmination of the royal ascendancy, which led the major parliamentary parties to forge an alliance with the Maoists for ending what they called the "royal absolutism" with the objective to prepare the grounds for democratic rule. A series of negotiations conducted between the NC, CPN–UML, and the Maoist leaders in Nepal and India led them to conclude a 12-point understanding on November 22, 2005, in New Delhi.

Both the political parties and the Maoists agreed on holding the elections of the CA to establish a democratic order in the country. However, political parties preferred to mention the end of the "royal absolutism," while the Maoists made a pledge to establish a republic.

It could be observed that the understanding reached between the SPA and the Maoists produced electrifying effects on the movement launched by the SPA. The civil society played a crucial part in improving the image of the parties, which had lost their credibility due to their kowtowing before the king and because of their dismal failures while in government or in parliament. As the SPA–Maoist understanding rallied around a common cause against King Gyanendra's rule, the sluggish movement got a strong dose of mass support following the Delhi understanding that soon received both national and international legitimacy. All major countries of the world supported the movement despite some reservations on the issue of involvement of the Maoists. Most foreign governments were discontented with the king for not opening dialogue with the non-Maoist parties in opposition.

The peaceful movement supported by the Maoists gradually picked up its momentum from March–April 2006. Political parties that had lost credibility due to their dismal performances in the past also started getting support from all sections of the population. The participation of people was unprecedented both in size and intensity. It spread across the country with the same popular support bringing about a radical change. Although the parliamentary parties were not vocal on the issue of abolition of the monarchy, they could not resist the people's aspiration for bringing about a radical transformation in the society and power structure. So when the king was advised by some foreign powers to offer the post of prime minister to the SPA in order to restore the democratic order, the SPA leaders could not accept it as it was "too little, too late." So after three days of his proclamation, another proclamation came on April 24, 2006, accepting the major demands of the SPA. Calling upon the SPA to "bear the responsibility of talking the nation on the path of national unity and prosperity, while ensuring permanent peace and safeguarding multiparty democracy," King Gyanendra summoned the session of the restored parliament (House of Representatives) on April 28.

What was more significant was the parliamentary decision to strip the king of all executive, legislative, and judicial powers in addition to taking a number of measures that reduced his status fully. Later, all ceremonial powers vested in the head of the state were taken over by the prime minister to the extent that even the credentials of ambassadors were taken by the prime minister. The king's position was further reduced following the parliamentary decision to nationalize the property of the king and his family members. The RNA, which was always under the king, also switched its loyalty to the new government, though a sizable contingent of the army (now named Nepal Army [NA]) continued to remain within the Palace.

The 1990 Constitution, which was the product of a compromise between three power centers—the king, the NC, and the Leftist force—was replaced by the Interim Constitution prepared by the SPA and the CPN (Maoist). According to the Constitution, the CA election was planned; the restructuring of the Nepali state was to be undertaken in order to end all sorts of disparities existing in the country; inclusive democracy was to be ensured by accommodating different groups, communities, regions, and gender; and the future of the monarchy was to be decided by the first meeting of the CA by simple majority. The agenda of declaring Nepal a federal state also became prominent at a later stage, though the actual nature of the federal system would be decided by the CA.

Meanwhile, all the political parties but the parties of former *panchas* (royalists) passed resolutions for declaring Nepal a republic. The NC party, which was and still is considered a moderate democratic party having constitutional monarchy as its cherished principle, embraced the republican agenda due to the popular support calling for it. Only the split-away Rashtriya Prajatantra Party–Nepal (RPP–N) came out openly in favor of constitutional monarchy. The other two parties of former *panchas*, Rashtriya Prajatantra Party (RPP) and Rashtriya Jana Shakti Party, continued being fence-sitters—neither supporting constitutional monarchy nor the republic. They left this issue for the CA to take a final decision.

The SPA and the Maoists who had forged an understanding to hold the CA election in the summer of 2007 postponed it thrice without sound grounds. The Maoists who had joined the government to hold the election decided to leave it, which opened up the agenda for a republic and the election to the CA. The Maoists wanted the Interim Parliament to declare Nepal a republic contrary to the previous decision that the first session of the CA would decide on the fate of the monarchy by a simple majority. According to the Maoists, as the situation had changed due to the deferral of the CA election, the two preconditions—the end of the monarchy and a full proportional representation system—could be fulfilled before the CA election. Other parties did not accept such a changed Maoist stance and adhered to the previous decision reached by the SPA, including the Maoists. (Prior to the merger of the two Congress parties led, respectively, by G. P. Koirala and Sher Bahadur Deuba, it was an Eight Party Alliance [EPA].)

These two preconditions were agreed upon when the SPA partially consented to increase the percentage of proportional representation from 40 to 58 percent. On the issue of monarchy, the Interim Parliament decided to end the monarchy but the decision would only be enforced after the first meeting of the CA. For broad national and international legitimacy, such a formal approval was made to accommodate the Maoist demand. As a result, a new date, April 10, 2008, was fixed for the CA election. To the astonishment of both the nation and the international community, the CA election took place amidst widespread applause and happiness.

It should be recalled that many contentious issues, which arose in the post–Jan Andolan II period, are now more or less accepted by the political parties. The agenda is to restructure the Nepali state by declaring it a democratic republic, accepting a federal setup, and following the spirit of inclusive democracy in order to accommodate the deprived and marginalized sections of society and regions. Concerning the representation, the Interim Constitution has made provisions to distribute the seats of the CA on the basis of the size of population of each community and region. While preparing the closed list of candidates for the CA under the proportional representation system, the political parties are now required to include the following ethnic, regional groups, Dalits, and women candidates (see Table 1.1).

Table 1.1
Percentage of Social Representation in the CA 2008

Groups	Percentage
Madhese (Tarai)	31.1
Dalit	13.0
Oppressed communities, tribal, and ethnic groups	37.8
Backward region	4.4
Others (Hill Brahmin–Chhetri, Thakuri, Sanyasi, etc.)	30.2

Source: Results of Constituent Assembly, 2008, as cited in Hachhethu 2009.

Although the Maoist and some Madhese groups accepted the formula of 42 percent and 58 percent, respectively, for the first-past-the-post and the proportional system, some minor armed groups in the Tarai continue their struggle to achieve a full proportional system. One of their major demands was/is for the whole Tarai belt (from east to west) to constitute a single federal autonomous unit with the right to self-determination. As none of the other groups, including the major hill ethnic groups and the Tharus of the Tarai, find this an acceptable proposal, carving out federal units either on the basis of ethnicity as demanded by the hill ethnic groups or on the basis of Madhesh as a single unit seems to be difficult.

Some words such as "secularism" and "nationalism" are also country specific as Nepal, across its modern history, was neither secular in the modern context of secularism nor is its "nationalism" akin to the spirit of national unity or nation-state. However, all the arguments made so far by Nepali and foreign scholars about the secular characteristics of Nepali society point to a certain degree of moderation in the Nepali society. Being predominantly a Hindu state, Nepal's processes of Hinduization did not intrude into other religions' territories. Many strands of religion commingled, forming a kind of syncretic culture.

The patronage provided by the state made the state more narrow and parochial which extended its domain to language, culture, and construct of Nepali society along caste hierarchy and discriminatory state dealing in economic and other social areas. So whatever secular trends were evident in the Nepali state, they changed into a kind of segregation. Later it took the shape of forms of discrimination against ethnic groups, Dalit, women, and regions. Religion too became very ritualistic in order to reinforce the tradition of caste and class.

Nepal's political developments continue to be uncertain and unpredictable. It has been defying both systematic and systemic courses of development ever since the fall of the 104-year-old Rana family rule in 1951. I have also conceptualized it as "jump theory" of Nepali politics, which carries the historical baggage along with the elements of change. It is also significant that liberal democracy based on pluralism has perennially become the underlined objective of such uneven development. Sometimes it appears to be deceptive in form as modernity seems to plant innovative ideas for spurring political awareness even without creating minimum democratic infrastructure, i.e., political culture as a committed orientation for owning all-embracing changes brought to fore as a result of political mobilization by political parties and other relevant groups and individuals. It is also deceptive because all such changes seem to lead to nowhere but to produce political disorder and uncertainties, which, in turn, also turn into authoritarianism and other forms of personalized rule.

Rediscovery of a Nation-state

The psychology of Nepali rulers had always been guided by the idea that the assimilation of all minorities and social groups into the broad Gorkhali culture would be the rock bottom of the modern Nepali state. The conquest of the valley by the king of Gorkha had indeed laid the foundation of uniculturalism (monoculturalism) and absorption of all other cultural and social groupings into the so-called unified nation-state. Thus:

> ... the integration model established under the Shah and later under the Rana regimes differed from the "bourgeois" models of nation building emerging during the same period in the Western world in one fundamental respect: under the Shahs and the Ranas sovereignty remained *de jure* with powerful individuals and factions able to manipulate and/or represent the monarch. From the point of view of the rulers, the plurality of the Nepalese [Nepalis] society was conceived within a uniform socio-political framework; diverse castes and ethnic groups were incorporated into a holistic framework of a national caste hierarchy.[21]

Assimilation fitted into the Gorkhali agenda of domination by one group of people over the other insofar as the attitude of the modern Nepali state was concerned. Stretching this trend further, the Mulki Ain (Legal Code) of 1854, enforced by the first Rana Prime Minister Jang Bahadur, "placed all castes of comparable status of the hills higher in status than similar caste groups among the Newars and the Tarai Hundus." Prayag Raj Sharma further states:

> The Newar Malla rulers of Nepal were the people who first seem to have devised a complete social system in the 14th century. The caste hierarchy under this system is till followed intact among the Newar society today. The code of 1854 has partly adopted this hierarchy.[22]

It was thus against integration that "provides for the coexistence of minority cultures with the majority culture; assimilation requires the absorption of minority cultures into the majority culture. The aim of

[21] Drawing on the idea of A. Hofer from his book, *The Caste Hierachy and the State in Nepal*, Joanna Pfaff-Czarnecka has debated it in her article "Debating the State of the Nation: Ethnicization of Politics in Nepal—A position paper," Joanna Pfaff Czarnecka, Damini Rajasinghe-senanayake, Ashis Nandy, and Edmund Terence Gomez, *Ethnic Futures: The State and Identity Politics in Asia* (Delhi, 1999), p. 52.

[22] Prayag Raj Sharma, "Nepali Culture and Society: Reflections on Some Historical Currents" in Kamal P. Malla, ed., *Nepal: Perspective on Continuity and Change* (Kathmandu: CNAS, 1989), pp. 163–164.

assimilation is a monocultural, even a monofaith society; the aim of integration is a multicultural, pluralist society."[23] In the opinion of Rose, "a syncretic form of Hinduism, encompassing much that is Buddhist or 'animist' in derivation, therefore, is the dominant religious and cultural form throughout much of Nepal."[24] Yet the controversy persists between the Hindus and non-Hindus with the latter opposing the imposition of Brahmanic Hindu values over the rest. As the people were subjugated under the predatory state, their resentment at such imposition was mute. But the process cannot be considered as "painless."

Such an approach to the process of nation-state building could last for 240 years and the unitary state structure was taken as the model for maintaining the ethnic mosaic intact. The selective use of a few castes and ethnic groups demonstrated the discriminatory attitude of the ruler. Other groups such as Newar and the people from the Tarai were isolated from being included in the army, while the *janjatis* or hill ethnic groups were disproportionately recruited into various state services. As Mahesh Regmi states:

> The standing army of the Gorkhali rulers had a narrow social and territorial base. The subject populations of the Empire were divided into two categories, only one of which was eligible for recruitment. King Prithvi Narayan Shah had instructed his successors to restrict recruitment to four communities, namely, Khas, Magar, Gurung and Thakuri. The list does not mention such other communities as Khawas, Khatri, and Chhetri, who gained entry into the standing army in subsequent years.[25]

[23] A. Shivanandan, "Integration vs. forced assimilation," *The Hindu*, Delhi, September 14, 2006.

[24] Leo E. Rose, *Nepal: Strategy for Survival* (Bombay: Oxford University Press, 1971), p. 8.

[25] See Mahesh Chandra Regmi, *Imperial Gorkha: An Account of Gorkhali Rule in Kumaun (1791–1815)* (Delhi: Adroit Publishers, 1999), p. 69. This information has been taken by Regmi from the Royal Nepal Army Headquarters (RNAH). See for Prithvi Narayan's favor for certain castes and communities (Pandes, Basnayat, Pantha, Thakuri, and Magars) in Mahesh C. Regmi, *Kings and Poliitcal Leaders of the Gorkhali Empire 1768–1814* (Patna: 1995), p. xii.

It is interesting to note that despite a lot of changes made in administrative and political sectors, the discriminatory policy laid by the Gorkha and Rana rulers did not show any radical departure from the past. Although Nepal experienced a sudden break with the demise of the Rana oligarchy in 1951, the change turned out to be nothing more than the restoration of absolute monarchy after 104 years. The Rana had thrown monarchy into the political oblivion after the coup in 1846. Taking revenge against the Rana usurpation of power, monarchy, by joining the forces of revolution, could reincarnate itself in the post-revolution period due to the gradual weakening of political parties. It was also proved that Nepalis had ended the Rana rule but the subject political culture of the past continued allowing the kings to consolidate the Shah ascendancy. All revolutionaries, therefore, started looking upon the Palace as their safest constituencies, forgetting the basics of democratic governance. Personal allegiance to the ruler, the same discriminatory policies in more refined manners, and patronage routes to powers and privileges, etc., became the basis. Dor Bahadur Bista states[26]:

> The small number of feudal at the centre and the local chiefs throughout the country were given all the freedom to exploit the people and the resources of the community in any manner they liked. The caste principles developed on the basis of *Manusmriti* and other Hindu texts helped reinforce the stratification from the very beginning of the Rana period.

Such narratives are meant only to establish the connection between nation-state formation and the value premises of Nepali society in its entirety. It covers religious diversity, ethnic structure, regional variations along with caste and class structures. Although most authors of Nepali society, culture, religion, and their impacts on giving a distinct identity have tried to present positive sides for national unity and harmonization, these postulates, despite being valid to a great extent, are now under scrutiny. Such reexamination process has come up along with the surge of mass consciousness. The marginalized and oppressed sections of

---

[26] Dor Bahadur Bista, "The Structure of Nepali Society" in Pashupati Shsumshere Rana and Kamal P. Malla, eds, *Nepal in Perspective* (Kathmandu: Centre for Economic Development and Administration, 1973), p. 179.

society and regions reject the thesis of nation-state that built on the false notion of assimilation and integration.

First, the formation of a territorially defined state and its uninterrupted continuity, despite the shrinkage of territory, as a consequence of the defeat at war with the British in 1816, is a major factor in history. Creation of a territorially defined state provided its rulers (Shah, Ranas, and elites of parties) with a country. The founder of Nepal, King Prithvi Narayan Shah, formed the kingdom out of conquest as many other rulers had done to give a definite shape to their nation-state. Some common characteristics can be identified. Both the formative period and later as a full-fledged nation-state have the combination of:

> ... politico-military rule that, first, has a distinct geographically defined territory over which it exercises jurisdiction; second, has sovereignty over its territory, which means that its jurisdiction is theoretically exclusive of outside interference by other nation-states or entities; third, it has a government made up of public offices and roles that control and administer the territory and population subject to the state's jurisdiction; fourth, the government claims a monopoly on the legitimate use of physical coercion over its population, sixth, its policy, to a greater or lesser degree, on the obedience and loyalty of its inhabitants.[27]

A "defined territory" with all many of the ingredients of the modern nation-state is indeed an asset of Nepal's efforts for making a "national state" that makes a departure from the old concept of nation-state. Nation-state, as is evident in the historical developmental context of Europe where the systematic theory of nation-state developed is exclusive in nature, has a homogenization policy to assimilate other communities and minorities whose proximity to power is not possible due to the narrowly defined hierarchy within the state. The integration policy of the state only cursorily recognizes the existence of language, culture, and other ethnic and community identities, but they are only assimilated into the dominant group's identity in the name of forming a synthetic identity.

Taking some of these concepts, it can be said that the emergence of the Nepali state throughout the 18th and the 19th centuries was well

---

[27] Walter C. Opello, JR, Stephen J. Rosow, *The Nation-State and Global Order* (Delhi: Viva Books, 2005, second edn), p. 3.

within the common parameters of other nation-states of the world. From the very day of the process of unification by force and later by other methods of achieving allegiance of subjects, the state in its original ethos and methods continued to imbibe the characteristics of nation-state. The post-Rana political innovations also could not make any substantive transformation into making a national state where today's demands of inclusiveness; empowerment of people; and end of all forms of caste, ethnic, religious, and regional differences could be addressed. Parties that claimed to be progressive and democratic also paid no attention to mitigating state-embedded disparities. Even for giving 5 percent re-presentation to women under the much-touted democratic Constitution of 1990, the movement parties themselves seemed to be lackadaisical. Other groups' status also continued to be unchanged with the dominant castes—Brahmin and Chhetri with 30 percent population—continuing to be dominant in all spheres of the state. Such caste politics came along with the king of Gorkhas, who subsequently became the unifier of Nepal. Being Chhetri and Hindu, Prithvi Narayan Shah, his successors, and the Ranas, all reinforced the caste structure so much so that even the revival of multiparty system in 1990 and parliamentary exercises over a decade or so could not make any substantive change in the power structure and in political parties.

One of the serious problems confronted by the elites of "new Nepal" (post-2006) is the subordination of ideology to the emerging trends of ethnicization, regionalism, various forms of parochialism, and above all, engulfing anarchical behaviors of youngsters in the country. Now parties are increasingly becoming defensive on the issue of religion, making the orthodox Hindus, who want to retain Nepal's identity as a Hindu state, assertive. Although Nepali people did not at all show their resentment at the declaration of Nepal as a secular state by the Interim Constitution, this issue is likely to be exploited by the Hindu fundamentalists of India and Nepal.

Secularism

Unlike many South Asian countries, Nepal's secularization process can be examined at two levels: state and non-state. The Nepali state was never secular as the rulers of Nepal were die-hard Hindus, both in ritualistic and functional terms. The king of Nepal could only be a Hindu, and the other religious and social groups (caste and class) and minorities were all *raitis* and *duniyadars*, some of whom, especially the high-caste groups, could constitute the elite class. Yet, because of its seclusion from the rest of the world or perhaps due to the lack of social and political awareness, the Nepali state did not pass through the pangs of social change as many other countries of the world had been.

But the political underpinnings of secularism were manifested in the wake of prodemocracy movements and on the degree of freedoms provided by the state. During the campaign of referendum (1979–1980), the demand of secularism triggered some debates provoking the former prime minister and democratic leader to retort that to declare a Hindu state is a fraud. The Constitution awarded by the king himself in 1959 under which Koirala became the first elected prime minister was silent on the issue. However, the Constitution of Nepal (1962) that came into force after the royal coup resurrected the Hindu concept of Nepali state.

The concept of Hindu state was used by King Mahendra and later by his successors for legitimacy that could rally the Hindus across the world. Since his new regime was the product of a coup that denounced liberal democracy and pluralism as sources of threats to national unity and national independence, Hinduism was the best weapon for survival. Conversely, today secularism has become a symbol of national identity because secularism means an end to all forms of discriminations on the grounds of religion. Secularism is thus "accompanied by three processes—non-discrimination, the right to one's religious beliefs, and non-alignment of the state with a particular religion."[28]

Nonetheless, the 2006 mass movement and the political developments thereafter nullified the theocratic nature of the state. The Interim Constitution declared Nepal as a "multiethnic, multilingual, multireligious, and multicultural state." The social construct of Nepali society as well as the popular sovereignty espoused by the new republic are the

[28] Neera Chandhoke, *Beyond Secularism: The Rights of Religious Minorities* (Delhi: Oxford University Press, 1999), p. 82.

guiding spirit for declaring a secular state. The state would not profess any religion, though all religious groups would have the freedom to profess their respective religion. On the grounds of religion, no discrimination would be made by the state; so any person professing any religion can become the president or the prime minister of the country.

In India, the doctrine of secularism was adopted for both legitimacy as well as for securing the interests of minorities. As Neera Chandhoke states: "Majoritarianism challenges precisely this democratic project of allowing space and recognition for all identities. And today it is majoritarianism that despite all the preconditions built into the constitution, and despite the original spirit of the polity, threatens to overwhelm us."[29] The rights of religious minorities was/is not expected to be ensured by the "majoritarian" democracy.

Nepal is a plural state in social and political sense. The Nepali state, as mentioned by the 2001 census, consists of six broad religious configurations: Hindu (80.62 percent), Buddhist (10.74 percent), Muslim (4.2 percent), Kirat (3.6 percent), Christian (0.45 percent), and others (0.4 percent). But except the Hindus, the figures have slightly gone up during the period since 2001. Political pluralism in today's sense cannot be isolated from the power as freedoms and the regulative procedure of the democratic state are based on the freedoms of people. Moreover, the demand of social justice is a part of inclusiveness as all people living within a given territory are entitled to enjoy freedom that propel into power. The electoral mechanisms are so developed that people could access both economic and political resources.

The new thrust for inclusiveness and empowerment of people is intimately related to secularization. It allows people to embrace broad sociocultural and humane values, which can only be possible in democracy. Polities based on religion are narrow and sectarian. Why is it that Indian political leaders and constitutional experts adopted the idea of secular state despite India being a Hindu-dominated state? They knew that in a democracy no citizen's rights can be compromised on the grounds of religion.

[29] Ibid., p. 9.

Fractured Parties and Democracy

A trend of fragmentation of political parties on nonideological grounds is a common phenomenon. Nepal's political instability or democratic setbacks since 1951 and more specifically in the post-1991 period till today is interconnected to parties divisions. In 1994, the majority government headed by the NC's G. P. Koirala collapsed due to intraparty conflict. The leader of the 1990 mass movement, Ganesh Man Singh, revolted against his own prime minister and left the party. Other leaders and members were also vertically divided into two camps—for and against Koirala. Later, the NC was formally split with Sher Bahadur Deuba forming yet another party (Nepali Congress [Democratic]).

Two scenarios are likely to develop in the foreseeable future. First, the conventional style of conducting parties would not help the old parliamentary parties like the NC to invigorate its image. Its democratic credentials are suspect as it has not been able to cope with newer challenges for setting its own socioeconomic progressive agendas. Any party's survival would, from now onward, be determined by its performance and not by hackneyed claim that it was/is the real protector of freedom and democracy. The octogenarian leader's dominance is now eroding, and his likely successors seem to be incapable of understanding the guiding spirit of today's dynamics. Girija Prasad Koirala, negated with other parties on major issues, was more casual and irresponsible in his utterances rather than being a responsible leader of delicate transition. Koirala, who acted as a patriarch, was penchant for personalized politics, which obstructed the development of the NC as a democratic party. His one-point decision to induct his daughter first as a minister and then as deputy prime minister made him further alienated from the party with most central committee members turning against his decision that he took without the approval of the party. Although his past actions were invariably taken purely as his personal affairs, most of them remained formally unchallenged. Since he was too self-centered, he was just like a hero of a Greek tragedy.

The CPN comprised more than a dozen groups since the 1960s. Individual groups, registered as parties, have either died after some time or are in skeleton shape. But some of them, such as the CPN–UML and the

CPN (Maoist), have come to this stage after having gone through several alliances and alienations. Nevertheless, the CPN–UML has been able to stabilize its position after the 1991 election and was also in government after it became the first largest party in parliament in 1994–1999, displacing the NC. Yet, another split took place after the 1999 election with some senior leaders forming another party. Surprisingly, however, these breakaway groups have not been able to sustain for a long time, forcing some leaders to rejoin the mother organization, while some others continued to be in small parties formed by them.

Such a story is also applicable to other parties. The RPP, formed by the former royal supporters or officeholders after the restoration of multi-party system in 1990, has undergone several splits, but these divisions, as in other parties, were on nonideological grounds. The post-2006 politics, which is also dominated by individual leaders, is no less different from the past. The Tarai (Madhesh) parties—the Nepal Sadbhawana Party and the Madhesh Democratic Forum, just to mention a few prominent parties—are passing through the period of division and attenuation. The forum leaders who came from various other parties to give a shape to the new party broke away on individual grounds. Some wanted to become ministers, others opposed it. Moreover, the new Tarai parties that came into existence in the wake of the Madhesh movement are seemingly becoming agendaless as most demands of Madhesh have more or less been addressed. Now they are short of mobilizing issues. Taking a cue from the Maoist violent approach, several armed groups are now indulged in killing, abduction, and extortion. It has been disclosed by the government that there are altogether 109 armed groups among which many are criminal gangs who use the open India–Nepal border freely for taking shelter in India. Criminalization of politics and politicization of criminals have thus worked in tandem indicating no respite from such activities.

One of the problems of Nepal's democratic republic is that the "transition," which is expected to be smooth, goal-oriented, and more or less consensual, has become not only uncertain and turbulent, but is also likely to erase the political achievements made over the years. Heroes are produced by the movements but their attrition starts soon as if they are like the heroes of tragic dramas. Heroes or charismatic leaders are independent variables for limited time to set the future agendas and for making transition smooth.

In the given context, however, the leadership role is always elusive, though leaders of parties survive due to servile attitude of their followers. Girija Prasad Koirala of the NC, for instance, behaved like an authoritarian personality taking all sorts of irrational decisions, which were not conducive for institution building. Nevertheless, for the first time in 2009, he remained no more infallible as his subordinates did challenge his personal decision for appointing his own daughter as the foreign minister and then the deputy prime minister. Since she had been defeated badly in the 2008 direct election of the CA, there was neither rationality nor maintenance of minimum norms of democracy. What was more undemocratic of the NC's decision was the appointment of a prime minister from the CPN–UML—defeated from two places, one in the capital, Kathmandu, and the other in the appointed prime minister's own home district, Rautahat—despite the NC being the second largest party in the CA. Abdicating its own claim to form an alternate government by virtue of being the second party, Koirala's choice fell on the candidate of CPN–UML. Bent on appointing his daughter as deputy prime minister, notwithstanding the opposition of his party colleagues to his decision, Koirala obliged the CPN–UML candidate, Madhav Nepal, to become the prime minister.

The NC as a liberal democratic party has almost lost its former aura and acceptability because of its failure to institutionalize democratic process since 1951. The institutionalization was tried once in 1959–1960, but against the backdrop of the ascent of monarchy, multiparty politics, let alone the party system, could be revived only after 30 years. Again, due to internal quarrels and personalistic attitude of leaders, it suffered a setback in the aftermath of the 1990 movement. Leaders like G. P. Koirala seemed to be overconscious of the domineering position of monarchy contrary to the spirit of the 1990 Constitution.

The post-Koirala phase of the NC is likely to be more challenging since its traditional bases of popularity is ruffled owing to the emerging dynamics, ideological ambiguity, external penetration, lack of institutional cohesion, lack of understanding the shifting power balance inside the country, and above all, its image of being a status quo party that does not move forward unless it is under pressure from a variety of factors and compulsions. Its socioeconomic policies are blunted by the pulls and pressures of vested interest groups within the party. It has to face the Maoist challenge on the socioeconomic front while at the same time it maintains its links with the consumerist middle-class values. Bereft of people-centric programs along with the issue of retaining its democratic credential, the NC as a democratic party needs to be both forward looking and modest. Since its policy of liberalization would no longer be relevant to the changed context, poverty alleviation, end of all forms of social disparity, and its uncompromising spirit on the core values of democratic governance can salvage the party. Since everything is in shambles in the country, it would be very difficult to resurrect its credibility. Surrounded by ethnic, regional, and hostile political groupings like the UCPN (Maoist) and other splintered Left and Right parties, the NC's leadership role, which is now plural, would be crucial for steering its own course of democratic development. On the one hand, it has to maintain its identity as the single largest democratic party and on the other, its progressive face also needs to be preserved in the eyes of the people. Presenting the Maoist–other parties' dichotomous situation, a Nepali scholar has, thus, described:

> The peace process in Nepal proved simply a political expediency to all. For the majority of political parties, it was just a process to regain their lost power with the mechanism through which they lured the Maoists to enter the competitive politics political fray. They succeeded in their venture to a large extent by drawing the Maoists to participate in mainstream national politics by declaring an end to the "People's War". The end of the violent conflict and a government of their own with active participation of former adversaries was their triumph towards peace. Appeasement of the Maoists, thus, becomes the price of peace. On the other hand, the Maoists entered the peace process tactically, using it as a means to abolish monarchy through the cooperation of and support of the mainstream political parties.[30]

[30] Dhruba Kumar, "Nepal's Turbulent Quest for Peace and Stability," *Aakrosh* (Delhi), 12, 44, July: 2009, p. 41. For Prachanda's remarks, see the press conference on November 8, 2009, and his controversial speech delivered before the Maoist combatants in the Shaktikhor camp in January 2009.

It seemed that the motive behind the Maoist decision to change the line was "tactical."[31] It was also a vindication of the perennial reality that had been confronting the communist parties of Nepal since the very birth of the party in 1949. No communist parties, whatever the incarnations of revolutionary cliché, have eventually transformed themselves as players in multiparty politics. In the context of the UCPN (Maoist), however, it has been successful to achieve its two fundamental objectives—end of monarchy and the CA for drafting a constitution befitting the sovereign people.

The regional, communal, ethnic, and other trends have further hit political homogeneity within political parties. Its reflection can be observed in the parliament. The parallel election system—first-past-the-post and proportional—along with the absence of a threshold point for election of a candidate under the proportional representation (PR) system have given grounds to a multiplicity of parties where if they get more than 25,000 votes, they could be elected to the CA or the parliament. And all want a share in government.

External Influence

Nepali politics cannot remain fully insulated from its geopolitical surroundings. Its active interactions with the immediate neighbors since the time of unification in the 18th century continue today. Nepal's internal politics, however, remained undisturbed during the Rana period because the rulers' understanding of the geopolitical situation that tilted in favor of the southern neighbor, then a stabilized power, dictated them to be friendly. Surprisingly, the advent of the British rule in India left behind only a marginal impact on creating a liberal polity as was found in India. But with the winds of change blowing against the colonial power, Nepali rulers also felt the heat of it in the 1940s. Since China was not in the picture for a long time, the Rana enjoyed the blessings of the British so long as its rule continued in India.

[31] Ibid.

The post-1950 politics of Nepal has been greatly influenced by India. Indian preference to certain individuals and parties has, thus, become a perennial source of major controversy in maintaining domestic political equilibrium. Nehru's letter to King Tribhuvan in 1951 where he mentioned not to make B. P. Koirala the prime minister did cast a long shadow on the future course as well. Indian action had its reverberation in 2010 when India, backed by other non-Maoist parties of Nepal, could block the chance of Prachanda becoming prime minister in 2010. The Maoist impatience to "capture power" might have prompted India and other parties' leaders to thwart the Maoist move through the president; however, in case of B. P. Koirala, no similar situation prevailed. Except Nehru's perception of B. P. Koirala as a radical, there was no other reason for depriving him of the post of prime minister.

During the royal regime (1960–1990), Indian role in appointing a prime minister was not felt, although King Mahendra did not ignore the Indian request, if not pressure, for denying the Chinese to undertake projects in the Tarai region. Shrewd and calculative as he was, King Mahendra also knew his limitations vis-à-vis India and, hence, took timely decisions to pacify the southern neighbor.

Most Western countries prefer liberal democracy in Nepal. They are in common with India on this particular project. Nevertheless, India does not like the active involvement of other powers making Nepal its exclusive domain. Sometimes, India's overbearing attitude has been resented by Nepalis when the Indian policymakers become too transparent in influencing the political developments in Nepal. In the post-2006 Nepal, both India and China have become more active than ever before. Such activities, which are being seen against the background of the rise of China and India, have been able to draw the attention of the world.

Summing Up

The foregoing narrative has tried to present a mixed picture of the Nepali state and democracy. Although some strong foundational values are embedded in the Nepali society that has all along been absorbing epoch-making changes and trends, continuity in such intrinsic strengths may not necessarily be everlasting if the state continues to erode and political institutions do not strike roots and become vulnerable even to the slightest pretext of change.

The Nepali state has retained its essential features such as the army, police, bureaucracy, judiciary, and other agencies, but political mission and strategies are lacking to make it strong and legitimate. Nepalis used to blame the monarchy for all ills they encountered in the past, but now with the monarchy gone, parties themselves are subject to public anger. The Nepali people in general think that parties wage revolution but fail to sustain its gains. It does not mean that the Nepali state is static since a lot of changes are underway even in the midst of political chaos and atmosphere of uncertainty.

Is democracy viable in Nepal? This question needs to be answered against the backdrop of political developments. Though disjointed and unclear, Nepal's changes are both revolutionary and substantive. The Maoists, as other Left parties, have become democratic without ceasing to be Leftists, if one goes by their names and political rhetoric. Democratic values have therefore triumphed but remain blurred in absence of institutionalization. Unless the forces agree to abide by these universally accepted values making them relevant to governance, democratic exercise remains elusive.

2

Nepali State Revisited

Relevance of State

The Nepali state is now under close observation for determining its actual status. Has the state failed? Is it a failing state? Or is it just passing through a temporary phase for becoming a modern "national state" with all attributes of inclusiveness, empowerment of citizens,[1] and better national and international projection of being a democratic state? The shift in political paradigm both nationally and internationally and the declining capacity of the state to cope with such developments have given rise to these questions. Those who were/are accustomed to passing life under the unbroken traditional structures and functions of the state ruled by patrimonial or semi-patrimonial types of rulers and leaders of parties whose clout also did not go beyond the boundary fixed by former type of rulers would not like change. People were forced to live with such patterns until they indentified with the nation-state as their savior and rose in revolt against the rulers. These rulers enjoyed total control over all structures of the state—army, police, bureaucracy, and polity. The Maoist insurgency launched for overthrowing such an "exploitative"

---

[1] T. K. Oommen, "Evolving Inclusive Societies through Constitutions: The Case of Nepal." An unpublished paper presented at a seminar on Social Inclusion Policies in South Asian States (Kathmandu: CNAS, June 25–27, 2009).

state had, for the first time, posed a great challenge because it was a war against the state. The state responded to it with full might under its control and reach, but more than 13,000 Nepalis lost their lives and thousands were rendered homeless or displaced from their homes and villages. Its fallout was also evident in the rise of population in urban areas including the capital, Kathmandu. In the wake of armed insurrection on the one hand and erosion of parties and leaders on the other, people's sufferings increased unabated, spreading an atmosphere of despair and disaffection for the state. Although the Maoist war ended with the signing of peace agreement between the Maoists and the SPA but the degeneration of Nepali state continued unabated in the post-2006 successful mass movement.

The people took part in the CA election with the hope that now onward Nepal would enter into a new era of peace, stability, and progress. However, contrary to such expectations, Nepalis have noticed the decline in the capacity of the state as its writ is beyond repair in an unprecedented manner, producing not only the symptoms of political instability but also of the breakdown of social order.

Whether or not the ongoing Nepali political scenario is comparable to the pangs of changes in other countries of the world, Nepalis also thought that the spectacular changes brought about by the 2006 movement would indeed set to rest the scope of instability and sufferings. Many developing countries of the world "comprise hope more than reality; their citizens often do not belong to a single culture, that is, they are not yet nation states, and they are only in the earliest stages of creating an apparatus of state machinery."[2] In Europe and in other parts of the world also, states have been created out of sheer political ambition of charismatic leaders, military generals, or kings. Many states are the products of conquest and wars that were generally waged for expansionist purposes. In some contexts, however, states are also created by undergoing the processes of legitimization of rulers "through genealogies and marriage alliances, and they set out the process of acculturation

[2] John A. Hall, G. John Ikenberry, *The State* (Delhi: First Indian Reprint, 1997), p. 2.

to Sanskrit culture that became historical change." "The establishing of a state," as Romila Thapar observes, "in the form of a kingdom was necessary not only to asserting power and organizing an administration but also to welding the many diverse groups living in a region."[3] According to Thapar, "Recipients of grants of land were potential founders of dynasties. The requirement of founding a state was therefore not confined to conquest."[4]

Nepal's situation is incomparable because of its own historical trajectory and shifting regimes and political values. Historically grounded analysis and myriad of ideological formations and their convergence in liberal democracy and pluralism have added both complexity and newness to the political dynamics. Sometimes such paradoxical and often contradictory developments also give rise to questions as to how the Nepali state will be able to absorb them. However, these realities will enable us to understand the historical foundations of the Nepali state, its development, present nature, and futuristic perspective.

Generally, the central focus of state is not likely to be replaced even by the great impacts of globalization. As it has been said:

[T]he modernization paradigm takes the *state* as the central unit of analysis. Such issues as integration, nation building, social mobilization and even economic take off are taken to be central social, political and economic processes but they are all, in the final analysis, interpreted through a state-centric optic. That is, the state is taken as a given or an end point; the state is itself is regarded as a constant, not a variable.[5]

The state is traditionally defined on the basis of four elements: territory, sovereignty, government, and population. Without a defined territory

---

[3] Romila Thapar, "The Vamsvali from Chamba: Reflections of a Historical Tradition," The Mahesh Chandra Lecture, Social Science Baha, Kathmandu, October 14, 2009.

[4] Ibid.

[5] Neil Nevitte, "Analysing Intercommoned Conflict: Theoretical Approaches and Comparative Cases" in Dhirendra Vajpeyi and Yogendra K. Malik, eds, *Religious and Ethnic Minority Politics in South Asia* (Delhi: Manohar, 1989), p. 3.

and coercive power, it cannot get its identity. Similarly, for implementing its decisions or policies, it needs to be sovereign, an element which cannot be compromised, though the modern underpinnings demand it to be limited in order to be responsive to the wishes of the people as well as to the international community. It is more so in the case of a weak and small state whose overall maneuverability is limited due to physical location, geopolitical dynamics, and its own inbuilt conditions. Situated between China and India and having intimate relations with the southern neighbors in varied dimensions, Nepal faces enormity of problems and limitations. Although sovereignty in the conventional sense is accepted by recognizing states as sovereign entities of the international order, in practice, however, the hierarchies of states are determined by a number of qualifications. So, it has been said that

> sovereignty is longer what it used to be; the legs of economic, military and cultural self-sufficiency and near autarchy on which it once rested have been one by one and all together broken; sovereignty walks on crutches—lame and wobbly, staggering from one failed fitness to another.[6]

It is a universal phenomenon of the erosion of state and sovereignty. Smaller nations are more seriously facing such crisis of survival against the context of internal uncertainty and effects of globalization. Nepal cannot be an exception to such changes.

Nationally, the Nepali state is being transformed because of new popular demands for inclusiveness, empowerment, distribution of power, and resources through the properly redesigned state structure. All the elements of a nation are being asserted for making the state as truly representative in character. Though it is a daunting task to immediately transform an old semi-feudalistic, centralized state into a new system, the process, though amorphous, has begun after the 2006 Jan Andolan. The composition of the CA and the pressure being exerted on political parties and other agencies to be more inclusive is an indication for change.

[6] Zygmunt Bauman, *In Search of Politics* (Stanford: Stanford University, 1999), p. 40.

Yet, for making inclusive process more qualitative, the policies of the transforming state need to be people-centric so that all deprived or marginalized segments of society could access to power and resources. Given the struggle now underway between two trends of continuity of old semi-feudal structure and orientation of political elites, known as status quoists and pretenders of change, and real change agents, the 2006 movement also seemed to fail to transform fully the existing nature of the Nepali state. So the same political elites who were participants in the movement failed to cope with the new challenges thrown open to them after the movement. As a result, they soon returned to old values in making compromises with those who had perennially resisted the fundamental change in society and polity. It was evident when the leaders of parties did not enforce the decisions recommended by various commissions formed after the movement. All those responsible for violating human rights or who had committed crimes against the opponents of the former regime were now the new darlings in the post-movement politics. Its glaring example was the failure of leaders of parties to accomplish the task of constitution making within the stipulated two-year period. The fear of dominant class and caste groups who also run the governments has stalled the process of change. Parties like the NC and the CPN–UML have shied away from the radical transformation on an egalitarian basis. Although such a phenomenon is not peculiar to Nepal, similar situation prevails in India where "incongruence between a modern state engaged in a secular process of nation building and a highly fragmented society divided on lines of caste, *biradari* (kinship), tribe, religion and region continues to work."[7]

The Nepali political elites have almost forgotten the essence of egalitarian dimensions of democracy. Their preoccupation with getting into state power without being serious on ending the existing exploitative character of the society and state has made them irrelevant to the spirit

[7] Manoranjan Mohanty, "Towards a Creative Theory of Social Transformation" in M. Mohanty, ed., *People's Rights* (Delhi: SAGE Publications, 1998), pp. 15–16.

of the movement. The struggle between the Maoist and other parties is also a reflection of how the elites of "new Nepal" are hesitant to change. If the Maoists are too eager to change the structure of state, other parties are scared of such radical changes. But even in the case of the UCPN (Maoist), it is too early to make any final judgment on its future role. Its overall performance in the post-2006 period does not inspire the general people that it would really take up the agenda of transformation. Its democratic credibility needs to be tested because of its conflicting views on modern liberal democracy. Similarly, the manner in which the Maoist leaders started hobnobbing with the former royalists, calling them as "nationalists," or made compromise for power or conducted the government, making no departure from the past, show that it would be premature to certify them as real protagonists of change. Yet, their contributions to end monarchy as well as to educate the people to be cognizant of their rights should not be undermined. How the Maoists together with other forces would consolidate them within the democratic setup needs to be watched—for, political parties seem to be more concerned with the seizure of power rather than consolidate the gains of the movement. Such a trend has not only dimmed the prospect of democracy but also affected the efficacy of the Nepali state. Failures on all sides—politics, economy, and breakdown in social and regional harmony—have made people more pessimistic about overall prospect of prosperous Nepal. The unfolding developments therefore look paradoxical with trends of change as well as the crisis of institutionalizing democracy.

A Narrative of the Modern Nepali State

The traditional Nepali state suffered a jolt for the first time in 2006 by the awakening of Nepali people. Their demand for being equally treated as citizens at par with other class or high-caste groups, whose overall dominance has had been persistent since the very foundation of the modern Nepali state, had weight. Today it is not only the pressures of ethnics, Dalits, gender, region, and other deprived sections of society but also the poor high-caste Brahmans and Chhetris who want to find their space, though there has been a tendency to put all these have-nots into the same category of haves. Putting all into the same basket of privileged high-caste groups and bashing them in the name of caste, the society seems to be further fragmented rather than become cohesive to stem the multiple crises faced by the country. Politically unstable, economically weak, internationally dependent, coupled with the upsurge of regionalism, parochialism, and sectarianism, how could such a frayed state transform itself into a new order at a time when its own capacity is in question? Does it mean that the Nepali state is really collapsing due to the emergent crises and trend? Its answer would be both positive and negative. From one angle, such problems notwithstanding, capabilities of the Nepali state cannot be minimized. Some of the attributes of its strength are: Rural economy, social tolerance, adaptation to change, modesty and accommodation, and slow but steady economic growth.[8] The social fabric of Nepal is not fragile as many tend to judge against the rise of parochial trends. Political upheavals and ethnic and regional demands have not shattered the solid foundation of society. This is what constitutes the strength of the Nepali society. Yet the question arises, how long can such a foundation continue to absorb the invading negative trends manifest in political sphere? If politics continues to be fragmented and parochial, its impacts on disturbing societal harmony may be strong and insurmountable.

Nepal's present physical form is the product of such expeditions as were launched first by King Prithvi Narayan Shah and, subsequently, by his successors. Although the Nepali religious and cultural traditions had played no less significant role for creating ethnic and cultural mosaic that helped maintain the postconquest period, the political ethos of the conquering rulers however dominated the political landscape throughout the modern Nepali history. Mahesh C. Regmi attributes to the "social and economic motivations for the creation of the Gorkhali Empire." It became an empire due to integration of numerous principalities then spread over in the west and east. The empire can only be created after

---

[8] See Krishna Hachhethu, *State Building in Nepal: Creating a Functional State* (Kathmandu: Enabling State Programme, 2009), p. 13.

making a state, as had happened to the creation of what we understand today as Nepal. The conquest of the Kathmandu valley, which was/is endowed with a rich cultural heritage and civilization, was the greatest achievement of Prithvi Naryan Shah whose mission of making greater Nepal did not stop till he reached out to the western and eastern small kingdoms and tribe-dominated regions. So, Regmi describes the Nepali state as an "Empire" because:

> the term is used to describe a state of vast size composed of more or less distinct national units and subject to a single centralized will. That is today, it denotes an expansionist attempt or policy by one state or some of its citizens to influence, exploit, and dominate the people of another, usually weaker country by overt or covert political, military and economic and cultural means.[9]

The incorporation of Gorkhali language and religious traditions was simultaneously imposed on the rest of the communities. Although non-Hindu religions, culture, and languages were allowed informally, they were subordinate to the main Hinduized religious tradition, Gorkhali language, or Khaskura, which came with the victorious rulers, the Gorkhalis. Not only the Newars of Kathmandu valley but other tribes and communities across the newly integrated territories fell into the homogenized state-protected religion, culture, and other forms of socioeconomic systems, which perpetuated the built-in disparity gaps between the privileged and underprivileged caste groups, regions, gender, and the Dalit.

The process of assimilation, thus, fitted into the Gorkhali agenda of domination by one group of people over the other insofar as the character of the modern Nepali state was concerned. Stretching this trend further, the Mulki Ain (Legal Code) of 1854, enforced by the first Rana Prime Minister Jang Bahadur, "placed all castes of comparable status of the hills higher in status than similar caste groups among the Newars and the Tarai Hundus." Prayag Raj Sharma further states:

[9] Drawing on Dan Schmidt and Wolfgang, J. Mommsen's definition from their article "Imperialism" published in *Marxism, Communism and Western Society: A Comparative Encyclopedia*, 1973, Vol. 4, p. 211, Regmi has tried to use it in the Nepali context. See Mahesh C. Regmi, *Emperial Gorkha* (Delhi: Adroit Publishers, 1999), pp. xi–xii.

The Newar Malla rulers of Nepal were the people who first seem to have devised a complete social system in the 14th century. The caste hierarchy under this system is still followed intact among the Newar society today. The code of 1854 has partly adopted this hierarchy.[10]

The preunification Nepal indeed had provided a rich cultural heritage, which is still embedded in today's cultural activities. Religious tolerance, people's adoptability, and resilience are some of the strongest bonds of social harmony and secularization. One of the glaring examples of such resiliency is the peaceful change of Nepal from a Hindu state into a secular state after the parliament and later the CA made a decision unanimously in 2008. Such a resolution was in accord with the spirit of the 2006. Although some obscurantist elements not reconciled to such transformation have raised the voice of holding referendum on the issues of the end of monarchy, secularism, and federalism, it was nothing more than an attempt to reverse the processes of change.

Coming in the wake of making a new Nepal and also taking into account the obstructionist role of monarchy toward democracy building, the resolution of the abolition of monarchy was also taken without any popular resentment. The 240-year-old monarchy was identified with Hindu religion and hierarchical caste and class structures and was considered to be an integral part of the very existence of the Nepali state. But when the popularly elected CA took a decision, no Nepali citizens shed tears on it. On the contrary, monarchy itself had lost its legitimacy by going against the verdicts of the people time and again. King Mahendra's coup in 1960 against the Parliament and elected government and the imposition of a partyless regime on the country and later similar repetition by his son Gyanendra in 2005 and other obstructionist roles played by monarchy drove the Nepali people to abolish the monarchy itself. Such drastic changes had been taken with the backing of the people.

---

[10] Prayag Raj Sharma, "Nepali Culture and Society: Reflections on Some Historical Currents" in Kamal P. Malla, ed., *Nepal: Perspective on Continuity and Change* (Kathmandu: CNAS, 1989), pp. 163–164. See also John Whelpton, *A History of Nepal* (Indian edn, 2005); Krishna Hachhethu, *State Building in Nepal: Creating a Functional State* (Kathmandu: ESP, 2009).

My point here is to stress the strength of Nepali society and people who are least influenced by religious and cultural rigidity. Nor have they ever become religious fanatics killing each other within the same state boundary. Despite such positive aspects of the fabric of Nepali society, the state was based on narrow religion and class, though class in the strictly defined Marxian economic context was not possible, given the lack of economic infrastructure needed to divide people into classes. Marginally, however, the members of the Rana family and a small section of Nepali people, favored by the rulers, had the advantage of becoming rich. It was in essence a patrimonial system, which went on combining the elements of patrimonial and oligarchic systems.

So caste, one religion, and social practices, which were considered unifying for over 240 years, have now been challenged with the increased awareness of various communities. The policies of the state, which were nothing more than the means of exclusion of various communities and poor people from even minor posts and status, projected the Nepali state as exploitative both in nature and functions. The hierarchy of caste was not only a social phenomenon reinforced by both the Shah and Rana rulers but it also gave an economic dimension to it as land and taxation systems were accordingly determined in terms of caste and class.

Even language (Nepali) is identified with certain *parbate* (hill caste groups, Brahman, and Chhetri) because of the patronage received by this language from the Nepali rulers till today. The recent controversy over oath taking in Hindi by the Vice President Parmananda Jha is a case in point. Jha, a Tarai Maithil Brahman, took his oath of office in Hindi contrary to the interpretation of Supreme Court that a president or vice president was required to use Nepali as per annexure 1 (ka) of the Interim Constitution (2006). It may be recalled that this provision nowhere mentions Nepali language to be used by the president and vice president. It simply mentions the format prepared in Nepali.[11] Such format could also be translated into other languages for convenience.

[11] See articles 36 cha and 36 Jha connected with sub-clause (2) of the Interim Constitution 2007 (2063 VS), p. 87.

When this case was brought into the Supreme Court to determine whether or not a person could take oath of office and secrecy in Hindi, the apex court in its judgment stated that since Nepali is the constitutionally prescribed language for taking such oath of office and secrecy, Jha was mandated to take fresh oath of office in order to honor the constitution. Again with a view to reprimanding the defiant Vice President Jha, a full bench of the Supreme Court issued another order to retake the oath in Nepali within a week, failing to obey which Jha would cease to remain the vice president.[12] However, Jha defied the order repeating it as a "prejudiced verdict" handed down to him by the alleged enmity of the chief justice who sat on giving the verdict. It seemed that the language issue was being seen politically thus prompting most Tarai parties and the Maoists to back Jha for defiance. Nevertheless, a solution was found that allowed Jha to take oath in his own mother tongue, Maithili, thus avoiding the controversy over Hindi.

In a multilingual state like Nepal, the makers of the Nepali constitutions since 1951 have invariably put Nepali as the only official language. Although in parliamentary deliberations, Hindi was used by the members in the former parliament in the 1990s despite official ban on using it. The speaker kept it in low profile by ignoring such deliberations in order not to hurt the sentiment of the Tarai people. In the Interim Legislature Parliament, the two terms used for satisfying the ego of the Maoists, who opposed the word "parliament," and other parties that wanted to retain it (parliament), Hindi has been used by the Madhese parties (Tarai parties) in order to show their separate identity from the *parbate* language or a language of the hill people.

Language is both a creator and destroyer of a nation-state. The story of Bangladesh begins with the language issue. In 1948, immediately after the Partition of India, Mohammad Ali Jinnah, the architect of Pakistan, triggered off the controversy when he said in Dhaka, East Pakistan, that Urdu would be the national language of Pakistan. As the then East Pakistan/today's Bangladesh was/is predominantly a Bengali-speaking area, the Bengali nationalism fed principally by language and

[12] *The Kathmandu Post*, August 24, 2009.

culture, went beyond the parameters set by the rulers of West Pakistan. So the power of religion was belittled by the power of language nationalism that eventually led to the emergence of a new republic of Bangladesh.

A small incident or speech can sow the seeds of disintegration as is witnessed in the world. In South Asia, Sri Lanka's long ethnic war in fact originated from the language issue. Although it has been suppressed after 27 years or so, the enormity of the crises has been devastating. Many other countries of the world have passed through such traumas of nation building. Nepal has still maintained the ethnic harmony despite some outpourings against Nepali language, caste-dominated social structure, and feudalistic norms rampant in the Nepali rulers and in other types of socioeconomic relationships. Nevertheless, ethnic ideology and regional sentiments rose sharply during and after the 2006 movement and the complaints or even anger are not wholly unjustifiable. Since the state was identified with a particular set of rulers or dynasties, the deprived sections of society continue to be resentful against the hegemony of a few haves.

The Hindi language, despite its rejection by the rulers and other Nepali-speaking elites of Nepal, has continued to dominate the agenda of Tarai politics. First, in the 1950s, the Tarai Congress led by late Vedananda Jha demanded that Hindi be used as one of the national languages. It was resisted by the hill people branding it as an Indian language, which had nothing to do with Nepali people. In the 1980s, this issue came up sharply following the creation of Nepal Sadbhawana Parishad led by Gajendra Narayan Singh. It was subsequently transformed into a political party—Nepal Sadbhawana Party—following the lifting of ban on outlawed parties in 1990. Frederick H. Gaige, an American scholar, who had conducted a fieldwork in the 1960s, in his book *Regionalism and National Unity in Nepal* shows the importance of Hindi in the day-to-day life of the people in Tarai. He writes:

> Hindi is important in the Tarai because of its use as a second language by plains people who need to communicate across regional language barriers. It is the language in which business activity is carried on throughout most of the Gangetic plain, and it is used in the Tarai wherever itinerant traders or craftsmen meet the local people. One hears Hindi spoken in the village markets and in the streets of

the towns. It is the language used by the Tarai villagers when they travel to India, a relatively frequent experience for many who visit relatives or attend religious festivals.[13]

Hindi is spoken and understood across the country due to close contacts between the Nepalis and the north Indians. Moreover, exposures to Hindi films, radios (now television), and other forms of mass communication and contacts have made Hindi popular in Nepal.

Thus, internally, the Nepali state went on following a culture of homogenization of society and politics; externally, the state-led nationalism embarked on giving a separate political identity with which Nepal could jostle with other powers of the world. The Treaty of Sugauli was one of the major events for giving such an identity despite the compromise made under the duress of the victor, the British. Loss of the territory west of Kali (Mahakali) and some big chunk of the western Tarai and territory east of Mechi River was a major setback to the "Gorkhalis." Moreover, the Treaty could "cripple the Nepalese military power" by securing for the British some useful roads, especially the area across the Mahakali River. It has been said that these "territorial sacrifices were the necessary conditions of peace."[14] Though the Nepali rulers knew that it was a dictated treaty, they reconciled to it knowing the limitation of Nepal. This was also a signal of the rise of an imperial power in the south along with the decline of the Chinese power until its reemergence in 1949.

During the post-1816 period, the British needed to be concerned with the Chinese while the Nepali rulers, the Rana oligarchs, were also at ease with the protection of the southern power. No further expansionist expedition was taken by the Rana rulers nor did they go beyond the limitations dictated by the new realities. The family oligarchy produced kleptocracy by amassing wealth for the entire generations of Rana

[13] See Frederick H. Gaige, *Regionalism and National Unity in Nepal* (Kathmandu: Himal Books, 2009), p. 118.

[14] Ramakant, *Indo-Nepalese Relations 1816–1877* (Delhi: S. Chand & Co., 1968), p. 39.

family members but, at the same time, also provided stability without progress. As it has been stated:

> The Ranas wanted the British support to keep their hold on the Darbar against their rival factions and perpetuate their feudal system of exploiting the people of Nepal. And in this direction they received a ready support from the English Government in exchange of pro-British policy and the Gorkha recruits. The integrity and the seemingly independence status of Nepal could also be preserved, but, in reality, Nepal was well within the broad framework of the English imperial interests and always followed the line of foreign policy as suggested by the Indian Government.[15]

The 1923 Treaty concluded between British-India and Nepal further guaranteed Nepal's "independence" in "unequivocal" term. Projecting Nepal as an independent sovereign country before the world, the Rana rulers applied for the membership of the UN in 1948 but failed to be admitted into the world body due to the Soviet veto maintaining that Nepal was not an independent nation as required for the UN membership. Subsequently, the document prepared by the Rana government strongly refuted the charge giving full account of the attributes of an independent nation. Nevertheless, admission to the UN became an uphill task for an independent state, and it could get the membership only in 1955. Later, Nepal became the member of the Security Council twice. Its contribution to UN Peacekeeping Operations has had been acclaimed by the UN with Nepal sending troops to the UN peacekeeping missions regularly.

The question of independence and sovereignty is more clearly articulated by the Treaty of Peace and Friendship of 1950 concluded between the postcolonial government of India headed by Jawaharlal Nehru and the outgoing Rana rulers of Nepal. As the treaties and other factors concerning Nepal's external status would be dealt with separately in the next chapter, it was, however, a confirmation of Nepal's limitations on its foreign and security policies. So even being independent and sovereign, nation-states need to be concerned about their limitations in conducting

---

[15] Ibid., p. 357.

the affairs of the state. In addition, many other factors, both positive and negative, work for determining the strengths and weaknesses of a state. The following section would therefore raise some of such factors, which I call competitive structures.

Competitive Structures of State

Royal Nepal Army

Nepali state had remained cohesive and stable until quite recently. However, the scenario is now changed with the emergence of multiple forces and competing state structures. Its cohesiveness so far maintained by force or by the myth of monarchy—that it was the most effective unifying force—has now been shattered. Even during the so-called constitutional monarchical period (1991–2006), state structures themselves worked as rivals. The role of the RNA, now the NA, was always perceived as deterministic in view of its alliance with the monarchy. Anything related to the RNA was decided by the Palace, and not by the decision of governments either appointed by the king or elected by the people. In the post-1951 Nepal, until the end of monarchy, RNA continued to be the main component of the Nepali state. The RNA had been used to quell the NC insurgency in the early 1960s but the Palace and the RNA put certain conditions before the elected government for the mobilization of the army against the Maoists. They were national consensus, a state of emergency, and an antiterrorist law.

At the outset of the Maoist insurgency in Nepal, a former home minister and some former army generals were of the view that the fire of insurgency could be extinguished within weeks if the army were released from the barracks. Contrarily,

... the bushfire of insurgency has spread to engulf the state. The army stayed inactive and completely uninvolved in the bloody fracas burgeoning in the country for the six years between February 1996 and November 2001. Since then, even after three years of counter-insurgency mobilization of the security forces and over a year after putting the country under the Unified Military Command prioritizing national security, the state remains paralyzed and its military power imperfect, despite being far superior to the forces of insurgency both in men and material.[16]

Accusing the army of not assisting the police while they were fighting the Maoists in Dolpa, Home Minister Govinda Raj Joshi questioned the purpose of maintaining state army if it did not help the government during crisis.[17] The elected governments headed by the NC leaders, G. P. Koirala and Sher Bahadur Deuba, were also under the RNA pressure not to create an Armed Police Force (APF) independent of the army. Realizing the noncooperation of the army to the government, the NC-led government thought of creating the APF to tackle the growing Maoist menace, which was spreading across nook and corner of the country. It is said: "When the Nepali Congress government realized that the Royal Nepal Army (RNA) and the King were reluctant to get involved in the Maoists' activities, this security organ was established."[18]

Considering the ARF as yet another security agency that would belittle the importance of the army, the RNA eventually agreed on its formation under the Unified Military Command (UMC) of the army. Formed on November 4, 2003, it was defined as a concept "to gain optimum use of capabilities and resources of various security forces" from top to the district level under it.[19] Since it was a paramilitary force,

---

[16] See Dhruba Kumar, "Military Dimensions of the Maoist Insurgency" in Lok Raj Baral, ed., *Nepal Facets of Maoist Insurgency* (Delhi: Adroit Publishers in collaboration with Nepal Centre for Contemporary Studies, Kathmandu, 2006), p. 87.

[17] See *Nepal Press Digest*, Vol. 44: 40, October 2, 2000; and Lok Raj Baral, "Nepal in 2000: Discourse of Democratic Consolidation," *Asian Survey*, XLI, 1, January/February: 2001; and Dhrubahari Adhikakri, "Ke Sena Bhumikabihin Janashakti Ho?" [Is the Army a Public Force without a Role?] *Bimarsha Weekly*, Kathmandu, November 10, 2000; and Bishwanath Upadhaya's interview in *Kantipur Daily*, October 2, 2000.

[18] See Deepak Prakash Bhatt, "Public Security Challenges and the Effective Mobilisation of Law-enforcement Agencies" in Rajan Bhattarai and Rosy Cave, eds, *Changing Security Dynamics in Nepal* (Kathmandu: Nepal Institute for Policy Studies and Safeworld, London, n.d.), p. 123.

[19] See Indra Adhikari, "Nepal: Trends of Militarization (1996–2005)," *Nepali Journal of Contemporary Studies*, (NCCS), Kathmandu, 8, 2, September: 2008, p. 72.

it received kinds of weapons as desired by the army. And the kinds of weapons to be given to the ARF could be decided by the army. Since the ill-equipped civilian police were untrained in military warfare and since heavy casualties were recorded during the counter-Maoist operations, ARF was expected to play the role of a well-trained armed force for combat operations.

The failure of intelligence, army, and other organs of government became common in the wake of Maoist insurgency. Raising the controversy over the role of army, the general secretary of the CPN–UML said that the army should be under the control of the government. Although the Defense Ministry headed by Prime Minister Koirala tried to cover the story of army's noncooperation to the government, the resignation of the Prime Minister shortly thereafter on the same grounds of noncooperation of the RNA suggested that the latter was in fact under the control of the Palace. When Gyanendra pushed all political parties to the brink by imposing a state of emergency and by taking all powers into his hand, Koirala opened his mouth in 2002 at a Nepal Centre for Contemporary Studies (NCCS) program in Dhulikhel that the emergency rule was imposed by the army under army's own terms and conditions to which the king complied.

Following the Maoist attack on the army camp in Dang in November 2001, the government, headed by Deuba, used the army after it fulfilled the three conditions put forth by the RNA before. In addition, the army demanded an infrastructural development in the Maoist-affected areas in the western hills in order to project its good image before the people.

Since the Palace itself was engaged in secret negotiations with the Maoist leaders who, after the assassination of King Birendra and his entire family members on June 1, 2001, disclosed that they and the former king were in contacts for finding out a negotiated settlement of the insurgency.[20] It may be recalled that King Birendra and later King Gyanendra were not at ease with the curtailment of powers of the monarchy arranged under the 1990 Constitution. Although the 1990 change

---

[20] See Baburam Bhattarai, "Aghosit Karyagat Ekata" [Undisclosed Working Relationship], *Kantipur*, Kathmandu, June 4, 2001.

was made on the basis of the tripartite agreement between the king, the NC, and the ULF, all the three forces violated the spirit of the Constitution that stipulated a constitutional monarchy à la British model. In actual practice, however, it was a semi-constitutional monarchy with some special constitutional prerogatives granted to the king. Fearing the interventionist role of the Palace and thinking that the army was under its command, leaders of political parties did not venture to take any independent decision on Palace and the army. Taking it as a cue, the army seemed to influence even the constitution-making process in 1990. Prompted by the Palace, accompanied by some other generals, the commander-in-chief went to see the interim prime minister, K. P. Bhattarai, to force him to accept Nepal as a Hindu state, with King as the supreme commander of the army under whose control the RNA could function.[21]

If somebody raised any question or made some inquiries into the army, the elected government leaders avoided such remarks terming them as "sensitive." Any political persons or researcher who wanted to know about the army was/is still denied his/her right. In fact, the Nepali state continues to be dominated by military dimension as of today because the controversy over army versus other structures makes regular headlines. The leaders of political parties, except the Maoists, felt that the army should be cultivated in order to make democracy work. What was more perplexing was that all prime ministers with the exception of Man Mohan Adhikari of the CPN–UML kept defense portfolio with themselves, regarding it as the most "sensitive" organ of the government because of it being an arm of the king. For satisfying the king, the prime ministers made deals with the army by conceding most of its demand. The whopping increase in the defense budget as well as the phenomenal rise in number of defense personnel was done on the grounds of containing if not defeating the Maoists guerrillas. Within a short span of 10 years, the size of the RNA rose to 97,000 from about 45,000 in 1990, hoping for an increase up to 1,200,000 as some former generals of the RNA had suggested during the Maoist insurgency.

---

[21] *Nepal Press Digest*, 34: 29, July 16, 1990.

The military and Nepali state were organic to each other. Nepal was indeed a military state because it was the mainstay of political power. All the Rana family members received military titles from their birth, and some of the Chhetri family members, who acted as courtiers, were appointed in junior military positions by the Ranas. Such a tradition could only be broken for the first time by the appointment of a *janjati* (ethnic community) Chhatra Man Gurung as the COAS in 2009, following the retirement of the controversial COAS Katawal. It is said that the "history of Nepal, in one sense, is largely a history of the RNA."[22] In 2009, International Crisis Report writes that the Nepali army "envisages a powerful role at the heart of the state, formally advising on any matter tangentially related to national security through powerful army-dominated institutions and informally advising politicians on all fundamental policy issues."[23]

The change in 2006 has definitely curtailed its unchallenged role in determining the politics of the country. The fear psychosis that haunts the politicians because of their own lack of confidence and perhaps due to much interventionist role of some external powers for keeping the army as an effective deterrent to the Maoist power in the country is not yet fully under the control of elected government. In the absence of the king, leaders of political parties, except the Maoists, seemed to encourage the president to put the army under its command. The conflict between the Maoist-led coalition government in the post-2007 CA election and the COAS leading to the resignation of the government suggested that the spirit of the old Palace politics was being replayed in the new context. Since the prime minister wanted to remove the Army Chief Rukmangud Katawal on the grounds of his defiance of the government order and also because of his utterances trying to mobilize the

---

[22] See the *Nepalese Army: A Force with History Ready for Tomorrow* (Kathmandu: 2008). Despite the transformation of the RNA into the NA in 2006 by the Interim Parliament, politicians have not yet come over their inherited mindset that the army ruled the roost.

[23] See International Crisis Group Policy Report, 2009, *Nepal Future: In Whose Hands?* (Brussels: August 13, 2009), p. 15.

non-Maoist parties for not accepting the Maoist agenda of integration of the Maoist guerrillas into the NA, the other coalition partners and non-Maoist parties went to the Presidential Palace to urge him not to accept the prime minister's move for sacking the army chief. It was alleged that the president was also acting at the behest of both the parties and some foreign powers who wanted to frustrate the alleged Maoist agenda of "controlling the army." The president, instead, sent a letter to Katawal to continue in office as before despite the prime minister's order of termination of his service.

In the history of Nepal, hardly a situation such as this had occurred with the two COASs, one appointed by the government and the other by the president, sitting in the same building. But after the presidential letter, the government appointee, Lieutenant General Kul Bahadur Khadka quietly opted out, while Katawal continued. Later, addressing the Parliament, Prachanda said that he preferred to resign in order to avoid the bloodshed in the country, which the retrogressive and pro–status quoits forces wanted to unleash in the name of thwarting the Maoist design of capturing total power.[24] In this context, one of the top generals confided to the author that the army had been politicized by General Katawal who did not miss any opportunity to mobilize leaders of national parties and foreign elements for his survival. Fearing that the Maoists would establish control over the army, leaders of parties favored the army chief. They (parties), therefore, took the shelter of the president and through him of General Katawal. It was also a blessing in disguise for those who wanted to see the rift between the Maoists and other parties. The intrepid handling of the situation by the Maoist leaders were no less responsible for creating a mess, but its agenda of putting the army under "civilian supremacy," though a contested issue among the political parties and others, would be a live agenda for the future.

It could be observed that some COASs in the post-1990 change, particularly in the context of the Maoist insurgency, made such statements that contrasted with the government. The prime ministers and the other leaders of parties could not dare to take the bull by its horns fearing that

[24] See *Indian Express*, May 7, 2009.

the king and army alliance would go against them. After 2006, fearing a backlash, Prime Minister Koirala, who headed the Interim Government until the CA election, appointed Katawal as the COAS, contrary to his tainted image of being an accomplice for the royal regime as well as for the violation of human rights during the Moist insurgency. Katawal, during his farewell speech (he retired on September 9, 2009), did not miss to warn that there could be no politicization of the Nepali army in the name of "integration," nor could any party's doctrine be imposed on the NA. He had all along been repeating during his tenure as COAS that the NA would only, as in the past, honor the legitimate authority and work for safeguarding national sovereignty, territorial integrity, and democracy.[25] But the track record of the army until the 2006 change was just opposite to it.

The issue of legitimacy today centers on "popular legitimacy" or "rational-legal" legitimacy that is derived from the sovereign people. The 1990 Constitution had only theoretical acceptance of Nepali people as sovereign as it simultaneously restricted the power of the people on the question of monarchy. The four preconditions—monarchy, sovereignty of people, multiparty system, and freedoms—could not be altered by the Parliament, thus, recognizing the king as one of the power centers as per the compromise reached between the NC, the ULF, and the king. As a result, leaders of political parties looked upon the Palace for guidance or even for intervention. The RNA could naturally find the king as the power center contrary to much-touted claim that it was constitutional monarchy. In fact, the veto power used by the king and the abuse of Article 127, which was related to remove inconveniences while implementing the constitution, proved that monarchy backed by the army ruled the roost. Such steps could have been possible due to the weaknesses of political parties that always tended to miss the opportunities to

---

[25] See *Himalayan Times* and *Rajdhani Dailies*, September 6, 2009. Criticizing the outgoing general for his uncalled-for sermon, the *Annapurna Post* (daily) wrote an editorial that the farewell speech tried to open the old wound instead of healing it. It would only establish the fact that the NA was still not reconciled to the change process. See *Annapurna Post*, September 6, 2009.

assert when the actual crunch came. In fact, the politicians themselves goaded the king to embark on political adventurism. In the given context too, history may repeat with different excuses and interpretations of such words as "legitimate authority," "accountability," "order," and "nationalism."

The language used by the army chief that the latter would obey the "legitimate and accountable" authority was ambiguous. Did the army carry out the order given by the Defense Ministry not to make fresh recruitment in the army? Did it get any political mandate to recommend the holding of referendum on issues such as Hindu state to the CA? Has the army chief the right to say that the president could only dismiss him from office only on the basis of his being the "supreme commander" of the army? Is it not a blatant lie that the army in Nepal has always followed the policy of integration since its organization? How could the outgoing COAS challenge the popular legitimacy of the CA stating that "unless a stable government is formed through the general election, the NA should not be disturbed?"[26] It meant that the CA, which had been popularly elected to make a new constitution and which also abolished monarchy, was, in the general's view, incapable of taking any decision on the restructuring of the NA. Nor could the peace process that entails the supervision, integration, and rehabilitation of the Maoist combatants numbering 19,602 (verified figure by the United Nations Mission in Nepal [UNMIN]) be possible. One of the main objectives of the new peace process and restructuring of the state is democratization and "right sizing" of the NA. Yet, since the Interim Constitution was written in haste and amidst the wrangling of the SPA and the CPN (Maoist), it is full of ambiguities. It does not spell out how such underlined objective would be fulfilled within a timeframe (two years) set by them. Thanks to the interparty conflicts and cabinet heterogeneity, the army chief had been able to assert in such a language. Later, it was proved that the interparty conflicts and lust for power prompted the parties to extend the term of the CA for another year.

---

[26] See the speech of the outgoing COAS in *Rajdhani Daily*, September 6, 2009.

Interestingly, however, the new COAS, Chhatra Man Singh Gurung, departed from his predecessor when he, in course, briefing the prime minister, said that it was up to the political leadership to take decisions on the issue of integration and on other areas pertaining to the NA, without, however, belittling the professionalism of the army. Thus, he skillfully seemed to accept the much-touted "civilian supremacy" for which the prime minister had to resign.

Regarding the supervision, integration, and rehabilitation of the Maoist ex-combatants, the Article 146 of the Interim Constitution (Sixth Amendment) (2063 VS) reads: "The Council of Ministers shall form a Special Committee to supervise, integrate and rehabilitate the combatants of the Maoist army."[27] But this committee never took initiative to discharge its functions as stipulated in the Constitution. None of the three prime ministers—G. P. Koirala, Pushpa Kamal Dahal Prachanda, and Madhav Kumar Nepal—of the NC, UCPN (Maoist), and the CPN–UML, respectively, did show any enthusiasm to complete the process even when they knew that both the constitution making and peace process would not be complete without undertaking the task of integration. Then who should be blamed but the indifference of all leaders to making a new constitution? Lack of homogeneity within the cabinet and the manifest army assertiveness to set its agenda on the issue also led to the delay of the integration process.

The socialization of army officers, specially the top brass, and the former RNA's direct connection with the Palace did work as a barrier to make military as inclusive and responsible to the civilian authority. In a successful democracy, the army cannot use veto power for influencing its decision. If a general does not support the policy of the elected government, he has to quit his post. It does not mean that the army has no role to play for devising strategy and policies for meeting the national objective. It has been said that the COAS, General Manik Shah of India, could prevail on Prime Minister Indira Gandhi for postponing the Indian

[27] See *Nepalko Antarim Sambhidhan 2063* (With Sixth Amendments) (Kathmandu: Ministry of Law, Justice and Management of Constitutional Assembly, 2007).

military action against Pakistan until the dawn of winter. Prime Minister Gandhi wanted to take action much early, which, given the physical location of East Pakistan (now Bangladesh), from weather point of view, was not favorable for the target to be fulfilled. Thus, the war for the liberation of Bangladesh started in December 1970, and became successful to create a new republic by chopping off the eastern wing of Pakistan.

The record of the RNA for violation of human rights and for committing atrocities against the citizens had outraged the international community at large. Human rights organizations both inside and outside the country and other state agencies did come out with strong statements in pointing out such gross violations. The US Department of State stated that the RNA was responsible for a number of killings, including deaths in custody in which torture was credibly alleged the RNA continued to kill civilians telling lie that all those killed were Maoists.[28] The National Human Rights Commission of Nepal has also published occasional reports about the killings and other forms of harassment committed both by the RNA and the Maoists. During the Maoist insurgency, the figures of death were uneven with the RNA killing totaling 8,377 people, and the Maoists taking lives of 4,970.[29]

Nevertheless, the positive side of the RNA's role has been appreciated in connection of the two movements—1990 and 2006. It has been said, though unverified, that the army was partly responsible for not shedding blood during the peak hour of the 1990 movement as well as in 2006 Jan Andolan II that could prompt the king to yield to the popular demands, which in the latter's case, also led to the abolition of monarchy itself. With the monarchy sidelined, the RNA (now the NA) shifted its loyalty to the new political forces. Such a shift also proved to be beneficial for holding election to the CA and experimenting with the first Maoist-led government mandated by the people through the CA election.

---

[28] US Department of State, 2003: 3 as cited in Dhruba Kumar, "Emergency, Militarization and the Question of Democratic Recovery" in Lok Raj Baral, ed., *Nepal: Quest for Participatory Democracy* (Delhi: Adroit Publishers, 2006), p. 172.

[29] See INSEC Report of 2005 and 2007. Among those killed, 820 and 193 women were respectively killed by the state and the Maoists. For a more detailed figure of various categories of people killed by the state and the Maoists, see *Nepal Human Development Report 2009* (Kathmandu: UNDP, 2009), pp. 136–137.

However, the army–Maoist relations soured soon partly due to the Maoist mishandling and partly to the alleged disobedience of the COAS on many tangled issues, such as "monitoring," "integration," and "rehabilitation" of the Maoist combatant. Since the very word "integration" into the army has/had been resisted by the NA and non-Maoist parties for fear of Maoist domination in the army, the issue is becoming complex in the context of constitution making by the CA. Yet, the six-point agreement reached between the SPA and the Maoists on November 7, 2006, and the Comprehensive Peace Agreement of November 22, 2006, have categorically mentioned three bases to which some senior politicians, including G. P. Koirala, tried to reinterpret in their own terms. They say that in no circumstances can the Maoist combatants be integrated into the army but can only be absorbed in different other sectors, while the Maoists insisted on integrating the combatants into the army partly or wholly depending on the qualifications fixed by the appropriate committee.

The other agencies of the state are the police and the APF. The former number 56,000 and the latter are manned by 25,000. The government seems to be bent on increasing the strength of both the forces in order to establish law and order and create a climate of peace and security. Parties have invariably tried to politicize the police and other agencies of the state. Any government that comes to power starts reshuffling the police officers for various reasons. Conceivably, they run after politicians for favor. It has been alleged that financial deals are also generally involved. Most want to be in good places so that they could amass wealth any means. The Nepali press reports are full of such stories as even in smuggling, drug, and women trafficking, crimes of all sorts, police in one form or other are involved. Criminals, unscrupulous traders, and politicians work in tandem for enhancing such trends.

Politicians still think that if both the administration and police help them to win elections from the first-past-the-post system (direct election), it becomes easy for them to reciprocate. That is why every party takes the Home Ministry before the election. The two local elections held in the 1990s under the two different governments were better examples to prove the hypothesis just presented before. The first local-level election was held under the NC government, which was in a majority after the 1991 parliamentary election and had won 57 percentage posts in district, municipal, and village units. In 1997–1998, the second election held under the coalition government whose home minister was from CPN–UML had been able to trounce the NC by more than 57 percent. It had been observed that the home minister was hell-bent on maximizing the posts for his own party.

Although the situation has changed to some extent after the introduction of the proportional representation system and beginning of coalition politics, the Home Ministry continues to be one of the prime posts for any party. Education, which is so vital for the overall development of the country, remains the most neglected domain for political leaders and, hence, the education minister is invariably nominated from among the lesser political personalities. Hounded by the public and pressed by the politicians, the police in general are demoralized. If the senior officers manipulate good postings, the lower police personnel are ill-fed and clothed. Stories are often circulated in the local press that almost all police officers serving in the districts came to Kathmandu after the Maoists left the government in 2009, and a new coalition government headed by the CPN–UML leader, Madhav Kumar Nepal, took over. The beeline made by the police officers was simply a manifestation of how the Nepali state is run. Most of them thought that without camping in the capital and lobbying for good postings and promotion, they would be left out. Politicized for wrong reasons, almost all political parties are guided by partisan spirit as well as by the system of *bhansun* (to influence the concerned authorities through various sources). The *bhansun*, which in popular parlance is also called "source and force," is the most effective means of getting favor from authorities. In normal political science term, it is a patronage route which can be applicable to politics, bureaucracy, military, and police, and in all organs of government and semigovernment agencies. It is the legacy of patrimonial system and today's "political feudalism" that gets high premium in the politics of developing countries.[30] In such systems, irrational judgment rather than the criteria of achievement or performance reign supreme.

[30] Writing editorially on the campaign for the politics of inheritance in Andhra Pradesh following the death of Chief Minister Rajasekhara Reddy, the *Hindu* used this term. It opposed the manner in which an orchestrated campaign was launched to anoint the 36-year-old son of the deceased chief minister.

See *The Hindu*, Delhi, September 5, 2009.

During the Rana regime, administration and politics were inseparable as all appointments, promotion, and dismissals were carried out by the Rana rulers, and those who performed *chakari* and appeased the Ranas were rewarded. Although the Ranas plundered the poor country for amassing wealth, they had also set some norms for maintaining administrative purity. While appointing and reshuffling the government servants, the officials were administered the oath by making them put their hands on their heads by touching *saligram* (a religious stone found in rivers of Nepal), copper, and *Tulasi* (sacred plant for the Hindus).[31] Nevertheless, the government officials and the police, who were regarded with awe by the ordinary people, used to take *ghoosh* (bribe). Since they were poorly paid by the state, the people bribed the authorities for getting things done. Such a practice still continues in the 21st century Nepal. Now both the politicians and administrative agencies have encouraged in various forms graft, scandals, commission, and bribery, making the entire political processes corrupt.[32] All such negative phenomena have, thus, worked as termite for decay in the Nepali state.

The issue of competing agencies might not be fully applicable to the case of police and bureaucracy, but they are also responsible for breeding corruption, stalling the development works, and for harassment of ordinary people. Although it is not their fault in view of the vitiated political environment and inherited mindset and practices, the making of a *nouveau riche* and the petty bourgeoisie is possible due the combination of all elements belonging to politics, bureaucracy, security forces, business sectors, people working in nongovernmental organizations (NGOs), and international nongovernmental organizations (INGOs). Remittances from overseas Nepali workers have also contributed to change the lifestyle of a tiny section of the population. This is how Nepal is governed, and this aspect would be dealt with in greater details in other chapters.

[31] See Bhim Bahadur Pandey, *Tyash Bakhatko Nepal Part 2* (Then Nepal) (Kathmandu: TU, Centre for Nepal and Asian Studies), p. 212.

[32] For all kinds of scandals, stories of corruptions including the sale and purchase of the members of Parliament for garnering votes, use of money power during elections, and others, see *Sushashan Barsha Pustak 2006* (Good Governance Book 2006) (Kathmandu: Remac Nepal, 2007).

Non-state Actors

In the present world, state as the principal actor is facing stiff challenges from different areas. It is no more a monolithic agency that dominates politics, society, economy, and other fields. Nationally, the state is under tremendous pressure due to political disorder; social dislocation caused by intra-country and international migrations; rise of subnational and regional aspirations; violence triggered off for political, ethnical and regional, and even sectarian reasons; and crises of governance and decline of political ideology. International interventions, increased dependency on external resources for running the state, and growing nexus between the national and international terrorism have also made the Nepali state weak with all indications that the time ahead is likely to be more challenging than before.

Among the non-state actors, the NGOs and INGOs have created both positive and negative effects on the state. The mushrooming of NGOs and INGOs are the extension and expansion of the globalizing world with the intent of creating both formal and informal mechanisms for greater interactions between the state and external communities. Tired of dealing with the sluggish state machinery for speedy development, the donors and other international support groups have now preferred to work with the NGOs. It is also seen as inroads made by the north into the south (developing countries).[33]

In Nepal, the restoration of multiparty system and the development of NGO culture are intertwined. The scramble of enthusiastic donors has been the most striking feature of the post-1990 Nepal. As of October 2010, the Social Welfare Council has recorded 31,000 NGOs in addition to 25,000 not affiliated to it. It has been learnt that about NPR 28 billion

---

[33] See Chaitanya Mishra and Dilli Ram Dahal in their respective papers "New Predicaments of Humanitarian Organizations" and "Problems and Prospects of Relationship between Government Organizations and NGOs/INGOs in Nepal" in Krishna B. Bhattachan et al., eds, *NGO, Civil Society, and Government in Nepal* (Kathmandu: Central Department of Sociology/Anthropology, Tribhuvan University, 2001).

is invested, though its actual result is yet not known. What is more amazing is that both the donors and foreign embassies, especially the Embassy of India, dole out funds without being routed through the Government of Nepal.

The positive aspects of growing NGOs in the country are presented as follows: creation of awareness of people in general, and the rural population in particular; mobilization of people at local development; development of a sense of empowerment; promotion of both research and action-oriented projects; opposition to some Acts and laws that tend to undermine the freedoms of people; and efforts to end social disparity through awareness campaign, such as the end of gender and caste discrimination.

The negative impacts on the Nepali society and state are no less significant. First, NGOs have produced the *nouveau riche* with the flow of foreign money. The new class born out of the foreign money pretends to work for the poorest of the poor and for all those who are really deprived of all kinds of opportunities provided by the state and the donors. Since the donors and the new elites (beneficiaries) take decisions independently of the state, a large chunk of money goes into the pocket of the recipients. In many projects, the foreign consultant's remuneration far exceeds that of the local experts; it has, thus, created a psychological gap between the foreigners and the locals whose indigenous knowledge is no less superior to outsiders.

Among the Nepalis, only *tatha batha* or smart, active individuals are benefitted; thus, contributing to form a new hierarchy of elites. Most NGOs are not likely to last long once the foreign funding is stopped. Many of them are person-oriented that generate immediate programs on the basis of money received by them and die soon once such instant projects are over. Another phenomenon of "smart individuals" is that they work as consultants in several places and earn money. The honorarium paid by the government or other institutions are less attractive for the experts because of the huge gap existing between the money provided by the donors and the government or other native institutions. However, the state itself is increasingly becoming NGO-ized or INGO-ized as its own organs and agencies are dependent on foreign money.

Even for organizing a small seminar, the government-run institutions rely on foreign fund.

Second, the national institutions such as the universities have been deserted by their own man/woman power due to the increasing tendency of specialists to work outside. University teachers and other people working in different government and semigovernment organizations prefer to work outside due to low salary and lack of other facilities. Thus, the Tribhuvan University, which is the oldest and the largest institution in the country, is increasingly losing its significance because of its failure to produce competitive people power. Ironically, the same university employees are used by the outside agencies by paying handsome money to them. As a result, teaching and academic research have suffered. It has been believed that private institutions and NGOs and INGOs are better places for career enhancement than the government-funded educational institutions from primary to highest level. All such public institutions are perceived as factories whose products can hardly meet the requirements of competitive market.

Families belonging to the middle class or the "creamy layers of society" tend to send their children abroad. Programs generated in the name of poor and deprived sections just become ritualistic. Nevertheless, not all NGOs can be placed under the same category as some of them are effective in improving the conditions of the target groups. Opening of educational institutions in the private sector and opportunities made available to work in private domain should be taken as positive side of development. But care must also be taken for reducing the widening gap between a tiny privileged section and the general people.

Third, the NGOs and INGOs seem to become powerful to influence the government. It has been observed that government officials, advisors, planners, and politicians are directly or indirectly linked to various NGOs. Even while they are in government or in semigovernment organizations, their linkages with the donors have made them financially well-off. Since the country itself is donor-driven, the Nepali state can hardly ignore the role of foreign funding agencies. Thus, it has also contributed to making a new moneyed class either by design or by default.

Among the non-state actors that work for debilitating the state are terrorists and their organizations within and outside the country. Now/ there has been a tendency to develop linkages between terrorists working inside the country and international terrorist gangs. Such linkages have drained out resources of the government, creating negative impacts on the development of the country. In today's international politics, terrorism has dominated the agendas of governments across the world and joint efforts are also made for stemming it. So it is "difficult to imagine a world without terrorism in the foreseeable future, for it would imply a world without conflict and tension ... one must conclude that the world is now entering a new phase in its history, more dangerous than any before."[34] When the state and government curtails freedoms or monopolizes power and resources, denying other general people of every opportunity, people resort to violent means. The illegitimate state and government might then call such means as terroristic methods. The armed insurrection of the NC and the 10-year-long war of the Maoist against the state were branded as antinational and terroristic. The terrorist tag is still branded on the Maoist by the US, despite the Maoist transformation into a peaceful party. However, in the given context, terrorism in various forms and objectives is taken as the potential force against the state. In Nepal too, doused in violence and indulged in criminal activities, violent gangs continue to pose threats to the state and society. Generally, terrorist activities begin with public targets, but in course of time they tend to kill individuals without specifying any charge, as has been happening in the country today. Killing of politicians and other individuals for no reasons whatsoever is the regular phenomenon of Nepal.[35] Nepal is under the international radar for terrorism because the country is being

---

[34] Walter Laqueur, "Left, Right, and Beyond: The Changing Face of Terror" in James F. Hodge Jr and Gideon Rose, eds, *How Did This Happen? Terrorism and the New War* (New York: Public Affairs, 2001), pp. 81–82.

[35] See in detail, Lok Raj Baral, "The Specter of Terror and Its Impacts on the Democratic Process in Nepal" in Sridhar K. Khatri and Gert W. Kueck, eds, *Terrorism in South Asia* (Delhi: Shipra Publications, 2003), pp. 223–236.

projected as a corridor for regional and international terrorism. Thus, pressure is mounted on Nepal for not making it as the hub of terrorism.

External Dimension

The emergence of the modern Nepali state and external linkages has a symbiotic relationship. Prithvi Narayan Shah, the founder of modern Nepal, has himself conceptualized the constraints of Nepal's foreign policy, which needs to be adroitly handled by the rulers and concerned elites. Nepal's physical location between China and India (previously with Tibet as a buffer) and the rising aspirations and ambitions of the two neighbors to become global powers and the much intrusive roles being played by them as well as by other external powers in recent years have further made Nepal vulnerable. Such vulnerability further contributes to the weakening of the state. Nepal today is prone to internal divisiveness, fragmented state structures, and elite idiosyncrasies. The tendency of the elite to look beyond the borders for survival has also acted as a negative factor for the Nepali state. It has not only downgraded national independence but has also eroded the norms of international law that governs interstate relations.

In this context, I am reminded of my short encounters with late King Birendra in February 1996. After having been appointed the ambassador of Nepal to India, the Foreign Ministry had, as a usual practice, arranged my audience with the King. During the conversation, King Birendra advised me to follow certain guidelines that a diplomat of a sovereign country was supposed to follow so that it would be easy to maintain the status as the representative of the state. Such a suggestion came in the wake of my presentation that highlighted my own informal understanding about India since my student days and later as an academic. Such informalities were absolutely essential but, as ambassador, his other personality should not also be diluted. Today, however, Nepal's politicians scramble for visiting New Delhi in particular for enhancing their prospects of power at home. When they do not draw as much attention from the

Indian side as they expect, they cry hoarse against India or grumble for being ignored. Reports of violation of borders, harassment meted out to the Nepalis travelling to India by the Indian police, floods and inundation of lowlands in the Tarai, criminal activities across the border, use of free border by terrorists, and many such activities carried out by miscreants are the most frequently reported events in Nepal and India.

Old strategies for state survival do not provide any reliable guarantee, nor can the state-led nationalism alone forge unity among the Nepalis. For, in the state-led nationalism, the rulers demand that "citizens should subordinate all other interests to those of the state."[36] If the ruling and other political elites fail to widen the scope of nationalism and continue to rely on state-led nationalism, the elites would inevitably become the prisoner of the old.

Historically, Nepal has always been ambitious of expanding its territories or to extend its influence in its neighborhood. The policy of expansion was taken as the manifestation of Nepali nationalism, though, in modern sense, the real spirit of nationalism could only be promoted through the policy of empowerment of people. Since such approach was beyond the scope of the then rulers and their courtiers, Nepal took the policy of adventurism by opening up war fronts with both the northern and southern neighbors. Such risky games had often jeopardized Nepal's own existence but could also be described, to borrow Leo Rose's words, "strategy for survival."[37] How the post-monarchy Nepali elites will be able to play the game in the changed context of national, regional, and world politics needs to be seen.

The idea of the nation-state or "national state" is becoming more tenuous because of trends of deinstitutionalization and fragmentation

---

[36] T. K. Oommen, "Evolving Inclusive Societies through Constitutions: The Case of Nepal." An unpublished paper presented at a seminar on Social Inclusion Policies in South Asian States (Kathmandu: CNAS, June 25–27, 2009).

[37] Leo E. Rose, *Nepal: Strategy for Survival* (New Delhi: Oxford University Press, 1971).

of political cultures and state structures. If the traditional nation-state is being questioned for not being inclusive and participatory, the national state that we visualize and propagate is yet to be materialized. Twists and turns of politics and tendency of external powers to be more active and transparent have added complexity to making a viable state. Thus, many theories and prescriptions applied elsewhere are not likely to be helpful for Nepal because Nepalis alone are the best judge for steering the course of the state.

3

Quest for Status

Wars, Treaties, and Diplomacy

The history of Nepal is marked by wars, which were fought mainly for expansion as well as for promoting economic interests through internal resource mobilization and trade promotion. So it was the economic motivation that most Nepali rulers in the postconquest period paid their attention to when they opened trade routes to Tibet. They went to wars or took belligerent approaches in pursuit of these policies.

Nepal's war with Tibet and the expanding British rule in India were basically motivated by trade (Tibet) as well as expansion. How did such wars prove to be beneficial or costly for the national interest needs to be analyzed. The treaties concluded after these wars were no less significant for future Nepal. The Treaty of Sugauli (1815–1816), in particular, which was the fallout of the defeat of the Gorkhalis, had indeed shaped the course of political and diplomatic history of the country. For the southern power, the consequences of the Treaty could help stabilize the British rule due to Nepal's stable position that could work as a buffer between Tibet and China. Moreover, finding a reliable and weak ally in its neighborhood, East India Company—which was setting its foothold in South Asia—was now assured of its northern neighbor; of course to the detriment of Nepal's independent actions that it used to take in the past. Severe limitations were imposed on Nepal following the signing of the Treaty of Sugauli. The Rana rulers, starting with Jung Bahadur in 1846, were cognizant of Nepal's limitations and imperatives for blossoming Anglo–Nepal relations.

Theoretically speaking, Nepal's dependency syndrome grew due to two main reasons. First, Nepal's power elites needed to be perennially preoccupied with the attitudes, moves, and interests of the British rulers and, hence, the conduct of domestic and foreign policies accordingly. It guaranteed political stability, which was nothing more than the continuation of the Rana family oligarchy. The Ranas, therefore, continued it for more than a hundred years by pursuing the policy of appeasement, cajoling, and pretentious nationalism based on conventional meaning of independence and sovereignty. Although it fitted well into the parameters of national sovereignty, territorial integrity, and independence, it was devoid of today's spirit of development of the country by getting economic advantages through the cultivation of bilateral relations. How wars tried to demonstrate the motivation of rulers for achieving recognition of power and how wars and other interstate dealings worked for and against it can be understood by some wars and treaties that Nepal entered in the post-unification period.

Capture of trade routes to Tibet and the occasional conflicts that occurred between the kings of Kathmandu valley and the kings of Gorkha had dominated interstate relations prior to the conquest of the valley kingdoms by King Prithvi Narayan Shah in 1768–1769. Later, the greater Nepal's rulers were engaged in wars with Tibet and China for the same reasons. It has been stated by historians that the Malla kings of the valley had also entered into treaties with Tibet. King Pratap Malla, for instance, had concluded a treaty with Tibet and had the following features:

1. Establishment of a "joint authority with Tibet" for controlling the border towns of Kuti and Kerung.
2. Permission given to the Newar merchants of the valley to open trading houses in Lhasa.
3. Posting of a Nepali representative in Lhasa.
4. Exemption of custom duties to Newar merchants engaged in trade in Lhasa and other places in Tibet.
5. Minting of coins with the name of Nepali king by Nepal for Tibet. Tibet was required to pay to Nepal for it and circulate the coins within Tibet.

6. Utilization of Kathmandu route (instead of Sikkim and Bhutan or Tawang) for trade between India and Tibet.[1]

It was believed that the Treaty

> contributed largely to the commercial prosperity of Kathmandu. Kathmandu played a very strong and profitable intermediary role in trade between India and Tibet until early in the twentieth century, when the British opened the route to Lhasa through Sikkim and Chumbi Valley following the Young husband expedition of 1904.[2]

Throughout Nepali history, beginning from the medieval times, Tibet has always occupied a prominent place for interstate interactions between Nepal and its northern neighbors, Tibet and China. Fearing that the Mongols from the north might take the advantage in Tibet, the Ch'ing Dynasty of China eventually decided to enter Tibet in the 18th century establishing its suzerainty there.

The Treaty of Peace between Nepal and Tibet, 1856, has mentioned the Emperor of China of being showed respect by both Nepal and Tibet. Article 2 of the Treaty mentions that

> Gorkha and Tibet have both been regarding the Emperor of China with respect. Tibet being merely a country of monasteries of Lamas and a place for recitation of prayers and practice of religious austerities, should troops of any other Raja invade Tibet in future, Gorkha will afford such assistance and protection as it can.

Among other points included in the Treaty are: exemption from levying taxes on routes, duties on merchandise, and on the "subjects" of the country of Gorkha; exchange of captured soldiers, including the Sikhs; establishment of trade factory in Tibet by Gorkha; joint adjudication of cases in Tibet; surrender of criminals by both the two sides; no vindictive action to be taken pagainst persons who had joined the Gorkha Darbar

---

[1] Chitra Ranjan Nepali, "Nepal ra Tibet ko Sambandha" (Nepal–Tibet Relations), *Pragati II*, 4, 10. As mentioned in Rishikesh Shaha, *Modern Nepal: A Political History 1769–1955*, Vol. 1 (Delhi: Manohar, 1990), p. 41.

[2] Shaha, ibid., p. 30.

during the war or "of the subjects of Gorkha joining the Tibetan Darbar. Lhasa was also to permit the opening of shops, trade in jewellery, ornaments, textiles, and food of all kinds by the Gorkha subjects."

The Tibet–Nepal Treaty of 1792 clearly brought China into the picture, recognizing it as the "father to both Nepal and Tibet, who should regard each other as brothers." It also gave authority of the Chinese government to investigate the cases of plundering in Tibet and the return of articles to the Nepalis. Tibet and China would permit the Nepalis to travel, establish factories, and to carry on trade in Tibet.

Thus, the dynamics of geopolitics had indeed begun with the penetration of the Chinese into Tibet to which the southern rising power could hardly remain passive. Sometimes, the Chinese power declined making Tibet as a buffer between it and Nepal and British-India. After having gone through a period of decline, it emerged with a bang as a power following the successful Maoist revolution in China in 1949. Consequently, the smaller countries in the south of the Himalayas and India, now ruled by the native rulers, entered into treaties with India. In fact, such relations were only the continuity of the old British-India policy in a slightly modified form. Bhutan, Sikkim, and Nepal, thus, came within the Indian security radar so that the communist China could be resisted if the latter posed any security threat to these countries.

Nepal has not fought the Chinese since the 1792 war. Although in actual sense, it was not a long-drawn-out war because of its nature. Nevertheless, Britain always perceived China as a potential spoiler in Anglo–Nepal relations. So, even diplomatic maneuverability of the Nepali rulers, often used as a bargaining counter for not undermining their protocol or country's independence, was suspect for the British. Yet, Nepal did not dare to go against the vital interest of the southern neighbor.

Nepal's close interactions with the British started following the signing of the Treay of Sugauli in 1816. The conclusion of the Treaty and the loss of territory was a major setback for those involved in the war. Nevertheless, the Treaty of Sugauli had recognized Nepal's independence and sovereignty. The Rajah (King) of Nepal, by virtue of being sovereign, had signed the Treaty because Nepal had only lost the war, not its independence and sovereignty. Under Article III of the Treaty, "certain territories were ceded by Nepal." It is said:

> That cession of territory by agreement under a peace treaty has never involved or indicated a loss of sovereignty or independence otherwise than in relation to the ceded territories. If the treaties were the case, there would be few States which could be held independent and sovereign in the present time.[3]

Perceval Landon has strongly defended the sovereign status of Nepal while signing the Treaty. As it has been said: "The terms of this Treaty show that it was entered into as between two fully sovereign states. The Government of Nepal particularly refers to Article II by which the territory is expressed to be bestowed on the Maharajah of Nepal in full sovereignty."[4] While giving away the right over Sikkim and other territories in Mechi River in the east and Kali River in the west, Nepal's King had used the prerogative of a sovereign. It may be recalled, these territories were conquered by Nepal in the 1814 war with the East India Company. Regarding the recognition of a state while exchanging envoys of both the countries, it has been categorically stated by Landon in these words:

> The functions of the office in Kathmandu are entirely different from those of a Resident in India. In the latter place, the Resident is ultimately responsible for representing to the Indian Government any condition of affairs within the State which, in his opinion, calls for the intervention of the Indian Government, and he is the instrument used by the Indian Government in the event of their deciding to take action. In Nepal, neither the Indian Government nor any other Government has any right of interference or intervention or even of offering advice. Nepal is an independent State, and the functions of the Envoy are simply those of a friendly observer whose duties are confined to reporting the chief events and tendencies in Nepal so far as they affect Indian interests, to acting as the official intermediary between the two Governments.[5]

However, despite these attributes of Nepal's independence and sovereignty, the consequences of the Treaty imposed more constraints on Nepal.

[3] Avtar Singh Bhasin, ed., *Nepal's Relations with India and China: Documents 1947–1992*, Vol. 1 (Delhi: Siba Exim Pvt Ltd, 1994), p. 7.

[4] See Perceval Landon, *Nepal* (London: Constable, 1928), p. 101.

[5] Ibid.

The country for the first time realized the emergence of an imperial power to the south. After losing territories to the East India Company in the 1814–1816 war, Nepal now developed more formal relations and interactions with the southern neighbor. The maneuverability of Nepal was drastically reduced after the war. Analyzing Prime Minister Bhimsen Thapa's adventure to wage a war against the British, Asad Husain writes: "If half the energy and diplomacy he spent to keep the British at a distance had been used against the Pandes [his court rivals], he could probably have done much more for Nepal."[6]

Even after signing the Treaty of Sugauli, Nepal's independent action to open hostilities with Tibet or conclude treaties with Tibet and China was not curtailed. Its conclusion of the Treaty of Peace between Nepal and Tibet, 1856 or of 1792, were instances of such independence.

In the preceding years, China and Nepal were in constant touch so much so that the Chinese Emperor dispatched a small force to pacify Nepal when the British tried to push the latter to the brink. In Ramakant's opinion: "It might be recalled that Nepal had her political contacts with China since 1792 when the latter had intervened in the Tibeto-Nepalese war."[7]

Nepal's status of an independent and sovereign state was made clear by the "Treaty of Friendship between Great Britain and Nepal signed at Katmandu [Kathmandu], 21st December 1923, and Note bearing the same date respecting the importation of Arms and Ammunition into Nepal—1923." It was done during Prime Minister Chandra Shamsher's rule. Article I of the Treaty reads: "There shall be perpetual peace and friendship between the Government of Great Britain and Nepal, and the two Governments agree mutually to acknowledge and respect each other's independence, both internal and external." Article III has explicitly underlined the mutual security interest, which could also be seen as a prelude to the provisions of the 1950 Treaty of Peace and Friendship. This article states:

[6] See Asad Husain, *British India's Relations with the Kingdom of Nepal* (London: George Allen & Unwin, 1970), p. 286.

[7] See Ramakant, *Indo-Nepalese Relations, 1816 to 1877* (Delhi: S. Chand and Company, 1968), p. 65.

As the preservation of peace and friendly relations with the neighbouring States whose territories adjoin their common frontiers is to the mutual interests of both the High Contracting Parties, they hereby agree to inform each other of any serious friction or misunderstanding with those States likely to rupture such friendly relations, and each to exert its good offices as far as many be possible to remove such friction and misunderstanding.[8]

Article V has laid down the rules and procedures for importing arms and ammunition, machinery, warlike material, or stores as "required or desired for the strength of and welfare of Nepal..."[9] These military requirements could be imported from or through British-India with the approval of the latter. In fact, the Treaty worked as a double-edged sword: recognition of Nepal as an independent and sovereign country while at the same time imposing severe restrictions of the freedom of Nepal to import arms and ammunition independent of India.

In the 1940s, the Ranas tried to diversify Nepal's relations beyond India, reaching out to the US, France, the Netherlands, and others. In 1948, Nepal applied for the membership of the UN, but could not get it following the veto used by the Soviet Union raising the question of actual status of Nepal as an independent country. In a document prepared by the government subsequently, the Rana government argued strongly for establishing Nepal's independent status that was more than enough for the membership of the world body. Nevertheless, it was only in 1955 that Nepal entered the UN and has since been playing different roles as a member. Nepal became the member of the UN Security Council twice as a nonpermanent member and has been participating in the peace-keeping operations in different parts of the world.

Such British–Rana bonhomie seemed to have matured for enhancing each other's interests; for British-India, Nepal's stability and friendship could be used for its imperial interest, and for the Ranas it was a guarantee for perpetuating the oligarchy. So the fact was that "both the British

---

[8] Avtar Singh Bhasin, ed., *Nepal's Relations with India and China: Documents 1947–1992*, Vol. 1 (Delhi: Siba Exim Pvt Ltd, 1994), p. 14.

[9] See the text of the treaty in Asad Husain, *British India's Relations with the Kingdom of Nepal* (London: George Allen & Unwin, 1970), Appendix XVII, pp. 390–392.

and the Ranas needed each other for their own selfish ends and national interests. The alliance stood firm because, like all durable alliances, it was based on mutual selfish interest."[10]

In retrospect, it could be observed that following the death of Jang Bahadur in 1877, his successors were not clear about the actual international status of Nepal; whether it was under the British suzerainty or under Tibet or Chinese suzerainty was not clear. The British Government in India had stated that "all that one can gather in that a State 'under suzerainty' is one whose sovereignty is in some degree controlled by another Power, and which is not a 'recognized member of the family of nations' for the purpose of international Law."[11] The 1923 Treaty had, therefore, removed such confusion by projecting Nepal's independent status in the world.

Continued Framework of Relations: 1950 Treaty and Beyond

The Rana rulers, starting from Jang Bahadur (1846) to Mohun Shamsher (1950), understood the emergence of an imperial British power in India or the continuation of old British policy toward its neighbors in the post-independent India and, hence, took every step to hobnob with the southern neighbor. The Rana rulers did not give the impression that they were enhancing their family cause at the expense of the Nepali state. Preoccupied with the maintenance of international status of Nepal and knowing the relative decline of the northern power until the communist takeover in 1949, they tried to appease the British without compromising its territorial integrity, sovereignty, and independence. Since these were the hallmarks of nationalism in those days, the Ranas maintained the balance on the grounds of political reality.

From another angle, however, the conventional concept of national independence was safeguarded by the Rana rulers until the gust of democratic wind blew in South Asia. The same policy with a slight adjustment

[10] Ibid., p. 291.
[11] As cited in Husain, ibid., p. 293.

has been pursued by the post-1950 power elites no matter who the rulers were/are. Yet these policies, despite being substantively the same, differ in nuances and symbols depending on the context and time. The new rulers of independent India, particularly Prime Minister Jawaharlal Nehru, were more conscious of national independence, territorial integrity, and sovereignty. Nevertheless, India started consolidating its relations with the three Himalayan states—Bhutan, Nepal, and Sikkim—by concluding new treaties with all of them. About Nepal, Nehru was more explicit, and he said the following in the Parliament in December 1950:

> We assured Nepal that we would not only respect her independence, but we wanted to see Nepal develop into a strong and progressive country. We went further to in this respect than the British Government had done; that is to say, Nepal began to develop other foreign relations. We welcomed it. We did not come in the way, although that was something far in addition to what had been the position in British time. Naturally, and quite frankly, we do not like, and we do not propose to like, any foreign interference in Nepal.[12]

Sikkim, a protectorate until 1975, has now become a part of India following its integration into the Indian Union. The other two kingdoms (Nepal is now a republic, and Bhutan) continue to adhere to the treaties concluded with India in 1949 and July 1950. Although Bhutan and India revised some provisions of the Treaty, its spirit remains undiluted. Nepal, despite the political rhetoric of leaders of parties for either abrogation of the Treaty or its revision or a review, it has not been able to propose the annulment of the Treaty. If any contracting party wants to abrogate the Treaty, it can give one year's advance notice for annulment. It reads: "The Treaty shall remain in force until it is terminated by either party by giving one year's notice."[13]

But as of now, no such proposal has come from either party. India sticks to the spirit of the Treaty while Nepali political elites simply make a propaganda issue for projecting themselves as "nationalist." Some provisions

---

[12] Avtar Singh Bhasin, ed., *Nepal's Relations with India and China: Documents 1947–1992*, Vol. 1 (Delhi: Siba Exim Pvt Ltd, 1994), p. 44.

[13] See the Article X of the Treaty of "Peace and Friendship" between the GoI and the Government of Nepal, July 31, 1950.

of the Treaty—especially related to mutual security and privileges to be provided to the nationals of both the countries, equal treatment in participation in trade and commerce, movement and privileges of a similar nature—seem to be complex in view of the all-embracing relationships between the people of the two countries.

One of the points to be taken into account is that India has categorically recognized "complete sovereignty, territorial integrity and independence of each other" (Article II). The security clauses that demand joint efforts to avert any threat emanating from a third party (by implication China) and the letter exchanged with the Treaty was of "special" nature, though Nepali political elites, particularly of the "royalists" and the Left groups, made the Treaty an infringement in national independence and sovereignty. The letter exchanged with the 1950 Treaty states: "Neither government shall tolerate any threat to the security of the other by a foreign aggressor. To deal with any such threat, the two Governments shall consult with each other and devise effective counter-measure." The letter has also limited the freedom of Nepal while seeking foreign assistance in regard to the development of the natural resources or of any industrial project in Nepal. Nepal was under treaty obligation that the Indian nationals were to be given priority for the award of contract, etc.

Continuity in Nepal–India relations was reflected more in the Understanding on Import of Arms by Nepal. As it remained a secret untill an American scholar, Leo Rose, disclosed it in his book *Nepal: Strategy for Survival*, published in 1971, the Understanding signed by Nepal's Ambassador to India, Y. N. Khanal and the Indian foreign secretary on January 30, 1965, was disclosed by India through a feature article by D. P. Kumar in the *Statesman* (Delhi) in 1989. The contents of the Understanding tried to meet the requirements of the Nepali army by supplying arms and ammunition and other facilities including training, clothing, etc., India had agreed to meet Nepal's defense requirements during King Mahendra's visit to India in 1963.

According to the Understanding, India was the lone supplier of arms and ammunition, but in case the requirements of Nepal could not be met by the former, the US and the UK could also supply in consultation with the GoI. Clause V of the Understanding lays down that the "Government of Nepal shall be free to import from or through the territory of India arms, ammunition of warlike material and equipment necessary for the security of Nepal."[14] Both the US and the UK were required to supplement assistance in a "suitably coordinated" manner.[15]

The 1950 Treaty, which is the framework of Indo–Nepal relations in view of its scope and specialty, has generated much controversy ever since its declarations. Controversies and criticisms hovering over the Treaty are both the expressions of the spirit of postcolonial South Asia as the countries of the region seemed to be apparently bent on achieving independence and freedom in both symbolic and actual sense. Sometimes such expressions have turned out to be highly xenophobic, and sometimes they are the by-products of strategies that are deliberately used by the politicians for domestic consumption.

What the main criticisms of the Treaty are and how these criticisms have been able to create impacts on defining Indo–Nepal relations are important aspects. It has been stated by the Nepali side that it is an unequal treaty concluded just on the eve of the anti-Rana movement launched in the late 1950s. Since the tottering Rana oligarchy was counting its days under the pressure of the then developing movement, the beleaguered Ranas, who were under pressure from the GoI for clubbing together the Himalayan kingdoms within its security umbrella, had no option but to conclude the Treaty. By doing it, the Ranas were hopeful of retaining some sort of power as they had been doing in the post-Sugauli Treaty. Since the 1950 Treaty was only an extension of the spirit of 1923 Treaty, it tried to encapsulate the entire gamut of Nepal–India relations. The three major aspects in the treaty are: special security relations, relations among the two peoples including the free movement of people across the borders without any passport and visa, and economic aspects.

Although the Treaty continues to keep the spirit of the old British-India policy toward Nepal, it is more extensive and inclusive in view of

[14] See the texts of the letter accompanying the 1950 Treaty and the agreement signed in New Delhi on January 30, 1965, in S. D. Muni, *India and Nepal: A Changing Relationship* (Delhi: Konark, 1992), pp. 191 and 196–197.

[15] See, ibid., pp. 196–197.

the wide-ranging, close, and deep bilateral relations. Also, considering the geographical situation of Nepal and permanent dynamics evident in bilateral relations, Nepal is under pressure to be much more dependent on India than on any other country of the world, including its northern neighbor, China. Thus, both geographical setting and geopolitical dynamics have posed greater challenges to the policymakers of Nepal. How Indian leaders and others often misunderstood Nepal's difficulty in maintaining a proper balance between China and India have perennially influenced Nepal–India and, to a limited extent, Nepal–China, relations.

Second, it has been assailed that it is an imposed treaty by India. An objective analysis of the then emergent geopolitical reality prompted the rulers of both the countries to be closer to each other in view of the emergence of communist China in their immediate neighborhood. The paranoia with which the noncommunist world was reacting to the rise of communism in the world, any Nepali ruler, regardless of their regimes or political orientations, could have reached such a decision. In case of the Rana rulers, in both national and political context, that was likely to go against them in future and the presence of the People's Republic of China in Tibet had led them to be closer to India, a countervailing power. It was, therefore, a decision based on the then developing scenario, which no power could ignore. India too was bent on reinforcing its strategic relations with the Himalayan kingdoms of Bhutan, Nepal, and Sikkim.

Finally, domestic considerations were no less pressing for the Ranas. India, now a free country, was concerned about peaceful change toward democratization of Nepal's regime. Jawaharlal Nehru, prime minister of India, who wanted to see a smooth transition to democracy in Nepal, said in the Parliament in March 1950:

> We have advised in all earnestness the government of Nepal—in so far as a friendly power can advise an independent nation. We have advised them in all earnestness that in the inner context of Nepal, it is desirable to pay attention to the forces that are moving in the world—the domestic forces, the forces of freedom—and to put oneself in line with them, because not do so is not only wrong according to modern ideas but unwise according to what is happening in the world today.[16]

[16] See ibid., p. 34. See also Leo E. Rose, *Nepal: Strategy for Survival* (Bombay: Oxford University Press, 1971), p. 185.

As it has been stated:

> In view of this possibility of change, it were [was] the Ranas who were more than willing to accommodate the Indian viewpoint on the question of new Treaty that was being negotiated. There was even a specific reason behind this. The leader of the Nepali Congress and the anti-Rana forces in Nepal, B. P. Koirala had gone to the extent of proposing a Treaty that integrated Nepal's foreign and defence policies with that of India's, almost in the form of a military alliance in order to ensure complete Indian support in favour of the democratic forces in Nepal's anti-Rana struggle.[17]

It is not only the international status of Nepal which is being raised often, but the domestic politics has also been perennially dominated by the 1950 Treaty ever since its signing. The Nepali politicians who want to link it up with nationalism assail the Treaty provisions for being unequal. In their opinion, it smacks of colonialism as Nepal has been tied to Indian security doctrine that keeps the Himalayan countries as its spheres of influence. Economically, equal treatment to be given to the citizens of both the countries is interpreted as harmful to the long-term interest of Nepal because of the demographic considerations. Moreover, the open border existing from time immemorial and the free movement of people across the border is likely to create political, social, and economic imbalances. Nepal whose demographic structure is determined by both internal and external factors, free movement of peoples and equal treatment to both the peoples are not fair deal.

Nepali politicians who raise alarm at the overwhelming presence of Indians in Nepal grabbing economic and other opportunities say that the Indians would eventually outnumber the Nepalis, triggering off inter-state conflicts on such issues that were never imagined in the past. Pointing out this aspect during his official visit to India in 1995, Man Mohan Adhikari, the first communist prime minister of Nepal, said in Delhi: "The number of Nepalis working in India is like a drop in the Indian ocean. But if Indians come into Nepal in the same proportion, this will create a major problem for us. That is why we want changes in the 1950 treaty." But Indian response was not positive as Prime Minister

[17] Ibid.

Narasimha Rao said, "Yes, changes have taken place. But neighbours will remain neighbours. Nepal and India are close neighbours. There is no need for any change in their cordial relations."[18]

Even in the 1980s, the Royal Government of Nepal had formed a study team headed by Harka Gurung, a former minister of state and Planning Commission vice chairman, to recommend measures for regulating migratory trends in the country. Popularly known as Gurung Report, it created havoc when it prescribed some steps for regulating the India–Nepal border. Three stages were recommended: (a) registration of people crossing the border, (b) issue of identity card, and (c) issue of passport. The people of Tarai (Madhese) denounced the Report for being biased against the Tarai people. The formation of Nepal Sadbhawana Parishad (Sadhbhawana Council), which later turned into a party following the restoration of multiparty system in 1990, aimed at creating awareness in order not to be exploited any more by the policies of what they called *pahadia* (hill people). They not only opposed the Gurung Report tooth and nail but also raised the issue of exploitation of the Madheses by the Pahades because of the discriminatory character of the hill-dominated Nepali state. The demand of federalism also came along with this demand for the emancipation of the Tarai people.

In today's context and given the erosion of the clauses of the 1950 Treaty, both the Nepali and Indian political elites seem to be unnecessarily bogged down on the issue of the Treaty. From security point of view, the Treaty spirit has been diluted when Nepal did not consult India while importing arms from China in the 1980s. Other powers, especially the US, the UK, and the European Union (EU), have been taking unprecedented interests in Nepal's affairs, both domestic and foreign, to the chagrin of India. India encouraged establishing diplomatic relations with China in the 1950s after it accepted Tibet as the Autonomous Region of China. However, it did not like Nepal to be too close China because of India's own close relations with the former. Nepal's relations with Pakistan and Israel were no less significant in view of the estranged relations these countries had with India. India recognized Israel only in

---

[18] *Nepal Press Digest*, 39:16. April 17, 1995.

the 1990s while Pakistan has had remained as one of the major preoccupations of the Indian Government. So the Treaty did not prevent Nepal from looking beyond India despite its own limitations by virtue of being sandwiched between China and India.

Nepal's imposition of work-permit system on the Indians boomeranged following India's strong reaction to it. Both Indians and Nepalis from the Tarai were put together in trucks by way of discouraging Indian laborers in Kathmandu. It was a indeed a prelude to the work-permit system subsequently enforced half-heartedly by the Nepali Government. Later it was said that such measures were taken from a security point of view taking into consideration the South Asian Association for Regional Cooperation (SAARC) summit of 1987.

Nepal's decision to grant citizenship to as many as 2.5 million people in the Tarai—during the rule of Interim Government formed after the 2006 Jan Andolan—and permission granted to non-Indian contractors for import of goods from third countries, contrary to Indian objection to overflow of goods that allegedly find their way into India, are not to the tune of the 1950 Treaty. The only benefit now being enjoyed by the Indians is the open-visa regime. In the case of Nepalis, the Treaty is far more encompassing as the Nepalis enjoy a lot of facilities in India.

The Indians view the 1950 Treaty as unequal for them, and the manner the Nepali politicians raise this issue is not based on reality. For Nepal it has become one of the issues for political mobilization, and politicians use this strategy when they are short of issues. What would happen to those 8-million-plus Nepalis working in India if the Treaty is abrogated in reaction to the Nepali demands? Can Nepal take back all those people if India decides to terminate the Treaty provisions whose beneficiaries are the Nepalis? It is said that the poorest people would be the worst sufferers if such crisis ever develops in India–Nepal relation. People from the western hills of Nepal trek to India when natural calamities occur, insurgency develops, and drought conditions prevail. What about the recruitment of Nepalis into the Indian army? Udhhab Pyakurel's observations that Nepalis would be the greater sufferers by the annulment of the Treaty deserve to be examined in order to find a better perspective of the Treaty. For, Nepalis are the principal beneficiaries in education, health, and employment sectors.[19] Myron Weiner, an eminent American scholar on South Asia, wrote in 1971 that India was a "safety valve" for Nepal because of the employment of a large number of Nepali nationals there.[20]

Now it has been realized in India that if the Nepalis were really anxious to make certain adjustments in the Treaty, there should be no qualms on the Indian side. However, what kind of relationship the Nepalis want needs to be explicitly spelled out. As a former chief of the army staff of India has stated:

> To establish relations between the two countries on a more positive and transparent footing, an essential prerequisite is a revised and restructured Indo-Nepal Treaty that equitably balances the interests of both countries and even allows for a degree of positive toward Nepal as a smaller entity, while always maintaining India's own irreducible core national interests.

If Nepal wants a more independent kind of relationship for demonstrating its independence and sovereignty to which some of the lobbies in Nepal have had been demanding, the general said:

> Nepal's recruitment for the peerless Gorkha rifle regiments of the Indian Army would certainly be an issue here, frequently raised by lobbies in Kathmandu as demeaning to national sensitivities. Here India should have no hesitation in putting the issue in full perspective by firmly stating that should Nepal desire to terminate the present arrangement, the entire complement of human resources for the 40 battalions of the Gorkha Rifles in the Indian Army could be found from within India itself, without any recruitment from Nepal.[21]

Has the 1950 Treaty compromised the sovereignty and independence of Nepal? Is it responsible for perennially straining Nepal–India relations?

[19] For a different interpretation of the 1950 Treaty, see Uddhab Pyakurel, "Rashtriyatako Kasima 1950 Treaty" (1950 Treaty in the Context of Nationalism), *Kantipur*, February 24, 2010.

[20] See Myron Weiner, "The Political Demography of Nepal," *Asian Survey*, 13 (6): 1973, pp. 617–630.

[21] See General Shankar Roy Choudhury, "Indo-Nepal bhai bhai," *Deccan Chronicle* as produced by *Republica*, Kathmandu, March 24, 2010.

Such questions need to be addressed with greater degree of objectivity. No country in the world is sovereign in absolute sense, nor is it dependent fully. It is indeed an interdependent world where even the "Lilliputians" have some roles to play. Moreover, having structural security and other arrangements made for common interests do not constitute subordination of independence and sovereignty to a particular nation. Japan and the US or other countries have similar relations forged for promoting common interests but all of them are independent sovereign nations.

In the given India–Nepal context, it can be said that no leaders of confidence can ignore the long-cherished national independence. The entire Nepali history is a testimony to the fact that rulers regardless of their regimes—patrimonial, oligarchic, authoritarian, or elected—have always tried to assert their independence despite misunderstandings that arise from time to time. Such mistrust arises due to divergent perceptions developed by the leaders of the two countries.

Nepal's Peace Zone Policy and the 1950 Treaty

I would like to call it a peace zone foreign policy because of the mobilization of both national and international resources to get endorsement from as many countries as possible. The entire foreign policy machinery was geared to making it the top foreign policy agenda that needed to be supported by all. Since the proposal was mooted in a dramatic manner without having any consultation even within the government, let alone the other neighbors, those who extended instant support to it also did it as a good gesture. King Birendra, on February 25, 1975, during the reception held in honor of foreign delegates then attending his coronation, declared:

> And if today, peace is an overriding concern with us, it is only because our people genuinely desire peace in our country, in our region and every where in the world. It is with this earnest desire to institutionalize peace that I stand to make this proposition—a proposition that my country, Nepal, be declared a zone of peace.[22]

[22] See His Majesty King Birendra Bikram Shah, *Proclamations, Speeches and Messages* (Kathmandu: Department of Information, 1975).

Trying to rationalize the reason for declaring it as a zone of peace, he underlined peace, security, and development as the components of peace zone proposal. It could be assumed that China, the Soviet Russia, and Pakistan promptly endorsed it that very day or some days later, while many others waited to examine it fully. As Rishikesh Shaha observes:

> The reaction of India's two adversaries and competitors in the region was predictable. The proposal, if put into effect, would embarrass India by making untenable some obligations and practices under the existing Nepal-India treaty.[23]

With a view to clarify its position on peace zone proposal, the Royal Government of Nepal came out with a seven-point agenda after seven years of the declaration of the proposal by King Birendra. The major points in it were: adherence to the policy of peace, nonalignment, and peaceful coexistence; no resort to the use of force, which might endanger the peace and security of other countries; peaceful settlement of disputes; noninterference in internal affairs; no permission for hostile activities within Nepal, and in reciprocity, states supporting the proposal would not permit any activity hostile to Nepal; honor to obligations of all the treaties so long as they remain valid; no formation of military alliance in conformity with the policy of nonalignment. Other countries supporting the proposal would also not enter into any kind of military alliance, nor would they allow the establishment of military base in their soil directed against Nepal.[24]

Such assurances and declarations did not work to convince India. Moreover, the political dissidents then working from across the India–Nepal border opposed the peace zone move as a ploy to neutralize their roles that were mainly conducted from India. Political dissidents that represented a variety of spectrum were in common to oppose it as well as to persuade India not to fall into the regime's trap. It was interesting to note that even the US supported the peace proposal in an indirect

[23] See Rishikesh Shaha, *Politics in Nepal 1980–1990* (Kathmandu: Ratnapustak Bhandar, 1990), p. 116.

[24] The seven-point offer was declared by Prime Minister Surya Bahadur Thapa in 1982. See *Review of Development in Nepal's Foreign Affairs (1973–1983)*.

way, that too in theoretical sense. During the state visit of King Birendra in 1983, President Ronald Reagan advised the Nepali monarch to open dialogues with Nepal's neighbors for making the proposal a "reality."[25] It indicated that without Indian endorsement, the peace proposal was not likely to effective.

For 15 years, the royal regime concentrated its attention on getting endorsement from all the five powers of the United Nations Security Council besides other powers of the world. One hundred and sixteen countries, some of them with vaguely worded statements and some others with more clear positions, endorsed the peace proposal.

Prime Minister Indira Gandhi of India asked Nepal, "which country poses a threat to Nepal's security" that prompted Nepal to be a zone of peace.[26] One of the major arguments advanced for reading into the motivation of the Nepali monarch was related to the 1950 Treaty that undermined Nepal's independence and sovereignty. So it was interpreted as a strategy to be free from India's security umbrella. K. Subrahmanyam, an acknowledged security expert of India, and a host of others, both in the media and individual scholars, interpreted Nepal's peace zone proposal as having elements of jeopardizing India's security. An Indian daily wrote that the proposal was "untenable" in view of the integral security and social, economic, cultural, and religious relations, thus, making the structure of relations "special."[27] Some Indian experts cautioned Nepali leaders against opening the 'Pandora's box' (1950 Treaty) without taking into account the entire gamut of bilateral relations. Muchkund Dubey, former Foreign Secretary of India and a scholar, has stated:

> In my view, the review or revision of the Treaty is not a priority issue in Indo-Nepal relations. There are other issues—like water resources, economic development of Nepal, imparting strength, resilience and stability to the democratic process in Nepal etc., which deserve priority attention. I am afraid, undertaking a review of the Treaty would open a Pandora's box [that] will cloud all other important issues

[25] *Rising Nepal*, December 9, 1983.

[26] See *Rising Nepal*, February 12, 1983.

[27] See K. Subrahmanyam, "Sub-continental Security: Some Perceptions," *India's Foreign Review*, 18, 2231, September: 1981, pp. 15–30.

and may adversely affect relations in the medium run if it is not handled properly. And given the emotive character of the issue of the review of the Treaty, it is not at all going to be easy to come out unscathed from the review.[28]

It can be argued that Nepal's proposal would have already lost its momentum if India would have been more forthcoming for accepting it immediately after its proclamation. As Rose has also remarked that "demands for revision of the Treaty were voiced almost immediately after its ratification, and the Ranas were accused of 'antinationalism' for having accepted the treaty."[29] So in real politick, symbol does not matter; obtaining reality guides the state policies.

Nepal as an independent, sovereign state also needs to be mindful of the changing context. Mahendra did it in spite of letting down his own image as a "nationalist." When the Nepali rulers failed to comprehend Nepal's constraints of geopolitics and socioeconomic interrelatedness, problems have had arisen in its relations with immediate neighbors, China and India. It happened during King Birendra's rule during 1972–1990. In 1975, his proposal that Nepal be declared a zone of peace suffered a setback after India's refusal to endorse it. India perennially asked the Nepali side: which country posed a threat to Nepal? Such a question was asked against the context of the 1950 Treaty and the letter exchanged with it since these provisions underline the joint response to any threat posed to them by any third party. In India's calculation, Nepal's peace zone proposal was nothing but an indirect attempt to undercut the special security provisions, which were/are exclusively designed for bilateral action. China was the first country to endorse the peace zone proposal followed by other 115 countries, including the US. However, during King Birendra's visit to the US, President Reagan in 1983 said that the US was theoretically committed to the proposal but to make it "a reality," Nepal was urged to get the endorsement of its neighbors, i.e., by implication, India.

[28] See in particular, Muchkund Dubey, "Some Reflections on India-Nepal Relations" in Lok Raj Baral, ed., *Looking to the Future; India-Nepal Relations in Perspective* (Delhi: Anmol Publications, 1996), pp. 47–57.

[29] See Leo E. Rose, *Nepal: Strategy for Survival* (Bombay: Oxford University press, 1971), p. 187.

Frailty of the Nepali state was also demonstrated by the unnecessary display of "nationalism," which, in the Nepali context, was and still is a kind of arousal of anti-Indian sentiment. In absence of any mobilizing ideology, political rhetoric and tendency of rulers to project them as true nationalists gave rise to false perceptions that Nepal was tilting toward China or India. The Nepali state was unduly under pressure when King Birendra's peace zone proposal became a "peace zone" foreign policy full of sound and fury, but signifying nothing. As all the diplomatic resources were mobilized to spread across the world, India continued to be suspicious of each move. In the 1980s, Nepal's decision to import Chinese arms into Nepal (through Nepal–Tibet border) led India to conclude it as a violation of the 1950 Treaty, which binds Nepal to import such arms from only three countries—India, the US, and Britain. The last two countries were to supply necessary arms and ammunition if India showed its inability to supply. But imports from these countries could only be done with Indian consent.

Imports of Chinese arms and some other factors, both personal and perceptual, seemed to create distrust between the Indian power elites and the Nepali king, provoking India to take a unilateral decision not to extend the Treaty of Trade and Transit. As a result, Nepal faced severe economic crisis owing to the restrictions put on the supply of essential items. However, the Nepali side managed to survive it for about nine months. Its consequences were many, the most significant of which was the collapse of the 30-year-old partyless regime led by the king. Political parties, which had all along been opposing the regime that lacked popular legitimacy, could take the advantage of the situation by mobilizing almost all political parties of India for making the anti-regime movement a success. In February 1990, the movement was initiated by the NC. Other Left parties also joined the fray by forging a ULF.

It seemed that King Birendra wanted to make the proposal a symbol of national independence. Whether it could also bring about a qualitative change in Indo–Nepal relations was questionable. Nevertheless, each country's foreign policy tries to achieve both symbol and substance in the comity of nations. By rubbing soldiers with heads of states or government of other countries, the rulers tend to show their legitimacy at home and abroad. Moreover, a small state needs to rely on its foreign policy more than on its military power. In the given context, however, symbol alone does not matter much if substance of relationship becomes a hostage of rulers and politicians. Short of any mobilizing ideology or programs, politicians in Nepal raise the issue of review of the Treaty. Some even go to the extent of abrogation of it when they are in trouble with India. Politicians who sport themselves as *rashtrabadi* (ultranationalist) even refer to the 1815 Sugauli Treaty, which, in their opinion, had compromised Nepal's territorial gains in the east and west. Even the Maoist Party chairman, Prachanda, joined the chorus with other *rashtrabadis* for avenging the loss of territory after Nepal was defeated by the then East India Company.

In hindsight, it can be said that all such expressions coming from the Indian side were/are nothing more than its continued adherence to the structure of relations as underlined by the 1950 Treaty and the letter exchanged with it. Thus, the 1950 Treaty still continues to be dominant in Indo–Nepal relations no matter how vigorously some sections of politicians of Nepal have had been trying to raise their voices for its review or even abrogation. At the same time, there has also been effort to moderate their positions keeping in view the intricacies of the relationship between India and Nepal. Yet even on the agenda of the trade and transit or on the sharing of water resources, India's security concerns figure prominently. In 1989, the unilateral decision of India to terminate the Treaty of Trade and Transit was influenced by the import of arms by Nepal from China. Prime Minister Rajiv Gandhi's strong reaction also encouraged the outlawed parties to mobilize support against the royal regime. India–Nepal relations was normalized following the restoration of the multiparty system in 1990 and by the visit undertaken by the Interim Prime Minister K. P. Bhattarai shortly thereafter. The joint communiqué published by the two sides on June 10, 1990, revealed that the spirit of the 1950 Treaty continued to be the underlined guidelines for future relationship.

In 1969, the Royal Government of Nepal went to the extent of rejecting the very spirit of the Treaty, maintaining that the Indian version of "special relationship" no longer existed with India not consulting Nepal when the former was with wars with China and Pakistan. The letter and the secret document signed by the two sides in 1965 had further reinforced the 1950 Treaty as Nepal could import arms and ammunition only from India or from the US and the UK after consulting India. In 1969, the Royal Government of Nepal asserted that Nepal was no longer obliged to honor the past treaties with India and the provisions for allowing Indian security personnel posted at the security checkpoints on the China (Tibet) border and urged India to withdraw them. India complied with it by withdrawing its security posts. However, during Prime Minister Kirtinidhi Bista's visit to India in the post-Bangladesh liberation war, both the countries reiterated that the 1950 Treaty continued to exist. Moreover, King Mahendra's last-hour decision to abstain from the voting by the UN that was convened for asking India and Pakistan for a ceasefire demonstrated the limitations of Nepal's foreign policy maneuverability. India did not accept the UN ceasefire resolution by 104 members and eventually succeeded in carving out an independent Republic of Bangladesh. As Nepal had all along been maintaining developments in East Pakistan as an internal affair, its abstention was taken as a diplomatic retreat from its avowed policy of neutrality between India and Pakistan or between India and China.[30]

Nepal–India relations continued to be strained in the 1980s with the former importing from China and the latter showing all indications of annoyance at such a decision. Eventually, India used the Treaty of Trade and the Treaty of Transit as a weapon for taking the Nepali ruler to task. India's unilateral decision not to extend the treaties along with the "economic blockade" imposed against India further soured Nepal–India relations. Its impact on the Nepali economy was enormous for the country. It was also felt that China, Nepal's next-door neighbor, cannot become an alternative at a time of difficulty with the southern neighbor because China was not in a position to supply petroleum and other heavy industrials from the north despite a great expectation that China would do

[30] For details, see Lok Raj Baral, *Oppositional Politics in Nepal* (New Delhi: Abhinab Publications, 1977), and Rishikesh Shaha, *Politics in Nepal 1980–1990* (Kathmandu: Ratnapustak Bhandar, 1990), p. 116.

so in crisis. The oppositional forces then trying to mobilize against the regime found it as a good opportunity to mount the movement. The NC, thus, took the lead in 1990 and decided to launch the mass movement from February 1990. Other parties also joined the movement later in order to restore the multiparty system in the country.

The reasons for picking up the momentum of the movement were both internal and external factors. Internally, the royal regime was isolated due to desertion of the former panchayatocrats who had skimmed the authoritarian regime by showing unstinted loyalty to the king. Many of them who had played key roles for consolidating the royal regime since the 1960 coup now turned the table against the king. Only a few of them, those too with less political clout within the regime, supported the system during the crisis. Second, the regime lacked both political and performance legitimacy contrary to the promises made by the kings (Mahendra and Birendra) that the country would be transformed into a developed one. Neither the personalized rule could sustain it ideologically nor did the promises made by the rulers prove its worth. Demoralized and divided as the elites were, they came to the conclusion that the king had no other options but to talk to the leaders of parties. Thus, the regime collapsed in April 1990 paving the way for a multiparty system.

The second important factor for the collapse of the royal regime was its failure to garner the support of the international community, particularly India. Annoyed with the king, Indian political parties supported the movement for the restoration of democracy, though the GoI's position was somewhat dubious on the issue. It was in a dilemma whether or not it should lend its support to the parties whose control over the people was not yet fully measured. Indian policymakers thought that a movement launched by disparate parties and leaders might go far enough for abolishing monarchy, considered as a symbol of national unity and stability. Later when they knew that the movement was going to be successful, they supported it on the condition that monarchy (constitutional) is retained. Since no parties had ever thought of ending the monarchy, it was easy for them to accept the offer.

Yet, for the royalists, constitutional monarchy meant a republic as all the powers of the king, both de jure and de facto, were to be transformed to the elected bodies. It was expected to be similar to the British monarchy despite the limited demand—restoration of multiparty system—put forward by the movement parties. How the Constitution was drafted and on whose terms and conditions it was framed are questions to be discussed later.

Other functionaries of the state—army, police, bureaucracy, and state-controlled media—become effective only when the core elites continue to keep a grip on the overall situation of the country. Politics, which is the key element of maintaining all the state structures intact, fails to show its rejuvenative capability, ideologically as well as practically, resulting in the demoralization of the subordinate sectors. The RNA, which was considered to be the most dependable ally of the king, had allegedly counseled him not to precipitate the crisis in 1990 by resorting to military solution. As the parties were united due to internal conditions and external support and the disgruntled members of the panchayat had both latent and patent support to the movement, the king was forced to yield. Even during the transition until the new constitution was promulgated by the government, the army, of course at the behest of the king, helped the government pacify the police force that went berserk in reaction to the killing of six policemen by the vigilante groups.[31] Moreover, the army, which again became active due to steady decline of the role of political parties vis-à-vis the king, the RNA once again worked in tandem with the Palace.

Ironically, however, monarchy continued to remain as the center of Nepali politics, whatever the provisions and spirit of the Constitution. Since the objective of the 1990 movement was confined to the restoration of multiparty system in the country after 30 years, the movement leaders thought that they would make a deal with the king if the latter agreed to be a constitutional monarch under the new constitution. But the failures of politicians once again made monarchy more assertive, thus, violating the very spirit of the new Constitution. Being successful for inserting the concept of Hindu monarchical state in the Constitution and knowing the steady decline of the appeal of political parties, which

[31] See *Nepal Press Digest*, 34: 18, April 30, 1990.

were instrumental in forcing the King to accept the change, the king once again became successful to share power. The tripartite agreement reached between the king, the NC, and the ULF and political schisms shown by the leaders of political parties made him assertive within a short time. Both the flawed constitutional arrangement and complex developed by the politicians vis-à-vis the king led to the gradual erosion of the constitutional processes in the country, thus, dashing all hopes, once again, of consolidation of democracy.

The prime ministers were invariably haunted by the Palace ghost and continued to look upon it for its opinion while making crucial decisions. When the elected government wanted to use the RNA against the Maoists, the king and the RNA put forth certain preconditions that indirectly disapproved the government's decision. The noncooperation of the king and army was clear when the home minister resigned blaming the army for not cooperating with the government for averting the Maoist threat. Later, Prime Minister G. P. Koirala resigned on the same issue though he did not come out with any statement disclosing the fact.

The Palace massacre in June 2001 and the accession to the throne by Gyanendra, the brother of the slain King Birendra, hastened the process of monarchical absolutism. First, the new king wanted to get a clean chit on the issue of the palace massacre that he was not involved in it. The two-member investigation commissions consisting of the chief justice and speaker of the House of Representatives put all blame on the Crown Prince Dipendra for undertaking such a bloody massacre, killing altogether 10 members of the royal family including the king and the queen. It may be recalled that the leader of the opposition, Madhav Kumar Nepal of the CPN–UML, had initially agreed to be a member of the commission but later, under the pressure of his party, retracted his decision. It was interesting to observe that the two-member commissions did not go into details except in interviewing some members of the palace and coming out with findings that made the Crown Prince the sole culprit. Who the other masterminds were behind the massacre still continues to be a mystery inside an enigma. Famous for his notoriety and misdeeds, Gyanendra's son Paras was anointed as the Crown Prince only after some time, that too during the Durga Puja festival when the people mostly remain disengaged and are in festive mood.

Taking advantage of the weaknesses of political parties, the new king embarked on taking power into his own hands. He not only started breeding conflicts within political parties but also appointed prime ministers of his own liking, bringing distortions in the constitutional processes in the country. Using the Treaty 126 of the Constitution that deals with the requirements needed for the endorsement of treaties by the Parliament concerning matters of national interest, King Gyanendra set out to destroy it by hiring and firing prime ministers and ministers without regard to other clauses that prescribe the procedures for making a government under the Constitution. Monarchy was, thus, brought into direct conflict with the political parties following the imposition of state of emergency on February 1, 2005, thus, polarizing Nepali politics into pro-monarchy and anti-monarchy camps. This move also drove the major political parties, then opposing the king's ascendancy, to move closer to the CPN (Maoist) for forging a united front for ending what they called "royal absolutism." The 12-point understanding concluded by the SPA and the Maoist (SPA–Maoist Accord) on November 21, 2005, was a historical watershed as it tried to address all outstanding issues raised by the Maoists for making a "new Nepal."[32] This refrain proved to be decisive to ignite the movement as well as the eventual end of monarchy.

[32] In short, the 12-points were: (1) establishment of absolute democracy by ending autocratic monarchy; (2) restoration of the Parliament with the force of agitation, by forming an all-party government with complete authority, holding election to a CA through dialogue and understanding with the Maoists and transfer of sovereignty and state power to the people; (3) establishment of permanent peace along with the solution to armed conflict by putting the royal army and the Maoist armed force under the supervision of the UN; (4) commitment to competitive multiparty system of governance, civil liberties, human rights, etc.; (5) Maoist commitment to create an environment, allowing the political activists of other democratic parties displaced during the course of the armed conflict to return to their former localities and live there with dignity, return their home, land, and property seized in an unjust manner and carry out their activities without hindrance; (6) no repetition of past mistakes by the Maoists; (7) seven political parties also not to repeat the mistakes *committed* in the past in the Parliament and in government; (8) respect for human rights and press freedom; (9) boycott of municipal and parliamentary elections to be conducted by the royal regime

Diplomacy: Past and Present

Prithvi Narayan Shah, the founder of modern Nepal, described his kingdom as "a *tarul* (root-food) between the stones." Such a description also prompted the rulers of Nepal to be adept at handling foreign policy of a country sandwiched between the two great countries of Asia—India and China. Leo Rose says that even in the days of Prithvi Narayan Shah

> Nepal's most formidable problem in formulation and implementation of foreign policy was the preservation of the country's independence in the face of the concurrent but separate threats posed by the newly emerging dominant power in northern India, the British East India Company, and a slowly but steadily expanding Chinese presence in Tibet. Present day Nepal thus perceives its critical geopolitical situation in terms of a long tradition as a buffer state and with some deeply ingrained attitudes toward the policies and tactics required to maintain its political and cultural integrity.[33]

Now much water has flown under the rivers in south of the Himalayas with the emergence of China as one of the potential world powers and India also becoming powerful in view of its development, size, population, military might, and nuclear capability. China's pace of development is spectacular that tries to catch up the US by 2050 or even much early. Its reach to the other parts of the world is fast increasing to which the only superpower—US—seems to be much paranoid. Tibet as the Autonomous Region of China since 1949 has also erased the buffer status bringing the two competitive powers, China and India, as Nepal's immediate neighbors. Even if these two Asian powers have been able

---

calling upon the people to make it a *failure*; (10) friendship with all the countries of the world, neighbors, especially China and India, and end of narrow nationalism of the regime; (11) call upon the civil society, professional organizations, various wings of parties, people of all communities and regions, press, and intellectuals to actively participate in the peaceful movement launched for democracy, peace, prosperity, forward-looking social change, and the country's independence, sovereignty, and pride; and (12) settlement of any problem that may arise between parties through peaceful dialogue at the concerned level or leadership level.

[33] Ibid., p. vii.

to maintain what is called "dynamic equilibrium" of both competition and cooperation, Nepal seems to feel the heat of both that try to set their strong foothold here. Such maneuverings are more transparent than ever before because of the unsettling political developments in Nepal. Political leaders who have been successful in making movements seldom give serious thought to redefining Nepal's relations with neighbors as well as with other countries that are much relevant to Nepal's economy. Nepal's dependency on foreign resources does not show any declining trend. Remittances of Nepalis working in some countries are also the sources of income.

It is also a truism that Nepal's relations with its two immediate neighbors—China and India—continue to be guided by geopolitical reality and the increasing trends of globalization. Nepal can no longer remain a Shangri-la isolated from the rest of the world as it is as much a part of the global system as it is integral to the South Asian region and China. Flow of tourists, communication networks, presence of Nepalis in all parts of the world and labor markets, etc., have reduced the gap between Nepal and other parts of the world. Such trends, nevertheless, do not necessarily change the basics of India–Nepal relations. India continues to be the "safety valve" for Nepal as its large population, especially poor and unemployed people, continues to trek to India for opportunities that are not available at home. Thus, Nepal's diplomacy is constrained by both the geopolitics and also by the newer trends, which are looming large in the conduct of domestic and foreign policies of the countries of the world. Terrorism, for example, is one of such trends or threats that most countries of the world are facing. How terrorism at home and in interstate relations can be tackled is also a challenge. Nepal in particular is also singled out as one of the sites of terrorist activities that are allegedly carried out by some groups against India. It has been frequently said by India that terrorists backed by the Inter Service Intelligence (ISI) of Pakistan use Nepal as a conduit for terrorist missions in India. Since terrorism has assumed international character, its networking across the world has enabled various terrorists groups to work in close collaboration in order to draw the attention of international community. So terrorism, which has emerged as a dominant non-state actor, has been able to sow discord between and among the countries of the region. Therefore conflicts also create "inter-state tensions, new alliances and bounds of cooperation, and redefine the strategic parameters of the region and its member countries."[34]

Since terrorism is replete with both domestic and external dimensions, violence is its guiding spirit, which is highly intractable for any response. Now terrorism and the politics of violence or what is called increasing trends of criminalization of politics have been able to side-track the major national agendas. Governance has been hijacked by politicians who pretend that they are running the government but in actual practice there has been a steady decline of the role of both government and state. As a result, political leaders seem to follow spirit of "make hay while the sun shines," i.e., caring little for setting people-centric action-oriented policies and programs. The domestic mess and inaction has been also reflected in foreign policy and diplomacy. Observers believe that no serious efforts were made to redefine Nepal's policy in the changing national, regional, and global context. Method of conducting foreign policy, particularly with neighbors, was highly personalized instead of making effort for institutionalizing foreign policy making or executing processes. In this context, paying tributes to the former prime minister and leader of the NC after his demise on March 20, 2010, a former Indian ambassador to Nepal was stated to have said "India committed the mistake of conducting personalized politics with the Nepalese leadership for the last 50 years. India will have to do fresh thinking of how to approach the new situation." Yet another former diplomat was of the opinion that G. P. Koirala had a long association with the Indian leadership but his domination of Nepali politics ensured that India–Nepal interaction became personal.[35]

Geography and history are the greatest tutors of Nepali diplomacy. Strategies follow on imperatives bestowed on the country. Sometimes when the rulers stretch geopolitical context too far without weighing its

[34] See S. D. Muni, "Introduction" in Muni, ed., *Responding to Terrorism in South Asia* (Delhi: Manohar, 2006), p. 27.

[35] See *The Hindu*, Delhi, March 22, 2010.

consequences, both the rulers and the country are endangered. Thus, strenuous relations are the product of political myopia and miscalculation adopted in the name of nationalism. Sometimes geopolitical pulls and pressures also make foreign policy difficult as had happened in the early 1960s and/or in 1989 or later. Since the rulers wanted to be projectionist for legitimacy at home and abroad, they deliberately displayed aggressive postures taking advantage of the adversarial relations then developing between neighbors. Domestic pressures similarly created strains in Nepal's relations with India. King Mahendra's 1960 coup not only imposed a ban on political parties but also terminated the first-ever elected government and parliament.

It can be argued that if India would have accepted the peace zone proposal without making any fuss of it, the proposal would already have attenuated. For, Nepal–India cannot be determined only by formal treaties; they go much beyond formal relations. But since India continues to see it through the prism of traditional formal relations that reflect both formal and informal dimensions, they continue to stick to it asking Nepal to point out the faults in the Treaty. Indian apprehensions that Nepal plays the China card when opportunity arises continue to influence Indian policymakers. Judged by the shifting stands taken by the Nepali politicians and rulers vis-à-vis India have also given grounds to such Indian misperceptions. It was expected that the new Nepali rulers in the post-1990 period or in the post-2006 Jan Andolan would formulate long-, medium-, and short-term policies toward neighbors and other powers much related to Nepal, but such policy formulation did not get any attention from any political party. On the contrary, parties, regardless of their political backgrounds or orientations, continue to be driven by old mindset and obsessions. Instead of developing cooperative and coordinated policy measures with India, leaders of parties did not show any courage and vision for developing Nepal's foreign policy, which is carried out by a successful diplomacy. It needed adequate studies and researches as inputs for policy measures.

Once Prime Minister G. P. Koirala had raised the issue of review of the 1950 Treaty in the Parliament in 1991–1992, but it had no follow-up action. Subsequently, his government abandoned this agenda to be picked up by Prime Minister Man Mohan Adhikari of the CPN–UML and later by other succeeding governments including those of the 1990s or by the Maoist-led coalition government headed by Prachanda in 2008–2009. Surprisingly, however, none of them went beyond review without spelling out what elements were needed to be incorporated into the Treaty or what alternatives Nepal had in case of the abrogation of the Treaty.

Triangular Relations: Continuity and Change

Changing geopolitics and shifting priority prompt rulers to steer relations between Nepal and its two neighbors, China and India, while at the same time continuing the traditional relations. The continuation of the 1950 Treaty and the letter exchanged with it or the secret agreements concluded in 1965 still continue despite recurrent strains in bilateral relations. However, when the opportunity arose, Nepali rulers or politicians seemed to be zealous in using foreign policy strategy for scoring their domestic agendas. Once it paid off, but at other times such a strategy backfired.

Such duality in Nepali foreign policy, especially with its neighbors, was more pronounced since the 1960 coup. On the one hand, King Mahendra was using China as a countervailing force to India in the post-1960 coup period until both Nepal and India seemed to change their strained relations that had developed in the aftermath of the 1960 coup to which India had not taken positively. The hit-and-run armed activities carried out by the Nepali Congressmen from Indian bases had also made Mahendra and his lieutenants paranoid with the alleged support to the anti-regime elements then condemned as "anti-nationals." Eventually, both China and the king used each other for enhancing their respective interests. Mahendra took a bold decision, obviously to the chagrin of India, by opening up the Himalayan route allowing the Chinese to construct a road linking Tibet with Kathmandu. Ridiculing Indian criticism, the king said that if communism did not travel on a mule, how could it come on a taxi?

China–India relations further worsened in 1962 when the border war broke out. Nepali rebels then operating from India were also under pressure with India fearing the possible Chinese incursions into Nepal on a pretext of driving out the Indians. Since the royal regime was nervous due to the intensified pressure from the NC rebels as well as from India, the Chinese foreign minister's statement that came on October 6 came as a rescue for Nepal. The statement stated that if any foolhardy attempt was made by any side on Nepal, China would come to the rescue of Nepal. Politics of reactions and developing of threat perceptions from each side also gave advantage to China. India's weaker positions during its border conflict of 1962 and King Mahendra's intent on taking advantage of such a power disequilibrium helped consolidate his absolute rule to the annoyance of India. Moreover, Chinese Foreign Minister Chen Yi's statement that China would come to help Nepal in the event of an aggression against it yielded unexpected result when the NC decided to suspense its anti-regime insurgency conducted from across the India–Nepal border. The Chinese reaction implied that the NC insurgency was being conducted with the support of India with whom China was already engaged in border conflict. India's weaker position caused by the lack of coordination within the various organs of government and also due to the Chinese aggressive statements made in support of the royal regime, made India put pressure on the NC leaders to suspend their armed movement. India feared that China would take the NC insurgency as a pretext to work against India. But India's enhanced military and diplomatic profiles during the Indo–Pakistan War of 1971 or what is called the War of Liberation of Bangladesh prompted it to be more defiant of the Chinese threat of opening a new war front in Sikkim within 48 hours, despite Pakistan's hope of such rescue mission. Erasing the past image of India, the defeat of Pakistan and the creation of the new Republic of Bangladesh presented India as a power to reckon with in South Asia. Truncated Pakistan, a leftover in the western part only, had been a comparative point for showing the power balance. Nevertheless, the creation of Bangladesh through the midwifery role of India could not make much difference in power balance following the emergence of both India and Pakistan as nuclear powers. Yet, from other perspectives, India is ahead of Pakistan insofar as the credentials of a regional power are concerned. The strategic balance of countries can show such a power imbalance if one tries to see the requisites of power in international politics.

Although Nepal's foreign policy parameters remain basically the same, other intervening factors that influence relations need to be adjusted. By doing it, sometimes it also becomes expedient for scoring certain immediate objectives which are not necessarily guided by the larger interest of the nation. But these intervening factors also play. The same strategy used by King Mahendra in 1961–1962 vis-à-vis India and China did not work in 1989 and 2005 when King Birendra and King Gyanendra tried to emulate their father's game, respectively. Birendra's decision to import Chinese arms without consulting India backfired following Indian unilateral decision to terminate the Treaty of Trade and the Treaty of Transit and the fallout of it in form of Indian support for restoration of multiparty system in 1990. Nor could China replace India for the supply of goods and petroleum or by provide massive economic aid during crisis. It demonstrated that China had its own limitations and even calculations that might have prevented it from coming out fully in aid of beleaguered royal regime in 1989. It also proved that India–Nepal relations are incomparable with any other power including China. Nepal's landlocked position facing south and severe constraints imposed on it geographically together with other factors cannot be seen only in isolation.

King Gyanendra's proposal for membership of SAARC to China after India proposed Afghanistan in the November 2005 Dhaka Summit did not go well with the Indian policy. Discretely showing its annoyance to the King, who had already become a bête noire following his decision to impose a state of emergency in Nepal on February 1, 2005, India was allegedly unhappy with his move for bringing in China in the SAARC. Whether it turned out to be one of the principal reasons not for shifting Indian attitude toward the royal regime or not, the royalists do not fail to attribute it to the end of monarchy in Nepal.

The US, the EU, and India worked in tandem to stop the supply of arms and ammunition to the beleaguered king, who was fighting the Maoist insurgency. King Gyanendra, by courting China, might have expected that the northern neighbor would come to his rescue by supporting him, but that did not happen. The Chinese government never used the word "terrorist" for the Maoist rebels, nor did it go extra miles for reciprocating relations with Nepal. China pursued the usual approach neither to criticize the regime nor to encourage the king's opponents. However, in the post-2006 period, Chinese visibility in its dealings with Nepal increased due to a multiplicity of power centers represented by the main political parties such as the NC, the CPN (Maoist), and the CPN–UML. The post-movement political landscape was new due to the emergence of many regional parties in the Tarai (Madhesh), which had remained the constituency of the two parties NC and CPN–UML. Now the regional parties with the strong backing of the Tarai people could show their strong presence in the CA. The two parties Madhesh Jana Adhikar Forum (Madhesh People's Rights Forum) and Tarai–Madhesh Loktantrik Party (Tarai–Madhesh Democratic Party) became first and second parties in the CA from the Tarai. Later, the Madhese Janaadhikar Forum (MJF) split into two, to be led by Upendra Yadav and Vijaya Kumar Gachhadar, respectively.

Monarchy, which had been perceived by foreign powers, including the Chinese, as a stable reliable institution, was no more; nor had other parties been able to impress on Nepal's foreign friends. Thus, it was natural that the foreign powers, in particular India, the US, the EU, and China, became active in Nepal. During the Maoist insurgency, all these powers did not hesitate to supply arms and other kinds of support to the royal regime. But India and the other Western powers discontinued such military and political support urging the king to open dialogue with dissidents who had fallen from the grace of king Gyanendra after his decision to take all powers into his hand in February 2005. Considering it as a setback to the democratic process, India and the Western powers had withheld military support to the regime. Yet China did not join others and continued its own type of relations with the Palace.

Open remarks and hectic diplomatic activities carried out by India and other Western powers also emboldened the Chinese to be indiscrete in its behavior. Not only the frequency of Chinese delegations increased at diplomatic and military levels but the Chinese visitors or even ambassadors became vocal about Nepal. China seemed to depart from its traditional practice of establishing state-to-state relations by reaching out to the leaders of various political parties thinking that not a party was in command of Nepali politics. Chinese participation in the MJF conference held in Birganj and the absence of Indian political parties gave the impression that Chinese are really bent on influencing the region of Nepal. Upendra Yadav, himself a Tarai leader and very close to the Maoist party until he broke away on the eve of the 2006 movement, was misunderstood for having established close link with the Chinese. It has been understood that the Chinese want the same type of privileges in Nepal–China relations as India has, which means the open border and other facilities that are accrued to Indians. Nepal–India relations cannot be put on equal footing with Nepal–China relations due to extensive, close, and deep relations between Nepal and India.

Nepali diplomacy is primarily related to its relations with neighbors. However, this is becoming more complex due to highly unpredictable behaviors of leaders of parties as well as by the developing international power politics whose effects are likely to be more challenging than before. So even if the triangular relations continue to be interactive as in the past, the emerging global power dynamics need to be taken into consideration by the new power elites of Nepal. China's emergence as a potential world power is multidimensional—with pronounced economic, military, and internal cohesiveness as its stable components. Yet, China has also its caveats such as overflowing impacts of global economic relations, particularly with the US and other countries, which are liberal democracies. China's economic prosperity also needs to be inclusive that enables people in general to be empowered.

Nepal–India relations can no longer be understood through the conventional prism. The fast-changing regional and international developments and trends such as the rise of ethnic, regional, and nonideological factors and their impacts on domestic and foreign policies have tried to reshape bilateral relations. The role of smaller states to manage both national and international trends has also shrunk in recent years. Since the old maneuverability does not exist to the extent that as it was in the past, Nepal is constrained to adjust to the new realities. Nevertheless, some key elements seem to constantly engage them in defining their relations. They are: political, economic, sociocultural, strategic, and perceptual.

Politically, India has all along been pursuing a consistent policy toward Nepal. In 1950, it put pressure on the Ranas to radically democratize the system despite the imposition of the same Rana rulers as copartners in the new dispensation. Later, the standoff between the Ranas and the Congress leader changed course, paving the way for monarchical absolutism. India did not support the December 1960 coup staged by King Mahendra against the first-ever elected government and parliamentary system,[36] despite conflicting opinions being expressed in support and against India's approach to democracy issue.[37] Consequently, the

[36] Conflicting opinions were/are being circulated in Nepal. Some are of the view that the coup staged by King Mahendra in 1960 had the tacit backing of India, especially Prime Minister Jawaharlal Nehru. Ganesh Raj Sharma, a senior advocate and confidante of B. P. Koirala, prime minister during the coup, accepts such a view stating that "... it is impossible to escape the conclusion that Nehru not only had the prior knowledge but had also consented to the change." In support of this hypothesis, Sharma refers to Rishikesh Shaha, then the King's emissary to Nehru, that Nehru in fact wanted to remove Prime Minister B. P. Koirala without dissolving the Parliament. Shaha is stated to have confided in Sharma that "he was confronted by an angry Nehru who said that he had agreed to the removal of B. P., but not for the dissolution of Parliament."

See Ganesh Raj Sharma's preface to M. P. Koirala: A Role in a Revolution (Kathmandu: Jagadamba Prakashan, 2008), p. xii.

[37] Prime Minister Nehru's statement in the Parliament on December 20, 1960, and the Indian government's overall attitude toward democratic movements in Nepal contradict the views of those who saw India's consent to King Mahendra's action of dismantling parliamentary democracy. For Nehru's statement in Parliament, see Muchkund Dubey, "Some Reflections on India-Nepal Relations" in Lok Raj Baral, ed., Looking to the Future: India-Nepal Relations in Perspective (Delhi: Anmol Publications, 1996). The responses to Ganesh Raj Sharma's view that India was behind the coup has been strongly refuted by S. D. Muni when he writes:

If Nehru wanted B. P. to be removed, why did he ask for the restoration of status quo ante? Further, why did he let the Nepali Congress wage a war against King Mahendra, even at the cost of allowing Chinese influence grow in Nepal, if he had already consented to the King's move? There is a tribe of analysts, commentators, public men and politicians who see India's hand behind almost everything that goes wrong in Nepal.

See S. D. Muni, India's Foreign Policy: The Democracy Dimension (Delhi: Cambridge University Press, 2009), p. 41.

democracy issue had always remained a pinprick in India–Nepal relations, though India continued to work with the partyless regime led by the absolute king, realizing that too much psychological distance to be created by mutual hatred, developed over democracy, and Nepal's China policy would go against the long-term interest of India. Since 1964, India, therefore, started developing a rapport with the king by sending a more conciliatory ambassador to Nepal in 1964. India followed a two-track policy toward Nepal by showing sympathy for the political dissidents, and also by developing rapport with the regime with massive Indian aid to Nepal. By the end of 1960s, India topped the list for doling out aid to Nepal. Moreover, it also played a small role in securing the release of B. P. Koirala after the latter supported the statement of Subarna Shamsher, then acting party president who was working from India. Subarna had offered the cooperation of the NC to the "development of the constitution (partyless panchayat)." Later B. P. Koirala changed his position that argued for the necessity of an armed movement for turning Nepal into a full-fledged democracy.

It seemed that the Indian policymakers or even its intelligence agencies had failed to assess the changed landscape of Nepali politics following the 12-point understanding reached between the SPA and the Maoists. The Government of Nepal was forced to change its previous position on Nepal's developments, prompting it to depart from its two-pillar policy (constitutional monarchy and multiparty democracy). India finally accepted the people of Nepal as the only legitimate deciding factor. India's open defiance of King Gyanendra's emergency rule and encouragement given to the political parties to be closer to the Maoists were some of the instances.

The former royalists, however, do not see the Nepali people playing any role in ending monarchy, but point out their fingers at India for allegedly supporting the movement against monarchy. According to them, King Gyanendra's move to make China a member of the SAARC during the Dhaka SAARC Summit in 2005 annoyed India, which eventually proved fatal for monarchy.

Second, Nepal's landlocked position facing the southern neighbor and close economic interdependence (dependence?) does not allow Nepal to be fully independent of policy decisions. Nor can China provide alternatives to it. In 1989, when India took unilateral decision to withdraw the trade and transit treaties, Nepal's economic difficulties could not be addressed by the Chinese despite rhetorical statements then coming from the Nepali ruling elites for Chinese favor.

Third, the civilizational linkages are so strong that they can hardly be influenced by politics. Sometimes, the religious issue gets politicized as it happened recently while changing the priests of the Pashupatinath temple. Political parties both in India and Nepal seem to overplay such issues. The Nepalis are by comparison more flexible to delve into the depth and height of Indo–Nepal relations, but the obscurantist elements on both sides of the border try to manipulate them to score their own interests.

Fourth, Nepal, being placed in the strategic zone of the region, particularly between China and India, needs to play a more moderate and balancing role between the two neighbors. Moreover, the burgeoning India–US relations, the straining of India–Pakistan relations, and the role of China to placate Pakistan vis-à-vis India are likely to put much pressure on Nepali rulers. It has been remarked that the US may try to consolidate its relations with both old allies like Japan and emerging power like India to strike a balance against China. Since Nepal is integrally connected to the Gangetic region of India, which is also India's heartland, Nepal should be cognizant of the vital security concerns of India. Similarly China's major concern is Tibet, to which the Nepali side needs to be serious. Now with the enhanced regional and global power position of India and China along with the trends of checkmating China's rise to that status, strategic dimensions are likely to be more complex. How China is increasingly showing its concerns over Nepal's internal and external developments has been vociferously raised as an issue by visiting Chinese dignitaries and representatives of its diplomatic mission in Nepal. The Chinese proposal to update the Treaty has to be seen in this light.

Finally, perceptions rather than substance also make elites of Nepal and India unnecessarily hypersensitive. The psyche that India is the key factor for bringing about changes either in the government or in the regime make Nepali politicians jittery. So are some political sections of India that try to interpret any event or action of the Government of Nepal as unfriendly to India. Lack of culture of empathy, thus, gives rise to distrust on both sides.

It seems that difficult days are ahead for Nepali policymakers. Internal situation is in a mess with the major parties responsible for bringing about a radical change quarreling for no substantive reasons. Economic, regional, ethnic, and governance crises are looming large indicating no concerted effort to resolve them. If Nepal fails to maintain a minimum level of development and keep its own house in order by consolidating representative institutions, its aspirations to be an independent and sovereign nation would also be undermined. Above all, minimum level of consensus among the major political forces, internal development, peace, and stability are the prerequisites for a sound foreign policy.

4

Democracy, Peace, and Development

Politics, whether based on people or on personalities—oligarchy or dictatorship—is about power. Power has varied forms and is judged according to our own respective value positions. For, unless we try to confine ourselves to single out a particular type of power, we have risks of being lost in power wilderness. My purpose here is to relate power to democracy as I have understood it in both universal and national contexts. As "elite" is a word which is ubiquitous in all types of regime transcending monarchy, authoritarian, tutelary democracy, or democracy, its variation also needs to be appropriately discussed. In monarchy, one-man rule prevails with the help of his courtiers who become elites in the modern sense. In democracy, elites need to be accountable and transparent, while in other regimes such standards are normally frowned at. Although totalitarian dictatorship is another form where power is exercised at the absolute will of a leader or committee members as was evident during the Stalin era in the former Soviet Union or in Germany and Italy during Hitler and Mussolini's era before World War II, such regimes now are diluted in forms of authoritarian rules. Some of them are absolutist and others swing between limited freedoms and absolutism.

My own understanding of democracy has undergone a change. Democracy as I understood until a few years ago was limited in horizon. I heard this word in Biratnagar in 1950 when I was a student of class III. When I saw the pamphlets thrown from a Dakota Aeroplane in November that year, they spread the message against the Rana oligarchy that scuttled democratic rights of people for more than a century and

117

against which the NC was going to launch an armed movement. Its declared objectives were first to dismantle the Rana regime and then to establish a democracy. By that time, democracy was understood as an import from outside because most Nepali leaders who were in the front had their political socialization in India. I have been trying to understand democracy ever since I read these pamphlets and also trying to update and contextualize my thinking. How many of my premonitions were false is now being reexamined. Normally understood, democracy is a universal value centered on people—their inculcation of culture of moderation, tolerance, recognition of worth of each individual, struggle for justice, indomitable courage, end of all forms of exploitation, development of cognitive and evaluative domains, change of government through legitimate constitutional and legal means, and security and peace. Without peace of mind and feeling of security, democracy can neither be practiced nor will it be sustainable. Whatever the definition of democracy, it is basically the rule of people's representatives who are elected periodically through suitable mechanisms designed for specific country or countries.

"Electocracy" versus Democracy

Democracy and election are integral to each other. Nevertheless, election qua election alone cannot ensure democracy because elections are increasingly exploited by selfish and power-hungry politicians or mafias in countries where the spirit of democracy is not internalized by political elites and their henchmen. If one believes that holding elections successfully is a test of democratic system, he/she is doubly wrong as the administration, police, money, muscle, and mafia rule the roost in name of elections and ensure the victories of their candidates. If democracy is principle, election is a tool without which modern democratic practices become impossible. Election is also a method with which democratic aspirations and democratic exercises are realized. What kinds of mechanisms are used by countries is a different matter. In developing countries, however, electoral politics that begins from declaration of election dates, manifesto preparation of political parties, candidate selection, resource mobilization, campaigns and coordination at both organizational and national level, counting of votes and declaration of results are various aspects of election system. Adherence to the code of conduct enforced by the election commission is also important for making election a success. In addition, the finale of the electoral system is the composition of legislature and election of executive either directly or indirectly through parliament depending on the types of executives arranged by constitution. Broadly, there are three types of Western political systems: "Anglo-American political systems (exemplified by Britain and the US), Continental European political systems (France, Germany, and Italy), and a third type is not given a distinct label."[1] However, within such broad types, variations are found in parliamentary, presidential, and semi-presidential types with country-specific modifications and innovations. Within the Westminster model also, many changes have been added in order to make it relevant to the country's own requirements. The Indian parliamentary system has retained the basic features of parliamentary type but it has also undergone changes. The election system is a crucial variable for making democracy work or fail as political elites indulgent in electoral politics are, to a larger extent, responsible for success and failure of democracy. As Larry Diamond has stated:

A country *cannot* be a democracy if there is no freedom of speech and association and no rule of law. But is this because elections themselves cannot be free and fair under such circumstances, or because free and fair elections are not enough for a country to be a democracy?[2]

Today's democracy demands "enthusiastic" or active participation of people irrespective of class, caste, ethnic loyalties, region, and gender.

[1] Gabriel A. Almond, "Comparative Political Systems," *Journal of Politics*, XVIII, 8: 1956 as cited in Arend Lijphart, *Thinking About Democracy: Power Sharing and Majority Rule in Theory and Practice* (London: Routledge, 2008), pp. 1–279.

[2] See Larry Diamond, *The Spirit of Democracy* (New York: Holt Paperbacks, 2008), p. 21.

The spirit of inclusive democracy, therefore, shuns ritualistic participation that works as a handy tool for catapulting certain limited people (elite) into the decision-making processes. In Nepal or even in India or elsewhere, there has had been a tendency of making electoral process narrow and ritualistic. Thus, such a mechanism was/is neither able to resolve the issues of inclusion and empowerment of ordinary citizens in whose names votes have been generally garnered nor could democratic system strike deep roots. Although the Indian political system is relatively better than many countries of South Asia, democracy in India too needs to be further refurbished for establishing a symbiotic relationship of what is called "substantive" and "procedural" democracy. Stretching this point, further, Jayal states:

> Those who view democracy purely as a set of institutions ... encompassing free and fair elections, legislative assemblies, and constitutional governments arising out of these ... tend to be sanguine about India as the world's largest democracy (because electorate) has successfully voted out corrupt or repressive regimes. But to those whose mental construct of a democracy is a society peopled by truly equal citizens, who are politically engaged, tolerant of different opinions and ways of life, and have equal voice in choosing their rulers and holding them accountable, Indian democracy appears to be a poor candidate.[3]

Based on "fallacy of electoralism," inclusiveness and spatial extension alone cannot meet the requirements of democracy. Thus, democracy goes beyond voting and freedom of expression, though they are also the essential aspects of democracy.

In the given Nepali context, if democratic consolidation is in a state of flux, electoral system is also on trial and error approach with political stakeholders (parties and civil society) still not clear about the durability of a particular election method. The broken links of election process is coterminous with that of overall democratic development to which I call swings from one end to the other with a variety of experiments. In 1959,

---

[3] Niraja Gopal Jayal, "Introduction: Situating Indian Democracy" in Niraja Gopal Jayal, ed., *Democracy in India* (New Delhi: Oxford University Press, 2001), p. 3. For similar opinion, see also Ayesha Jalal, *Democracy and Authoritarianism in South Asia* (Delhi: Cambridge University Press, 1995).

the Nepalis for the first time participated on a nationwide scale for electing representatives to the Parliament. This experiment ended with the termination of multiparty democracy in 1960. The partyless regime led by the king did not allow formalized oppositional politics despite permission granted to express individual opinion without mentioning the king and the "fundamentals" of the new regime. Nevertheless, the royal regime did not go unchallenged as both the "extra-systemic" and "systemic" oppositions did their best to expose the undemocratic character of the regime. On the one hand, the outlawed parties, especially the NC and some factions of Communist Party of Nepal (NCP), mounted their opposition to the regime, its (regime) own functionaries and professional organizations opposed from within on the other.[4]

So the electoral process introduced by the regime in its early phase was a virtual selection of loyalists who had no political ideology but to be a thoroughbred conformist. The administration and police managed such selection of individuals. Only the national referendum held to ascertain the opinion of the people for choosing either a multiparty system or panchayat system with reforms were free to express opinion on political issues except monarchy. Subsequently, the adult franchise elections, which came in the wake of constitutional reforms following the mandate, albeit highly controversial, received by the regime in the referendum, allowed candidates to contest on an individual basis because of the continued ban on parties. Although the victory was for the reformed system, King Birendra took it as a mandate given to the "partyless" regime. However, the regime could not set the clock back by strictly imposing its discipline on them resulting in contradictions within the regime. Such a contradictory political situation changed following the restoration of multiparty system. The anti-regime movement in 1990 became successful to force the king to give in to the restoration of multiparty system abandoned two and half decades ago. It was expected that constitutional monarchy and multiparty system of the British variety would be consolidated under the Constitution of the Kingdom of

---

[4] See in detail, Lok Raj Baral, *Oppositional Politics in Nepal* (Delhi: Abhinav Publications, 1977).

Nepal (1990). Since it was a compromise document reached between the two movement forces—the NC and the ULF of some communist factions—and the king, its actual spirit remained ambiguous. For, on the one hand, the Constitution believed in constitutional monarchy and was expected that the Palace behave accordingly; on the other hand, it also acknowledged somewhat elevated role of the king due to his gestures that he had shown for transforming his role into a new position to be agree upon between him and the NC and the ULF. The preamble to the Constitution mentioned four main pillars—constitutional monarchy, multiparty system, sovereignty of people, and fundamental rights of people. What was intriguing were two contradictory elements. First, it was said that there would be no alternative to constitutional monarchy under the Constitution, and second, the people of Nepal were sovereign. Even the Parliament elected by the sovereign people did not initiate any debate on monarchy whatever role it played. Thus, there was no provision of amending the Constitution if a situation arose about the role of monarchy in the future. It has foreclosed the option that could only be changed through extra-constitutional means or what John Locke had suggested the right of people to revolution in case the contract broke down.

The third experiment with the multiparty Constitution was also traumatic in many respects. First, the political parties that had anointed monarchy after the 1990 movement thinking that monarchy would now onward accept the change for consolidation of multiparty democracy were proved wrong. Launched for achieving only a multiparty system, the 1990 movement itself remained vague with regard to the nature of polity in the future. However, by way of making the Constitution, the two forces—the NC and the ULF—became confident that parliamentary democracy was going to stay with the cooperation of the king. During the making of the Constitution, the chairman of the commission and the Interim Minister had been able to convince the royalties that their interests would be well safeguarded by making compromises in the constitution. Although the Palace was not happy with the limited position bestowed on the king by the Constitution, the Palace intrigues began with the announcement of the new Constitution itself. Instead of reading out the text of the speech prepared by the government, King Birendra took out his own text from his pocket and read it to the surprise and anxiety of people who had thought that the new era of stability and democracy had begun. Even during the drafting phase of the Constitution, the Palace had tried to ensure its sovereign position along with the retention of Hindu state. Some top-ranking army generals were sent to press on making the king as the de facto chief of the RNA as was the case in 1959 arrangement. It was perhaps thought that the army was the exclusive domain of the king. It may be recalled that King Mahendra had used the army to stage a coup in 1960.

Three elections for the Pratinidhi Sabha (Lower House) were held under the 1990 Constitution, the second one (1994) being mid-term election. All these elections were held on the basis of first-past-the-post system, which is being practiced in the UK, India, and a few other countries. Since it is called a majority–minority system with the winner taking all, despite its loss of popular votes, any winning party could form the government. In 1991 election, the NC got absolute majority by winning 110 seats in a House of 205, while the CPN–UML became second by winning 69 seats. In popular votes, the NC had only 37 percent followed by the CPN–UML with 30 percent. So for the first time in the history of the country, the Communist Party could make up from its previous position of four seats in the 1959–1960 Parliament of 109 members.

When the 36 members of his own party did not support the government to pass a vote of thanks, Prime Minister Koirala advised the king for the dissolution of the Parliament and went to the mid-term election. Angered by the role of party dissidents, Prime Minister G. P. Koirala advised the king for dissolution of the House to which the king obliged and declared fresh election. From a representation point of view, all the three elections of the 1990s and the negative politics that crept in were indicative of how parties missed the opportunity for consolidating democracy. High degree of political instability overshadowed many positive aspects as parties spent much of their energy on petty personal and partisan interest thus emboldening the kings to intervene when the opportune movement was at hand. Moreover, the three parliamentary and local elections did not at all indicate to make democracy more inclusive, which could make feel empowered.

The three elections held under the 1990 Constitution did not make any departure from the past insofar as the nature of composition of the

Table 4.1

Showing the Representation of Various Caste/Ethnic and Gender in the House of Representatives (1991, 1994, and 1999)[5]

Caste/Ethnic Groups	Population	Percentage	1991	1994	1999
Hill Caste Groups	702,320	30.89	114 (55.61%)	129 (62.93%)	122 (59.51%)
Dalit	1,692	7.11	1 (0.48%)	–	–
Kirat/Mongol Ethnic Groups	501,131	22.04	34 (16.59%)	24 (11.71)	28 (13.66%)
Newar	124,532	5.58	14 (6.83%)	12 (5.85%)	14 (6.83%)
Ethnic Groups of Inner Madhesh (Inner Tarai)	251,117	1.11	1 (0.48%)	–	–
Madhese Castes	3,464,249	15.24	18 (8.71%)	22 (10.73%)	29 (14.15%)
Madhese Dalit	904,924	3.99	–	–	–
Madhese Ethnic Groups	2,814,927	8.11	18 (8.78%)	14 (6.83%)	10 (4.88%)
Muslim	971,056	4.27	5 (2.43%)	4 (1.59%)	2 (0.97%)
Female	11,377,556	50.04	7 (3.41%)	7 (3.41%)	12 (5.85%)
Male	11,359,378	49.96	198 (96.6%)	198 (96.6%)	193 (94.15%)

Source: Central Bureau of Statistics, Kathmandu; National Planning Commission; Department of Census; June 2002. Tabulated from the results declared by the Election Commission of Nepal in 1991, 1994, and 1999.

Parliament was concerned. The new elites in various parties were not also different from past elites. Thus, the pattern of representation in various national legislatures and local bodies show the domination of the same hill caste groups in politics. The composition of three lower house of the Parliament in 1991, 1994, and 1999 demonstrates the unchanged picture of Brahmin–Chhetri domination.[6] Politically, however, the two

[5] Lok Raj Baral, "The Unclear Road Map: Parties and the Political Process" in Lok Raj Baral, ed., *Political Parties and Parliament* (Delhi: Adroit Publishers, 2004), p. 51. Table 4.1 shows the unchanged pattern of representation in the three elections held during 1991–1999.

[6] For a detailed picture of the representation pattern, see also Lok Raj Baral, Krihsna Hachhethu, and Hari Sharma, *Leadership in Nepal* (Delhi: Adroit Publishers, 2001).

leading parties could stabilize their positions either sitting in the government or in the opposition. The percentage of seats won and the popular votes received by them also indicated that the two parties—the NC and the CPN–UML—were expected to alternate their roles through elections, while the RPP, a party formed by former royalists after the 1990 movement, still far behind in strength both within and outside the Parliament, was expected to act as a balancer or even as a "wild card," depending upon the political context and power equation. The only corollary was that the combined parliamentary strength of all other parties as shown by the 1991 and 1994 elections, including the RPP, did not cross 30 members, i.e., less than that of the NC and CPN–UML. Such an analysis could lead us to conclude that the two elections had given strong indication for a two-and-quarter party system.[7] Interestingly, this scenario continued to dominate with slight change in the position of the RPP after it was split in the wake of governmental instability. The undivided RPP really played a "wild card" following the defeat of the NC in 1994. However, the NC could restore its lost ground in 1999 election reducing the size of the RPP and the CPN–UML. The CPN–UML too split on the eve of election contributing to ensure the NC majority in the Parliament. As a result, the splits reduced the role of both the RPP and the CPN–UML, enabling once again the NC to be at the center stage of politics.

From the point of view of political stability, the loss or gain in the elections did hardly matter to the Nepali parties. The NC with absolute majority in 1999 could soon break following King Gynendra's ascension to the throne after the Palace massacre in 2001. Intent on dividing the parties as did his father in the late 1950s, the new king contrived division within the NC while the other parties were already split. In 1994 election, the NC "supreme leader" Ganesh Man and his colleagues did not support the official NC in order to contrive defeat for the party led by G. P. Koirala. Personality wars have had been a recurrent subject in the politics of Nepal since the early 1950s. It needs to be watched how the parties behave in the post-monarchy Nepal. Judging by the intraparty

[7] Lok Raj Baral, "The 1994 Nepal Elections: Emerging Trends in Party Politics," *Asian Survey*, xxxv, 5, May: 1995, pp. 439–440.

and interparty conflicts, reminiscent of the past, as stated in the previous chapters, parties are not likely to be in proper shape for consolidation of democracy. So, a spate of splits or internal wrangling may afflict the parties and democracy.

CA Election and New Political Dynamics

The post-2006 political transition entered into yet another phase with the successful election to the CA on April 10, 2008, and its stunning results. The CPN (Maoist) that had waged People's War for about a decade surpassed the other national parties like the NC and the CPN–UML by becoming the first largest party in the CA. Of the total electoral seats of 575 allocated for both majority (first-past-the-post) and proportional systems, the Maoists wrested 220 seats, while its major competitors, the NC and the CPN–UML, respectively, getting 110 and 103 seats. The 26 members nominated to the CA on the basis of proportion have added further strength of respective parties. If the first-past-the-post system would have been accepted, there was great prospect of Maoist emergence as a majority party. How the CPN (Maoist) fared well in the direct elections could be seen in the numbers of seats it won.

Tables 4.2 and 4.3 that show positions of parties and social representation pattern in the CA make substantive change in making democracy inclusive.

In Table 4.4, a comparative view of the pattern of representation in the former parliaments and the CA (2008) will show the marked difference.

Compared to the previous elections held in the post-1990 multiparty era, elections to the CA were significant in many respects. First, it dramatically changed the pattern of caste domination, facilitating other social and regional groups to climb up the political ladder in at least quantitative sense. It could be done through the PR system as parties were given the rights to present their closed list of candidates, making the entire country as the single constituency. Since the parties had mandatory provisions for enlisting various social categories (*janjati*, Dalit,

Table 4.2

Parties' Positions in the CA Election Results, 2008

No.	Political Parties	FPTP Result	PR Result	Total
1	Communist Party of Nepal (Maoist) (CPN [Maoist])	120	100	220
2	Nepali Congress (NC)	37	73	110
3	Communist Party of Nepal–Unified Marxist Leninist (CPN–UML)	33	70	103
4	Madheshi People's Rights Forum	30	22	52
5	Tarai–Madhesh Democratic Party (T–MLP)	9	11	20
6	Sadbhawana Party (Mahato)	4	5	9
7	Janamorcha Nepal	2	5	7
8	Nepal Workers and Peasants' Party	2	2	4
9	Janamorcha Nepal	1	3	4
10	Independent	2	0	2
11	Rashtriya Prajatantra Party (RPP)	0	8	8
12	CPN–ML	0	8	8
13	Communist Party of Nepal (United) (CPN [United])	0	5	5
14	Rashtriya Prajatantra Party–Nepal (RPP–N)	0	4	4
15	Rastriya Janashakti Party (RJP)	0	3	3
16	Rastriya Janamukti Party	0	2	2
17	Communist Party of Nepal (Unified) (CPN [Unified])	0	2	2
18	Nepal Sadbhawana (Anandi Devi) (NSP)	0	2	2
19	Nepali Janta Dal	0	2	2
20	Federal Democratic National Fourm	0	2	2
21	Samajbadi Prajantantrik Janata Party Nepal	0	1	1
22	Dalit Janajati Party	0	1	1
23	Nepal Pariwar Dal	0	1	1
24	Nepal Rastriya Party	0	1	1
25	Nepal Loktantrik Samajbadi Dal	0	1	1
26	Chure Bhawar Rastriya Ekata Party Nepal	0	1	1
	Total	**240**	**335**	**575***

Source: Election Commission of Nepal, Kathmandu, 2008.

Notes: *Twenty-six members would be nominated from various sections of society to make a 601-member CA.

FPTP-First-past-the-post.

gender, region, and other minorities), they, accordingly, prepared a close list of candidates in order of preference. The result was determined according to the countrywide votes polled by each party.

Table 4.3
Social Representation in the CA

Population Groups	FPTP Result	PR Result
Janajati (Indigenous nationalities)	59	88
Janajati (Madhesi)	18	27
Madhesi	48	76
Muslim, Churaute (Bangle dealer)	7	9
Dalit (Madhesi)	2	11
Dalit (Hill)	5	29
Others (Hill) Brahmin, Chhetri	101	95
Total	240	335
Women	30	160

Source: www.election.gov.np as cited in Nepal Human Development Report 2009 (Kathmandu: UNDP, 2009), p. 74.

Note: FPTP- First-past-the-post

Table 4.4
Societal Representation in the Parliament in the Past and in the CA at Present

Caste/Ethnicity	Population (%)	House of Representatives (% of 205 seats)			CA	
		1991	1994	1999	No.	%
Hill high caste	30.8	56	63	60	200	33.3
Hill ethnic	28.5	24	18	20	159	26.5
Madheshi caste	14.8	9	11	14	123	20.4
Madheshi ethnic	8.7	9	7	5	53	8.8
Muslim	4.3	2	1	1	18	3.0
Dalit	12.9	0.5	–	–	48	7.9
Total	–	–	–	–	601	100
Women	50	3	3	6	197	33.77

Source: Adapted from Krishna Hachhethu, *State Building in Nepal* (Kathmandu: ESP, 2009), p. 89.

Nonetheless, such PR system as practiced in 2008 was flawed in many respects, but the question was paramount in the given context. Members who came from the PR system and members representing their constituencies through the direct election method seemed to develop a psychological gap with the former having no constituencies of their own for maintaining direct contact with their constituencies, while the latter felt that they were in fact the real representatives of people as they could win elections in competitive system. The persons listed in the PR system were perceived as nominees of parties who were not required to fight election in person. However, in all legislative businesses, both types of representatives enjoyed equal treatment. The two-year-old exercise in the CA, which also works as the parliament, has shown that members who came from far and wide of the country and had no previous backgrounds in legislative exercises are not wasted. Members who were in constant interactions on various issues such as forms of government, federalism with special reference to Nepal's own sociocultural and regional settings did improve a lot qualitatively. Many chairpersons of the committees, who did not know anything about parliamentary committees, soon developed as better parliamentarians, showing that democracy is learning-by-doing process.

Parties, Crisis of Governance, and Geopolitics

Crisis of governance in today's Nepal is related to ideology, parties, and leadership and the universe they create for their roles. In addition, the role of the external players to influence events, process, and actors has also contributed to the crisis. During the royal regime it was easy to pass the buck saying that all misdeeds flowed from the Palace. The post–2006 Jan Andolan elites blame each other because of their lack of vision, experience, and tendency of flouting the norms of governance. Consequently, all the organs of the government—bureaucracy, police, APF, and army—and government-run corporations have been affected by partisan politics. The prime minister cannot establish his leadership in the government due to two things. First, the loose cabinet system of government consisting of divergent parties and individuals has made the prime minister's position very weak. Incapable of taking decision, he has to keep quiet even if his colleagues defy him. As no parties command majority support in the Parliament nor is there any possibility of one-party dominance system in the future due to the mixed electoral system—the first-past-the-post and proportional—the prime minister has/will become weak to establish his leadership. Even in the case of Maoist-led government headed by Prachanda in the aftermath of the 2008 CA election, the role of the prime minister failed to project his image by providing effective governance. For, pressures from within his own party and also from other coalition partners seemed to limit his role. How the Maoist-led government was forced to resign when the prime minister took decision to sack the chief of the army staff has been discussed in other sections.

The crisis of governance came in sharp focus following the installation of Madhav Kumar Nepal–led coalition government. Defeated from two constituencies (from his home district , Rautahat, and capital Kathmandu), Nepal became prime minister with the support of the second largest party, the NC, the breakaway MJF (democratic), the NSP (Mahato), and the T–MLP along with some small parties. Technically, Madhav Nepal was member of the House through the nomination of his party under the proportional system, but he had in fact forfeited his legitimacy to head the government after his defeat from two constituencies in direct election.

Second, the polarized personalities, parties, and ideologies cannot make a prime minister effective. Its negative consequences could be seen in the constitution-making process despite being the first priority of each party. Defiance of the prime minister by his colleagues including those of his own party, lack of strong will power, tendency to be more compromising on issues so vital for establishing the institution of the prime minister, failure to formulate policies, and pervasive crisis of governance created by other intervening factors have affected the working of the government negatively in today's Nepal. The peace process, which was to be completed soon after the formation of the first Interim Government (2006–2008), has turned out to be most contentious issue for taking ahead the road of democracy and peace. Against this background, the so-called controversies over the role of external powers and the UNMIN can be examined.

The Government of Nepal's handling of Machine Readable Passport (MRP) issue was marked by ineptitude. First, the government awarded it to India and then withdrew its decision in the midst of strong criticisms of the CA members for granting the printing of the MRP to India without any bid. Finding the French group as the lowest bidder, the government went in favor of the decision made by the ministry despite strong opposition of Foreign Minister Sujata Koirala who wanted to give it to India. She not only opposed this in the cabinet but also came out with a strong statement lashing out at the officials of her own ministry for what she said keeping her in the dark on the whole issue. Nevertheless, the cabinet authorized the prime minister, notwithstanding the opposition of the concerned minister, to settle the issue by accepting the deal offered by the French company to make passport within the stipulated time. What was surprising was that how a foreign minister could continue in office despite being so strong a critic of the entire passport episode. Prime Minister Nepal had also confronted an awkward situation when his foreign minister, Sujata Koirala from the NC party, boycotted his official visit to India at the eleventh hour when the he showed his reluctance to appoint her deputy prime minister on the request of her father, G. P. Koirala, then the NC president and a strong political personality. Defeated from her own constituency in Sunsari district and also being opposed by most senior leaders of the NC or of its working committee, Sujata was imposed from above. Hence, the initial reluctance of Prime Minister Nepal not to appoint her as deputy prime minister was understandable but eventually complied with the order of G. P. Koirala.

How the government in the "new republican Nepal" works is also demonstrated by the "helplessness" of the prime minister. The controversy of the UNMIN typifies such state of affairs. The UNMIN came to Nepal on the joint request of the government headed by G. P. Koirala and the CPN (Maoist) leader, Prachanda. Sent by the UN Security Council decision to support Nepal's peace process, with specific tasks related to the monitoring of arms and armies, both the NA and ex-Maoist combatants. Its term had been extended four times as no parties involved, including the Maoists, gave priority to the three tasks—monitoring, integration, and rehabilitation (MIR)—of the Maoist combatants. Similarly, the NA was also put under its radar:

> ... in order to hold elections to constituent assembly in a peaceful, free, and fair
> . environment and for democratization and restructuring of the Nepali Army as per

the feelings expressed in 12-point agreement, eight-point understandings, 25-point code of Conduct and five-point letter sent to the United Nations.[8]

However, as time dragged on without any decision on the three tasks to be completed by the Maoists and the government after the successful election to the CA in 2008, the Maoist and non-Maoist parties started picking up quarrels on the issue of the MIR. With the increasing loss of trust and mutual cooperation between the three major parties, the UCPN (Maoist), the NC, and the CPN–UML due to their overindulgence in power game, no substantial progress could be made but the identification of about 19,000 combatants and their placement in seven camps spread across the country.

Parties that worked in tandem during the 2006 movement and subsequently until the CA election started parting company. The first party to break relations with the Maoists was the NC. It did not support the Maoist party by becoming a coalition partner as other parties did after the CA election. On the contrary, it decided to sit in the opposition until Prachanda was ousted on the issue of dismissal of the COAS. Other parties too changed their position along with the NC in order to pave the way for an alternate government. Surprisingly, however, the NC, which was the second largest party next to the UCPN (Maoist) did not form the government but, instead, facilitated the CPN–UML after having reached an understanding that Madhav Nepal was acceptable to the NC, not Jhalanath Khanal, the parliamentary party leader and CPN–UML president.

Parties' Role and Uncertain Future

Notwithstanding some positive features of the post-2006 Nepal, prospects of democracy remain more uncertain than ever before. As vehicles of democracy, parties are becoming weaker due to the lack of

---

[8] See the six-point agreement between the Seven Party Alliance and the Maoists in Uddhab Prasad Pyakurel, *Maoist Movement in Nepal: A Sociological Perspective?* (Delhi: Adroit Publishers, 2007), p. 175.

organizational solidarity, strong leadership, commitment to the basic values of democracy, and failure in institutionalization. Power-hungry leaders who swear by the quintessence of democracy during the movements or during their election campaigns seldom remember their tall promises they made in the past thus preparing the grounds for democratic backlash. When the atmosphere of political uncertainty starts haunting the people, changes made for consolidation of democracy tend to be attenuated. Some sections of society who have not reconciled to the changes think that any reverse wave in democratic consolidation would automatically make people nostalgic of the past. They think that monarchy can be restored as in England or in other western democracies, or Nepal as a Hindu state would also be back because of the predominant Hindu population (81 percent). However, it can be safely said that, given the awareness of people and monarchy's own loss of credibility that it showed during its personalized rule in different phases of history, any return of monarchy and Hindu state appears to be wishful thinking. Even if the leaders of parties try to change their positions for reversing the decision made by the CA, the non-Hindu population and secular-minded forces will oppose it to the hilt.

Some Indian sadhus in collusion with obscurantist elements in Nepal try to whip up this sentiment in Nepal. Encouraged by the response they get from some elements including the former king, a few politicians and Indian lobbyists want to keep Nepal a Hindu state in the world but fail to convince the Indian people why India opted for a secular democracy despite being dominated by the Hindus (81 percent). It has been found that some of these sadhus who try to mobilize the Nepalis for restoring the Hindu state were frauds.[9] Nevertheless, such efforts and rumors spread across the country have no popular backing.

Nepali Congress, Other Parties, and Democracy

Since our running theme is state and democracy, the role of the NC needs to be adequately treated. Its tumultuous journey itself provides

[9] *Himal Khabar Patrika* (Kathmandu), March 29–April 13, 2010.

a broad contour of Nepali democratic history. Most Left parties in the scene continued the politics of reaction as they were not independent variable in the past. Although the Maoist insurgency could help transform Nepali politics substantially, the NC had come eventually to lead this transformation too. As a democratic party, it, therefore, continues to represent even the present struggle for democracy.

In retrospect, the major reason for democratic uncertainty can be attributed to the weakening status of parties committed to democracy. The NC, which claims its liberal democratic commitment since its organization in the 1940s and continued its struggle for achieving democratic freedom despite occasional setbacks it suffered for achieving its goal, does not show any credible role for democratic consolidation. It has had all along compromised its basic principle since 1958. It departed from the CA in the name of pragmatism but suffered humiliation at the hands of the kings when they themselves set the terms of reference of the model of democracy into which they could be fitted. Personal liking and disliking of India and the kings led to the wars of two stepbrothers, B. P. Koirala and M. P. Koirala, leading in turn to the rise of absolute monarchy. Thus, ironically, the 1950–1951 change itself proved to be a vehicle for restoration of monarchy, which played its active and semi-active role till its end in 2006.

In the 1950s, the NC's changed political stand on the CA election could however be understood in positive light hoping that the parties would get enough *space* to widen their strength under the Constitution awarded by the king himself and, hence, its decision to contest would in course of time prove to be conducive for democratic development. Such a changed position paid off with two-thirds majority in the 1959 election. The NC ran the government for 18 months until the ambitious king, whose insatiable lust for power was beyond the control of parties, intervened for discarding the multiparty democracy itself.

In retrospect, the NC could have retained its basic ideology of popular sovereignty if it had not compromised its principle of the CA. How the party in exile picked it up again after it decided to wage a violent movement in 1961 and reaffirmed it in May 1967 could become a lesson for us. Its greatest lesson was that the party could neither protect its ideological image nor did succeed to broad-base democratic infrastructure by accepting the Constitution awarded by the king as a royal gift. The NC leadership also failed to read the vaulting ambition of King Mahendra who went to the extent of killing his own creature—the Constitution of the Kingdom of Nepal 1959—by using the NA to terminate multiparty democracy.

The NC's strategies for pressurizing the kings were characterized by both violent and nonviolent means. Since the royal regime was geared to enhancing the image of the king as nation builder in both symbolic and actual political sense, he was only the "supreme, active and dynamic" leader as his members of the entourage tried to describe. So violence, according to the NC's resolution passed in Patna in 1961, was the only option left to it and, hence, the start of the armed insurrection conducted from across the India–Nepal border. Stigmatized as "anti-national elements" by the regime, the NC and India were denounced together as if India was behind the anti-regime movement. It became clearer when India put pressure on the NC leaders then in India to suspend the movement following the Chinese threat that China would come to the help of Nepal if any country made attempt to invade the latter. Thus, despite being disgruntled with Indian pressure, the NC had to suspend its armed movement in 1962.

It is worth mentioning the U-turn of the NC in 1968 when the party in exile decided to cooperate with the king for "further development of the constitution" (panchayat) where upon its president B. P. Koirala and leader Ganesh Man Singh were released and amnesty was granted to the NC activists then living in India. The climate of rapprochement between the NC and the king proved to be momentary, though the cost for undoing its past decision of the CA was reminiscent of the 1958 Birganj conference where the party had decided to accept election to the Parliament and the Constitution to be offered by the king.

Bishweshwar Prasad Koirala, who felt humiliated by the regime when he tried to meet the king in person but failed, decided to take up arms once again rationalizing the thesis that in authoritarian traditional monarchy where other democratic channels of expression of dissent were closed, armed movement was the only option for him. He declared it in India and went into action. The NC which was already divided into camps, despite being theoretically one, the armed action proved disastrous with heavy casualties on the NC's side. Meanwhile, B. P. Koirala once again changed his position by deciding to go back to the country stating that democracy and nationalism were inseparable and the king's role in maintaining national unity was also important. In fact, the imposition of emergency in India by Indira Gandhi in 1975 and restrictions put on the activities of the NC activists prompted him to come to such a conclusion. He, thus, returned and talked of reconciliation with the king, as his "neck and King's were tied to each other." Both the Indian emergency and the rise of communist force in Nepal were likely to be detrimental to Nepal's independence and democracy.[10] Such a ding-dong battle continued until the end of monarchy, but the party did not take up arms after the return of Koirala in 1976. Activities conducted peacefully inside the country could be more effective than the armed struggle launched three times in the NC's history. The first in 1950 became successful due to combination of a number of factors, both internal and external. Internally, the divided Rana family members themselves helped develop the anti-Rana movement. Second, the wave of democracy was blowing across South Asian region due to India's triumph of freedom movement and democracy. The NC leaders and others who were educated in India could form the party to fight against the native Rana regime. The NC's decision for armed insurrection and tacit support extended by Indian leaders and activists, barring some hard-core Gandhians, helped a lot for the NC-led movement. Four, King Tribhuvan's decision to take shelter in the Indian embassy in Kathmandu to be flown to Delhi worked effectively to foment the movement. It created legitimacy crisis for the Ranas as the infant grandson of the king was put on the throne in order to show the world that monarchy was still maintained in *de jure* for getting recognition from other powers. Finally, the GoI was instrumental in the change, though its mission to establish a constitutional monarchy failed shortly thereafter

---

[10] See in detail, Lok Raj Baral, *Nepals's Politics of Referendum: A Study of Groups, Personalities and Trends* (New Delhi: Vikas Publishing House, 1983), pp. 35–41.

Two other movements (1990 and 2006) succeeded because of the formation of coalition between the NC and Left forces. Since both the movements were peaceful, their consequences were, however, unexpected. In 1990, the single demand of the restoration of multiparty system eventually ended in "constitutional monarchy," however deceptive term it might be in the context of the post-movement politics. As its details have already been discussed, it is nonetheless worthwhile to mention the failure of politics of compromise in the politics of Nepal since 1950. All compromises ended in absolute monarchy, because the monarchs, who were thrown into oblivion by the Ranas after the bloody Kot massacre (1846) or even earlier by other powerful courtiers and generals, made conscious bids for restoration of monarchy. So when the opportunity arose, democracy and elected governments or parties were singled out for elimination. King Birendra's decision to hold referendum in 1979 and participation of all political parties in it as if it was going to be a kind of "political integration" became futile when the referendum result was declared by the king. After the defeat of the multiparty side, the NC put up a small demand—end of mandatory provision for taking the membership of one of the class organizations (youth, ex-soldiers, peasant, women, labor) that were created within the partyless regime—but the regime ignored it going alone for holding elections to the National Panchayat without the NC and other parties (banned) on individual basis. The NC boycotted it and started launching the peaceful movements.

What was more fascinating was the plight of the regime's prime minister, a mastermind for making the partyless system a success in the referendum, who went into the poll without the cooperation of parties and became the first elected panchayat prime minister. His life too was shortcut as the royals conspired again to oust him for monarchy's interest. Never tired of citing the example of Jang Bahadur who had usurped power in 1846, they circulated the rumors that Prime Minister Surya Bahadur Thapa was no less ambitious than Jang. Forgetting his role for serving the royal interest by ensuring the victory of the regime in 1980, King Birendra, on the promptings of his brothers and courtiers, contrived his defeat in the National Panchayat by issuing order from the palace to defeat him. Obeying the hint (they used to say line), Thapa, who had the support a few hours ago, was ousted from the government in less than two years.[11] Such shortsighted approach, which relied more on traditional conspiratorial politics than on modern democratic practices, in fact, started the process of ending monarchy itself. In 1990, the partyless nature collapsed and in 2008 monarchy itself came to an end.

Democracy is, thus, a permanent casualty. Sometimes it has been hit by the traditional rulers, sometimes political parties themselves are responsible for making it unsuccessful. The NC is now bereft of strong leaders who are expected to take democracy ahead. Strong leader also tends to be more authoritarian as has happened to the NC. Girija Prasad Koirala, who emerged as the strong leader after he elbowed out his former detractors, did not help develop party as democratic institution. His fighting instinct and revengeful character and organizing ability paid him rich dividends, albeit at the cost of the party. His death has left behind a big void in the NC as no so-called new generation leaders could match the commanding height of G. P. Koirala. His strong leadership role could also prove to be more positive for settling many crucial problems including the successful negotiation he conducted for bringing the Maoists into mainstream multiparty politics. Girija Prasad in return also yielded to the demands of the Maoists for ending monarchy as well as for holding the CA election, despite his wavering statements that he often made for some sort of a symbolic monarchy. Dictated by circumstances and humiliated by the kings in and out of government, he went along with other parties for the abolition of monarchy.

[11] The author had a long conversation with Thapa few months before his ouster. He gave the hints that he was likely to meet the same fate of any other prime minister of Nepal. The king's brothers and courtiers were extra-constitutional power centers. Later, after his defeat, Thapa told me he had two options: to commit suicide or to face the National Panchayat for his natural death. He told this while responding to the king who wanted his resignation. According to Thapa, the king said that he appreciated his split for facing the vote of no confidence in the National Panchayat, despite the king's brother, Gyanendra's, objection to vote of no-confidence which, in his opinion, is not the spirit of partyless system.

See Lok Raj Baral, *Nepal: Problems of Governance* (Delhi: Konark, 1993), note 34, p. 64.

At a time the country is at a critical juncture due to lack of direction and political uncertainties and other crises, a moderate party—the NC—is becoming weak. The Left upsurge, particularly the emergence of the Maoist as the first party in the CA on the one hand and failure of parties in general to forge consensus for order, peace, and democratic consolidation on the other, have further added complexity. It seems that the NC would not be able to project its image unless it tries to assess its new role in the changed context. Its progressive agenda and democratic credentials should be the guiding spirit for revamping the party. Since the party has lost its wide support base by ignoring its different constituencies—Dalit, ethnic, Madhesh, intellectual, peasant, and laborer—it will indeed be a daunting task for the party to compete with the other left parties.

The unsettling democratic terrain of Nepal is caused by the increasing trends of deinstitutionalization of political parties. The NC turned out to be a one-man party after some of its senior leaders were marginalized or dead. Trends of patronage distribution as had been generally done during the former royal regime had been repeated by the leaders in the post-1990 period. It continued until the death of G. P. Koirala. Resentment at, if not defiance of, his individual decision to make his daughter minister and, later, deputy prime minister was shown during his last days. Interestingly, party men grumbled for Koirala's decision to anoint his daughter, but could not pass any formal resolution on it because of his strong position. With the demise of Koirala, the NC has entered into a new phase of collective leadership. Still centered on personalities, the NC's homogeneity and institutionalization process may suffer setbacks. Time alone will test how the NC would stand up to the new challenges it encounters in the future.

The NC's decision to develop a working relationship with the CPN (Maoist) and other Left parties, like the CPN–UML, unfolded the nature of the movement. Both the Maoist and non-Maoist parties reached an understanding that first they should work in unison notwithstanding certain strategic constraints on the two non-Maoist parties to enter into a formal arrangement with a party that was still underground and had not terminated the insurgency. Nevertheless, angered by King Gyanendra's stubborn attitude and his penchant for discarding political parties, Koirala and the other CPN–UML leaders were prepared to end the royal absolutism first and then move on to the agenda of state restructuring. Prior to it, the Maoists were to accept the principles and practices of multiparty democracy departing from its orthodox Maoist line. In return, the other parties (SPA) would agree on such issues as holding of the CA election. Since the two demands—end of monarchy and the CA—were the benchmark for the Maoists, the SPA leaders, particularly Koirala, convinced the Maoists that all other demands but the immediate declaration of republic could be accepted instantly. It was believed that Koirala convinced that his thinking to establish a republic was ingrained in his mind since Gyanendra had sidelined him in 2001. But due to the practical difficulty, he thought that it would be easy to take up the issue after the CA election as it would be only competent body to decide the fate of the monarchy. So the 12-point agreement did not mention only the end of monarchical absolutism but also disguised the hidden agenda of republic. Yet it still needs to be verified against Koirala's own utterances on sort of a symbolic existence (baby king, etc.) of monarchy. However, such duality of approach ended following the unanimous declaration of the end of monarchy by the first session of the CA in 2008. Such historic resolution was moved by the NC leader and Home Minister Krishna Prasad Sitaula.

First the restoration of previous parliament and announcement of the CA election along with a number of other radical steps including all the end of vestiges of absolute monarchy including the renaming of the RNA into NA did show Koirala's skillful handling of the volatile situation. However, Koirala who in fact was a party in himself did not pay attention to introducing basic principles of institution building. His personalized style and myopic decisions did not help the democratization processes regardless of his role as a crusader of change.

Ironically, King Gyanendra first used Deuba by appointing him prime minister after the latter formed his own NC and then removed him from power blaming that he was "incompetent" prime minister for holding election. Overwhelmed by the royal gesture shown to him later, Deuba said that the Gorkhali king did justice by anointing him again. The CPN–UML too joined the Deuba government maintaining *pratigaman* (regression) had been half corrected. In the wake of royal ascent, a series of making and breaking of governments had taken place until the imposition of emergency in 2005, which was also the culmination of the rise of royal absolutism in the post-1990 multiparty era.

Democracy's survival is in question due to the emergence of heterogeneous ideological/parochial trends, which are fed by high doses of ethnicization and regionalization. Ideology has been debased in numerous ways. On the one hand, the Left parties, at least in conventional sense, are communists for tactical reasons only as it becomes difficult for them to depart from the logo and slogans they carry since their birth and on the other hand they are within the multiparty liberal system. They pretend to be Left or progressive for being populist so that people could be attracted toward them. Ideology is used for tactical purposes or just to be different from other parties. The Maoist party is parliamentary in practice and anti-parliamentary in theory. Parliamentary system as is being practiced in the UK or in India might not be a carbon copy for Nepal because of its own context but in many respects its essential features are adopted even in other types of system. The Interim Constitution (2007) did adopt the parliamentary type but just to satisfy the Maoist ego, it was decided to call Byabasthapika-Sansad or legislature-parliament. As the two words in fact convey the same meaning but in order to be different from parliamentary system and by way of striking a deal with the Maoists, both words were inserted in the Constitution.

The Maoist image of a party that can bring about qualitative change in the life of the Nepali people is also on the slippery slope but, compared to other competitors, it still has a clout to mobilize people, because the Maoists are yet to be tested in power and pluralistic politics. Since the party was heading a coalition government with different strings being pulled by the other parties and also because of its own inexperience of highly individualistic politics conducted by other leaders of parties in the midst of mutual suspicion and fear, the Maoist party was forced to leave the government. Although the Maoist leaders did not understand the complexity of Nepali politics that has had been influenced by various real or psychological factors, their bold decision to quit the government in 2009 on the grounds of "civilian supremacy" (army should be under the control of the government) could be appreciated. If the Maoists would have made a compromise with other parties by not taking action against the army chief, the Maoist-led government could last longer. But the Maoist move, to all intents and purposes, was read by non-Maoist parties and external communities as those whose objective was *satta kabja* (power capture), a popular Maoist expression in the post-2006 Nepal. Although any political party is organized for capturing power, there was nothing new to it but the speed with which they worked frightened their competitors, who did not like to disturb the army at a time when the whole country was in transition. Moreover, since the Maoist-led government was created with the support of many other parties but the NC in opposition, it had practical difficulties in taking independent decision. It was understood that many parties that supported it in the beginning subsequently retracted their position due to a variety of internal and external factors. Since then the Maoists have been organizing strikes, stalling the Parliament, and accusing India for its alleged meddlesome activities for influencing the course of events.

How the Maoist bogey is created by non-Maoist parties in the post-CA election (2008) has been well articulated by an analyst in these words:

> But the argument that Maoists will 'take over' is more a reflection of the NC and UML's own lack of faith in their political strength than anything else. If NC and UML spend all their time lobbying with the Indian embassy and NA to save them, the Maoists will of course become stronger. The transformation of the Maoists is a process, not an event.[12]

Such a process of transformation will take time but the other parties, including Indian policymakers, seemed to be paranoid and scared when the Maoists were in government after the CA election. The Maoist decision to remove the army chief, notwithstanding the Indian and other parties' pressure, proved to be costly for the UCPN (Maoist). It not only lost power but also rose in revolt against India for the alleged

---

[12] Prashant Jha, "Plain Speaking," *Nepali Times*, Kathmandu, May 7–13, 2010.

interference in internal affair. A Tarai analyst has commented that "it seems that India had helped the NC and CPN–UML alliance but this is not the reality. India had only helped the Nepal Army for which it used the NC and the UML."[13]

Some mixed signals about the Maoist transformation have made non-Maoist parties and the international community suspect, despite their high hopes for Maoist transformation into a systemic party. The conflicting statements regarding the political system and disbanding the ex-combatants (living in different camps under the supervision of the UNMIN) and their impatience for grabbing power as well as their reluctance to complete the peace process on the basis of agreements and understandings made earlier have give risen to mutual threat perceptions and suspicions. Relations between the UCPN (Maoist) and other political parties strained after they entered into political competition during and after the CA elections.

Although the UCPN (Maoist) has not done better than other parties either in projecting its image or in governance, its actual organizational strength will be judged only after the next elections. Second, the party leaders seem to be flexible to take even unpleasant decisions for what they call "public good" but their shifting strategies and tactical alliances have contributed to tarnishing its role. Yet, it has shown to the world that it can renounce violence in favor of peace with a view to transforming itself into the role of constitutional party. The Maoist party's decision to accept the advice of international community and the civil society has also been appreciated within the country and outside.[14] But in democratic commitment, it must prove its trustworthiness. If the largest party does not make its ideology clear and continues to dream of grabbing power by any means, it may damage its own future.

[13] Tula Narayan Shah, "Pheri Madhesh Chukdai Chha" [Madhesh Losing Again], *Kantipur*, Kathmandu May 10, 2010.

[14] For an analysis on it, see Radhakrishna Mainali, "Bartaman Sarkar ra Maobadi Rajniti" [Present Government and Maoist Politics], *Annapurna Post*, Kathmandu, May 10, 2010.

The enthusiasm and hope generated during the Jan Andolan 2006 and the Maoist decision to join the mainstream pluralistic system along with the acceptance of popular sovereignty is fast eroding across the country. If the Maoist party needs more time to be socialized in democratic politics and procedural technicalities, other two national parties, the NC and the CPN–UML, are likely to erode further because of their weakening contacts with the common people. Short of people-oriented policies and their effective implementation and their tendency to becoming parties of status quo, they will have tough time to sustain in competitive politics. One scenario can be drawn that both the NC and CPN–UML may continue to forge an alliance in case their individual capacity may not match the challenge thrown up to them by the Maoists. Certain irreconcilable approaches of the two big communist parties and the impacts of international players on keeping them apart may be detrimental to the democratic process.

The pre-CA election in 2008 did convince us that insofar as ideological framework was concerned, Nepali political parties were together. The election manifestos, barring some political rhetoric, have provided the contours of politics for the future. However, it should not be forgotten that such manifestos have all been remained on papers or as propaganda materials used for election campaigns and are hardly implemented by any political party, even if certain parties come to power on those agendas. Election manifestos are, thus, matters of rites for them.

Normally, the manifestos of parties work as "destabilizing populism," which come with sound and fury but signify nothing. However, political parties during the CA elections seemed to be more sober and pragmatic despite many caveats they encounter during the implementation of their manifestos. One of the important aspects of the whole exercise is that politically all parties are in common but the RPP–N which, unlike other fence-sitters, is upholding constitutional monarchy. Its preelection stand on monarchy and Hindu state is somewhat modified in the post-2008 CA election particularly following the decision of the CA to abolish monarchy and to declare Nepal as a secular state. Tempting to cash in on the people who are still nostalgic about monarchy and Hindu state, RPP–N questioned the decision of CA or parliament on such subjects adding that these issues including Nepal as a federal state need to be put on referendum for soliciting the opinion of all Nepalis.[15] The protagonists of referendum forget that in the UK, it was the Parliament that had taken all crucial decisions including the fate of monarchy. It was the king versus Parliament that eventually resulted in parliamentary supremacy enabling it even to determine the fate of monarchy.

On all other agendas, RPP–N is also in common with other parties. The NC has tried to contextualize itself to the ground realities with the agenda of republic with a ceremonial head of state (President) as is practiced in India. Yet its ambivalent position could be observed in statements of party president and a few other activists supposed to be close to him. Even today a school of thought believes that the NC's decision to endorse the abolition of monarchy was made in haste without any serious study in order to satisfy the Maoists. But such arguments seem to be too simplistic in view of the changed political landscape and republican idea ingrained in Nepali politics.

It seems that most parties are not fundamentally different from one another. The CPN (Maoist) wants to enforce land reform measures with the objective of land to the tillers. Whether its so-called economic radicalism pays dividends or not, it has set its economic target to be achieved within a timeframe. Moreover, it wants to transform the existing semi-feudal Nepali state into a progressive republic. The NC and the UML are no less vocal for such agendas but their past performances are not impressive as the general people had expected.

[15] It is interesting to note that some former COASs have demanded that the issues of monarchy, Hindu state, and federalism be settled through the national referendum. It seems that they wanted to dig out these issues challenging the CA resolution as if it had no power despite being sovereign in all respects. There are two ways of change—peaceful and violent revolution. In the Nepali context, it was the product of both as the republic first came from the Maoist insurgency and was, subsequently, accepted by all political forces in the country. The CA, which was the product of the movement, passed a unanimous resolution on all three issues closing all controversies. Nevertheless, each individual or group has right to express views on all of them because Nepal, unlike the former royal regime, is committed to liberal democracy.

On many other issues of restructuring of the Nepali state along the line of federalism, most major parties are together. The Maoist party committed first to creating 11 autonomous regions and three more sub-regions such as Mithila, Awadhi, and Bhojpuri on the basis of ethnic, territorial, and demographic settings. Even today the Maoists are not firm on numbers of federal units. The NC and the CPN–UML have not come with such divisions but stick to the federal system with three hierarchies—center, province, and local units. The Maoist manifesto does not show any reservation on giving the right to self-determination to the autonomous regions, while the SPA has diluted this issue in the agreement reached with the three Madhese parties prior to the CA election.

On the agenda of the structure of government, almost all parties, but the RPP–N, have chosen either presidential (Maoist), parliamentary with nominal head of state (NC), and prime ministerial system (CPN–UML). However, both the Maoist and CPN–UML are still unclear what kinds of presidential or prime ministerial system they could adopt. The CPN (Maoist) in particular is ambiguous about the presidential system in the context of pluralistic democracy where freedoms would be guaranteed as in other developed democracies of the world. It can only be assumed that it is less likely to prefer the North Korean or Cuban model, given the existing realities of Nepali politics. Is it, then, going to adopt the US model where separation of powers, check, and balance based on popular sovereignty is taken as the principles and functions of the system? In any vibrant democracy, accountability of rulers is a must even if the presidents or the prime ministers are elected directly by the people. It also applies to the CPN–UML model of directly electing the prime minister, though it remains vague unless the party comes out with more clear ideas on the issue.

Going by the manifestos of parties, except the RPP–N, the Janasakti, and some other mini-parties, Nepal has become the federal democratic re-public based on the principle and practice of inclusive democracy where ethnic groups, Dalit, gender, and Madhese and all other Nepalis would have self-rule and shared rule as one political scientist has said. It needs the restructuring of the state in order to ensure such self- and- shared rule through the PR system in various agencies of the state—army, police, administration, and government. Universal values of democracy have been vindicated in all these developments, but leaders of political parties have not been able to free themselves from the chrysalis of their entrenched past predilections and culture. So, despite radical structural changes brought about by the movement as well as by the impact of the 10-year-long Maoist insurgency, these changes seem to be undermined by the same elites.

Two scenarios are likely to develop in the foreseeable future. First, the conventional style of conducting parties would not help the old parliamentary parties like the NC to invigorate its image. Its democratic credentials are suspect as it has not been able to cope with newer challenges for setting its own socioeconomic progressive agendas. Any party's survival would from now onward be determined by its performance and not by hackneyed claim that it was/is the real protector of freedom and democracy. The octogenarian leader, who ran the party rather ruthlessly, died in March 2010 leaving behind a weak party. His likely successors are yet to be tested for their understanding of the guiding spirit of today's dynamics. Girija Prasad Koirala, who was negotiating with other parties till his end on major issues, was more casual and irresponsible in his utterances than a responsible leader of delicate transition was supposed to be. Second, the Left politics would in all probability be more conflict-prone in the time to come. It seems that the largest party—the Maoist—is struggling hard to retain its present position with somewhat dubious ideological posturing of being committed to pluralistic system and to "people's republic" without detailing the attributes of the latter. Such ambivalent position cannot continue for long, though its helplessness was understandable in view of the intra-party controversy on whether a revolutionary party should go in full swing with the liberal democracy of the Western variety or not. Such a contradictory attitude was also determined by its inability to be as much radical as it expected to do while in government. Other parties whose major preoccupation is Maoist fear cannot allow the latter to adopt more progressive policies in the given feudalistic structures and ethos. The mixed election system that prevents any party from getting majority and the lack of confidence to work together for stability and progress would only continue the politics of uncertainty and crisis of governance.

Another major Left party, CPN–UML, suffers from its so-called middle-way policy between what it calls "right" represented by the NC and "extreme left" of the Maoist variety. Yet, how these two terms "right" and "extreme" Left can be the political tags, respectively, for the two parties need to be examined. From such a yardstick, can the CPN–UML, a centrist party that claims to have played a moderate role for enhancing liberal democracy despite its shifting ideological stance that it has had taken from time to time, able to preserve its Left identity? In the past, both the CPN–UML and the NC have wavered in their core ideology to the extent of splitting the parties. The strong monarchy contrived divisions when opportunity arose. The last NC split occurred in 2002 as a faction of the party decided to join the King's camp. The CPN–UML leaders too could not resist the temptation to be in the government.

Nevertheless, the mainstream NC did not support King Gyanendra's rise to absolute power. Its opposition to the king's violation of constitutional spirit could eventually blaze a trail for democracy, despite the participation in the government of the breakaway NC (NC [D]) and the CPN–UML. At a time when the king wanted to appoint his prime minister by flouting the letter and spirit of the Constitution, King Gyanendra asked for application for the post of prime minister as if some officials were being appointed. Surprisingly, the CPN–UML leader, Madhav Kumar Nepal, was reported to have applied for the prime minister's post but failed to get. Instead, King Gyanendra became his own prime minister and the diehard royalists who had served the regime after the 1960 coup were his juniors.

Nepali political parties split not on the grounds of ideology but on personal rivalry and conflict. The NC is the worst sufferer of intra-party conflict since the early 1950s. Temptation to be close to the Palace led the NC leaders to part their ways. In the 1990s, personality clash between G. P. Koirala and the "supreme leader" Ganesh Man and G. P. and K. P. Bhattarai weakened the party considerably, although no new party was opened with the same name by the departing leaders. The 2002 split, however, made a difference with Deuba deciding to open another NC (D) after he preferred to be close to the palace with which he could stay in power longer. Later, Deuba and his colleagues rejoined the NC despite their homecoming being not so smooth and congenial. So the scar of split still continues even today with both pro-Deuba and the other camp competing with each other during organizational elections and in sharing responsibility.

The major Left parties'—CPN–UML and the UCPN (Maoist)—criticism of the NC's pro–status quo proclivities seems to be untenable given the resilience the latter has shown while changing the course of political development. Prime Minister Koirala became an eyesore to King Gyanendra who wanted to take all powers into his own hands but Koirala argued against such vaulting royal ambition. So the image of the NC (main) could be significantly restored following its decision not to kowtow to the king. Girija Prasad Koirala was, thus, a fallen leader in the eyes of King Gyanendra who once told him to resign for his depleted image (corrupt).[16]

In retrospect, however, parties' records in parliamentary politics were/are negative with all indulging in power game inviting political instability. Failure to abide by the letter and spirit of the Constitution, their hobnobbing with the former royalists who were not fully reconciled to the end of partyless regime, and who became the catalyst for instability further eroded their image. Revamping the damaged image was an uphill task for the NC as well as the CPN–UML. The civil society leaders helped regain it following the formation of the SPA to launch a movement against the king. Towering as he was both physically and politically, Koirala was accepted as the leader of the SPA. His role to open dialogue with the Maoist leaders, then underground, and the understanding reached on the 12-point program had electrifying effects on the movement. The NC's alliance with the Left parties was possible in 1990 despite the political standoff between the communist and the NC ever since the beginning of multiparty system in 1951. It has been argued that

---

[16] See G. P. Koirala's interview with the *Saptahik Weekly*, Kathmandu. In reply to King Gyanendra, Koirala said that the king's role was also in question due to the Palace massacre of June 19, 2001.

NC could work in tandem with the communists only after the death of B. P. Koirala who always opposed such alliance stating that it would end the democratic identity of the NC.

In the post-2005 change, never tired of repeating a middle-way approach hoping to negotiate with both the camps (the NC and the Maoist) so that many knotty problems could be resolved, the CPN–UML became a loser both in maintaining internal party cohesion and in playing an effective role for steering the course of national politics. Consequently, public perception of the CPN–UML was negative because of the ambivalent stand of the leaders, indecisiveness, and a lack of leadership. Party's division becomes clearer when it was/is in power. In 2009, the party nominated Madhav Kumar Nepal, defeated from two constituencies in the 2008 CA election, as prime ministerial candidate for heading a coalition government. It was believed that the NC President G. P. Koirala had also chosen Madhav Nepal in lieu of Jhala Nath Khanal, who is both a president and leader of the parliamentary party. Most ministers nominated by the NC and the CPN–UML were either defeated in direct elections or came to the CA (Parliament) through the PR system in which the party could put their names in the list. Interestingly, the defense and foreign ministers who represented the CPN–UML and the NC, respectively, and were both defeated in direct election, defied the prime minister on various policy decisions. Both the parties and the prime minister could not take on these powerful ladies lest the loss of support in the government. Some ministers of other parties too were left untouched for violating the basic norms of minister.

Tendency to cling to power and indiscipline within the rank and file of the party also tarnished their image. Clashes between the Youth Communist League (YCL), a Maoist youth wing, and the UML's student young—the Youth Force—on the one hand and pro-NC student organization on the other have become a routine affair. All such violent clashes occur not on ideological grounds but most take place on money matters or contracts to be given to certain bidders with whom they have connections. So it is increasingly turning into a fractured party, devoid of strong and decisive leadership. It is not only the top leaders of the party but its second rankers too who defy the top leaders, including the prime minister. The CPN–UML's credibility and also of the NC's have eroded because of the latter's support to the UML leader, defeated from two constituencies in the 2008 election, as prime minister. Such an unexpected position came to the party after the NC, despite being the second largest party in the Parliament, passed it on to the CPN–UML, a third party in strength, to head the government following the resignation of the Maoist prime minister, Prachanda.

The NC and the CPN–UML have however worked in tandem on the eve and after the 2006 movement. If the tall leadership of the NC could reach out to the Maoists, then underground, to join multiparty party politics in a new democratic setup, the UML, being yet another communist party by name if not by action, corrected its past mistake and rejoined the movement politics. It had been understood that the CPN–UML seemed to be making frantic efforts to persuade the Maoist leaders to shun violence. While finalizing the 12-point understanding with the Maoists in Delhi, CPN–UML leaders were privy to it. It was, subsequently, shared by the other SPA members for finalization.

Changing Landscape of the Tarai (Madhesh) Politics

The Tarai or Madhese politics took a sudden turn in the post-2006 movement. By that time, the NSP was the sole representative of the Tarai but it too failed to catch the Tarai sentiment when the SPA and the Maoists were accused of ignoring the Tarai issues. Some new Tarai groups, therefore, sprang up for articulating the interests of Madhese or people of Tarai. One of the serious charges was that no parties composed overwhelmingly by the Pahade (hill people) gave any attention to redressing the grievances of the Tarai because of the continued psychology of domination of the hill people. Fuelled by such deep-rooted complaints against the hill elites, who had been continuously ruling the country, it was high time to resurrect the Tarai sentiment so that the new Nepal envisaged by the proponents of change could become a reality. So the demand of federalism, autonomy to the ethnic and regional groupings, end of disparity in recruitment in NA and other agencies of the state, proportionate distribution of jobs, and granting of citizenship certificates to those who were "deprived of citizenship" in the past became prominent. It was argued by the Tarai parties that more than 4 million people were entitled to get the citizenship certificate. It was subsequently found that only about 1.2 million from the Tarai and 1.3 million from the hills could get the citizenship certificate.

The lenient policy of the Interim Government that was formed after the movement came under criticism for callousness with which it dealt with the issue of citizenship. It was alleged that many unqualified persons were granted citizenship right without any verification because of the tremendous pressure then put on the government by the Tarai leaders. Moreover, it was also the pent-up feeling against the discriminatory policies followed by the Pahade rulers of Nepal. The stringent citizenship measures incorporated into the 1964 Citizenship Act and the follow-up policies taken for discouraging the "foreigners" (Indian) further annoyed the Tarai people. The 1990 Constitution also "imposed" criteria based on "descent," birth certificates, and other documents including the language criteria but were not accepted by the Madheses, though the launching of a movement against such measures was still far off. In 1994, a government commission itself had reported that almost 3.5 million Nepalis did not yet have citizenship certificates. In November 2006, the citizenship law was amended, making anyone born in Nepal before 1990 and permanently resident eligible for citizenship. Naturalized citizenship is now open to people who can speak or read any language used in Nepal.[17]

Nepali political landscape was dramatically changed by the Madhese movement as well as by the mixed electoral system. As it has been said: "The Madhesi wave has also helped open the territory for other ethnic regional groups to pursue their agendas. Identity politics are unlikely to go away."[18] Nevertheless, such identity politics is not an exclusive Tarai

[17] See the Citizenship Act, 1964, Kathmandu: Ministry of Justice and Law, 1964, and the Constitution of the Kingdom of Nepal, 1990 (Kathmandu: His Majesty's Government, Nepal). See also International Crisis Group, Policy Report, *Nepal's Troubled Tarai Region*, July 9, 2007 (Brussels: International Crisis), p. 4.

[18] International Crisis Group Report, *Nepal's New Political Landscape*, Peking, July 3, 2008, p. 10.

phenomenon as it has seeped through the nook and corner of the country. The emergence of *janjati* (indigenous) movement, demand of Dalit and women and other poor people or caste groups such as Brahman, Chhetri, etc., have raised their voices for getting fair treatment from the new Nepali state. Such widespread movements have made them relevant to the power game because their numbers in different layers of power structure and practices need to be taken into account.

The PR system and allocation of seats on the basis of population were applied for both direct and proportional system. As a result, it increased the number of seats of Madheses significantly. In the House of 601, the four Madhese parties got 82 seats in addition to the seats allocated by other national parties. But the splits of MJF into MJF (Democratic), NSP into Sadbhawana (Mahato) and Sadbhawana (Anandi Devi led by Giri) in addition to the containing trends of splits of other Madhese parties have considerably weakened them. Now the MJP that had 52 seats in the CA has is now reduced to 25. Its breakaway MJP (Democratic) retains 27. The leader of the breakaway group is a former NC Tarai (Tharu) leader who broke the party for joining the non-Maoist coalition government. Indications are that other major Tarai parties are likely to be further fragmented in the future. Such divisions are nonideological with all leaders accusing others of betraying the cause of the Tarai.

Referring to federalism, all the Tarai parties demanded "one Madhesh, one Pradesh" by making the whole of Tarai (from east to west) as a federal entity. It, therefore, rejected the vertical division of the territorial units as, in their opinion, that would divide the Tarai.[19] Although the demand politics could be well understood against the faulty state structure and elite orientation against the Tarai since the formation of the modern Nepali state, how suddenly such a movement could flare up with new sets of parties and leaders was interesting. Surprisingly, however, most Tarai leaders who dramatized the situation by adding regional component in the national politics were not new leaders. They, in fact, joined the fray by quitting their own parties that had also catapulted them into

---

[19] See the agreement made with the Tarai parties and other related documents pertaining to Tarai movement.

different roles before the movement. The MJF led by Upendra Yadav had taken lead to blow up the Tarai agenda, which soon affected the nature of national politics as well. Later, other Tarai leaders also joined the fray by opening new parties such as the T–MLP. Upendra Yadav of the MJF and Mahanta Thakur of the T–MLP, respectively, came from the CPN (Maoist) and the NC. Even the oldest Sadbhawana Party created by Gajendra Narayan Singh is now split into four with separate identity as parties. One of the strange characteristics of Tarai politics is that even regionalism that propelled the movement to a new height is being divided along caste and class lines thus posing threats to the cohesiveness with which the Madhese parties had once been able to show their strength. The way the Madhese leaders changed their decision at the behest of India during the election of the prime minister from the parliament and did not cast their votes also became transparent in the eyes of the people.

Although the major Tarai parties had been able to catch the immediate sentiment during the movement and election, it seems now that these parties face major challenges for existence once the mobilizing ideology (broad-based identity politics) further starts eroding and new caste and class formations would intervene. Moreover, the challenges put up by other groups, most of them with criminal records, and the increasing trends of politics of criminalization and criminalization of politics have added multiple dimensions. If all the demands are fulfilled or nearly fulfilled and if the Tarai leaders fail to penetrate into the Tarai Dalits that too have different layers, other backward communities, and Muslim, the Tarai politics would be dramatically changed. It seems that the existing Madhese (Tarai) parties would no longer be able to mobilize people under the single Tarai banner as they had been able to do during the Madhese movement.

India has also been perceived as one of the obstacles for the independent development of Tarai politics.[20] Regular writings of some Tarai intellectuals in the national newspapers and their expressions in public

[20] Tula Narayan Shah, "Pheri Madhesh Chukdai Chha" [Madhesh Losing Again] *Kantipur*, May 10, 2010.

debates reveal how India is tempted to keep them at its beck and call.[21] In their opinion, the old mindset of the present Tarai leaders that they should not go beyond India will make them weak in course of time. It does not mean that they should be anti-Indian in their orientation in order to be confident.

How the national parties like the NC, the CPN–UML, and the CPN (Maoist) would be able to restore their lost constituencies in the Tarai is beyond our imagination. Nevertheless, compared to the NC and the CPN–UML, the Maoist party still maintains its rapport with the people at the bottom. Whether it can deliver or not would be decided by its future role. The fractious politics and losing credibility of all parties may not give them a decisive mandate to rule. Thus, for enhancing the prospects of power, coalition between the Tarai and other national parties is a must. The Indian scenario might be replicated in Nepal too, but with a difference: In India, regional parties have more or less maintained their strongholds, which in turn can become coalition partners at the Center. It has given much weight to the regional parties for being partners in both state and central politics.

Peace and Development

Peace, democracy, and development are exclusive to each other. Nepalis who had experienced peace without progress during the 30 years' of royal rule (1960–1990) and, later, now realize that peace and democratic stability are necessary for development. The 10-year-long Maoist insurgency and the state response to it (1996–2005) not only claimed more than 13,000 lives but also displaced people, destroyed social harmony, and economic infrastructure. Fear and anxiety coupled with unemployment and rural–urban migration swelled the population of towns and cities. It was reported that everyday about 1,500 people from the western hills trekked to India for employment, thus, leaving behind

[21] See also Prashanta Jha and C. K. Lal's writings, just to mention a few, in various newspapers and weeklies.

at home females and children. Situated as they were at crossfire between the Maoist guerrillas and the state force, people fled to safer places.

The Maoist *Janayuddha* or people's war had all the characteristics of the Maoist guerrilla warfare as if it was the carbon copy of Chinese Maoist revolution. Indoctrinated in Maoist doctrine, strategy, tactics, and technology, the insurgency was based on "protracted war" with three distinct stages: strategic defensive, strategic stalemate, and finally strategic counter-offensive.[22] Started with a gun and a small number of personnel, the Maoist insurgency could develop into a formidable force within a short period. Taking it lightly, the state, first, pressed the civil police into combat operations against the Maoists, and later, the APF and the RNA joined following the major attack in the Military Barrack in Dang. How the Maoists were successful in forging "working relationship" with the Palace before the massacre in the palace in June 2001 had been disclosed by the top Maoist leader Babu Ram Bhattarai when he wrote an article in *Kantipur Daily* immediately after the assassination of King Birendra and his entire family members, allegedly by the Crown Prince, Dipendra, supposed to be a maniac involved in love tangle with a Rana girl. It has been known that Dipendra's proposal to marry her was rejected by his parents (king and queen), and this is what drove him into this act of frenzy and revenge. Such a dramatic development worked as a catalyst for the end of monarchy itself.

It had been understood that the late King Birendra was also not happy with the limited constitutional role and, thus, used to take independent decision on many issues. Emboldened by the failures of parties to work effectively, he had started pulling strings against the elected government. Regarding the RNA, the Palace was least prepared to compromise and, therefore, did not allow Prime Minister G. P. Koirala to use the army against the Maoist. Later, his successor Gyanendra followed the suit stating that he would not like bloodshed caused by the mutual killing.

---

[22] Mao Zedong, *Selected Military Writings of Mao Tse-tung* (Peking: Peking Foreign Language Press, 1967) as mentioned in Dhruba Kumar, "The Military Dimensions of Maoist Insurgency" in Lok Raj Baral, ed., *Nepal: Facets of Maoist Insurgency* (Delhi: Adroit Publishers, 2006), p. 93.

It was taken as yet another way of undermining the authority of the elected government as the Palace had not, in fact, reconciled to the dilution of its power under the 1990 Constitution.[23]

A strong desire for peace by the people of Nepal had been contributed by the divided role of the state that miserably failed to cope with the Maoist threats as well as by the callous manner with which the Maoist guerrillas started creating havoc across the country. Was the Maoist insurgency an act of terror? The embattled Nepali Government leaders seemed to use these two terms—terrorism and insurgency—according to their conveniences. Prime Minister Lokendra Bahadur Chand had skillfully avoided describing the Maoists as terrorists in a discussion program held in Kathmandu in 2001 just on the eve of holding the second round of negotiation with the Maoists. Subsequently, however, the Deuba government put the terrorist tag to the Maoists following the first attack on the RNA camps in Dang, Syangja, and Solukhumbu districts in November 2001. For doing it, the government had to impose emergency, which was also a precondition that it had put before the G. P. Koirala government when the latter wanted to use it in the wake of the Holleri incident where as many as 70-plus police personnel had fallen into the Maoist trap. Declaring a state of emergency, Prime Minister Deuba said:

> In utter disregard to the government's efforts and people's goodwill, the Maoist terrorists carried out attacks on the innocent people, political party workers, civil servants etc. They even attempt to hurt the national integrity by assaulting the security personnel including police and army ... His Majesty's Government of Nepal has decided to declare a state of emergency in the country to prevent the worse situation ... from being further deteriorated. Maintenance of peace and order by mobilizing security agencies has become our foremost duty and necessity.[24]

---

[23] The ADC of King Birendra has himself disclosed the plan of royal takeover. King Birendra was toying with the idea of taking over power, and if the Palace massacre would not have occurred on June 1, 2001, the King's direct rule could have been imposed. See Vivek Kumar Shah, *Maile Dekheko Darbar: Sainik Sachibko Samsmaran* (The Palace I Saw: Reminiscences of Military Secretary) (Kathmandu: Yati Publications 2067 [VS], 2011).

[24] See the text of speech in Uddhab P. Pyakurel, *Maoist Movement in Nepal: A Sociological Perspective* (Delhi: Adroit Publishers, 2007), Annexes-II.

The 12-point understanding reached between the CPN (Maoist) and the SPA in 2006 ended the state of fear, allowing the people to heave a sigh of relief. Its point three stated the need of permanent peace along with a positive solution to the armed conflict. Making commitment to the values of competitive multiparty system of governance, civil liberties, human rights, the concept of rule of law, the Maoist leaders assured the SPA leaders that they would abide by these principles. More appropriately, the Comprehensive Peace Accord (CPA) reached between the Interim Governments headed by G. P. Koirala, declared the formal end of conflict with a promise that the modalities would be worked out for the "supervision, integration and rehabilitation" of the Maoist combatants. However, the agreement did not explicitly mention the integration of the former combatants into the NA, but the Maoist leaders later made it the principal condition for making a new constitution. With the passage of time and due to various intervening factors, both national and external, the three governments headed by three leaders of major political parties, the NC, the Unified Maoist and the CPN–UML, have invariably failed to end the issue of integration and rehabilitation. Stiff resistance of the NA, the major political parties and allegedly Indian resistance frustrated the Maoist plan of wholesale integration of ex-combatants (19,600) into the NA. Since the Maoists have made it a good bargaining chip for reentry into the government, other parties that worked in tandem during the CA election are opposed to the second Maoist-led government unless it tried to demonstrate its credentials by adhering to the basic principles and norms of democratic politics, by returning the confiscated property and lands, and by disbanding the YCL.

If the political parties fail to rebuild minimum level of confidence and trust and work together for taking the peace process ahead, return to confrontational politics seems imminent. Humiliated and hounded by other parties, the Maoists thought that a new war was being imposed on them and, hence, the Maoist preparation for a "decisive war." The Maoist perceived that all the anti-Maoist forces would rally behind the force of the state in order to quell the Maoist uprising. However, quixotic it might be, the Maoist party was isolated both internally and externally. The stubborn attitude shown by both sides has once again made the peace process uncertain. The Maoist penchant for its old armed strength despite being within the competitive party politics has not extricated its leaders from the old Maoist doctrine that "power comes from the barrel of gun." The party had decided to transform itself into the multi-party system, but not to pluralism, by abandoning its violent path after committing to the peace accord. This problem has created trust deficit between the Maoists and other non-Maoist parties and external powers that want to see the full Maoist transformation from its past hangover. The three divergent proposals moved by the three top leaders of the UCPN (Maoist) at the Sixth Extended Plenum held in November, 2010, at Palungtar in Gorkha district, demonstrated such a division. The three proposals presented, respectively, by party Chairman Prachanda, Vice Chairman Kiran Baidya, and Vice Chairman Babu Ram Bhattarai could not find an acceptable formula for synthesizing three views on whether or not the party should give up its previous decision to fully transform into multiparty politics (liberal democracy) or should move toward completing the constitution making and peace process as agreed upon in 2005 and later or adopt both the options (revolt and peaceful as twin strategies). Among the three leaders, Prachanda preferred to accept both the ideas of fresh revolt as proposed by Kiran and adherence to the transformation process until the deadline (May 28, 2011) set before by the CA for completing the constitution-making process. Unpredictable and elusive as he is, Prachanda have all along been speaking dubious language of revolt against the existing order and move along with all the agreements reached between UCPN (Maoist) and other parties. Among the three, Babu Ram wanted to continue the peace process and agenda of constitution making to reach a logical conclusion. Also, he did not like to declare India as the principal enemy of the party as the internal elements who resist the change should be declared as first enemies.

Yet, it has been explicitly mentioned in all the documents that the principal agenda of the Maoists is to capture power by any means, revolt and constitutional and other political methods, which other parties see it as the Maoist design.[25]

---

[25] Suspecting the Maoist strategy of transformation, serious debates have arisen in the country. Most conflicting statements coming from the Maoist leaders are interpreted as nothing more than cajoling other parties and general people. See also Gagan Thapa, "Maobad ki Loktantrabad" (Maoism or Democracy), *Kantipur*, December 7, 2010.

Nevertheless, the pragmatic approach of the Maoist leaders could catapult the party into the center stage of politics. It became the first party in the CA election. If the party leaders would have worked in low profile until the making of the constitution and holding fresh election, it could win the confidence of the people. Such a possibility was high given the declining popularity of other parties. For, the transformed Nepali politics, which no longer becomes the exclusive domain of the feudal monarchy, needs new attitude and new political culture for its consolidation. If the gains of the movement such as republic, sovereignty of people, freedoms and practice of inclusive democracy with full empowerment of people regardless of caste, class, gender, region, and ethnicity, etc., are not consolidated, the dream of a genuine democracy would never be achieved. At a time when the transition itself is in peril, the agenda of consolidation becomes only an afterthought. The successful making of a constitution and holding of elections to regularize the democratic process would begin the journey of democratic consolidation. Linz and Stepan are of the opinion that

> consolidation has been achieved when (1) no significant political actors try to achieve their objectives by creating a nondemocratic regime or encourage violence, foreign intervention, or secession; (2) the vast majority of the population believe in democratic government, and (3) conflicts are resolved within specific laws, procedures, and institutions sanctioned by the democratic process.[26]

Nepali democratic movements have espoused the principles of democracy since the end of the Rana rule in 1951. Multiparty politics and government by people were always the dominant agenda despite the setbacks it suffered during its actual practice. If the hard-core political leaders and their followers do not become democratic by temperament as well as by democratic exercises, politics strays in different directions, thus, putting it in peril. So, despite dramatic turn of events in Nepal, both democracy and peace are elusive in the country. Even if the Maoist and the state have silenced their guns and have covered a long distance for

---

[26] As mentioned in Robert Pinkney, *Democracy in the Third World* (New Delhi: Viva Books, second edn, 2008), p. 179.

bringing about unprecedented changes in the country, political violence and spread of gun culture have threatened both peace and democracy. It has been reported regularly that the Maoist activists, especially the YCL members and other non-Maoist gangs, have continued extorting money and confiscating property to which the affected people and the non-Maoist political parties have decried such Maoist behaviors. Stray groups, most of them criminals, have resorted to similar tactics. The Tarai is the worst-affected region where killings, lootings, abduction, and death threats have not only threatened peace and harmony but also stalled the democratic processes. The government's new security agenda has not worked successfully to curb all sorts of criminal and anarchical activities. A small incident paralyzes the country. The transport and industry sectors are the worst-hit areas; roadblocks and factory closures are regular features in the post-movement Nepal.

Development Picture

Development itself is an inclusive concept and activity. As in politics, it also aims to empower people relating to the structure and dynamics of power. Thus, the enormity of its scope and integral relationship with power has made development as a sine qua non for democratic consolidation. Strong demand for socioeconomic transformation is made for ending the structure and practices of exploitation. Now democracy and disparity cannot go together. Entrenched value systems and instruments of exploitation need to be overhauled by the inculcation of new values and by restructuring the state and society. Nepali revolution (2006) has laid out the agenda for such change but political actors seem to have forgotten the main agenda of democracy building.

Nepal has completed its 11 plans and is entering into the next soon. How the planning process with its beginning in 1956 has succeeded to substantially transform the social and economic conditions of people needs an objective analysis. Started with NPR21 crores, the first plan was more symbolic as it was just the beginning of the planning process. However, "the plan never played to give a sense of direction and coherence to a multi-faceted development effort."[27] The royal coup of 1960 set its own agenda of politics–economics fusion and produced a Third Year Plan. The panchayat system innovated by King Mahendra aimed at number of economic and social measures in order to impress on the people that the new regime patronized by the king meant business. The land reform program and reforms in Mulki Ain (legal code) were initiated in 1963 and 1964 and strategies for reducing economic dependence were devised. But some measures taken for trade diversification could not take off without having developed a sustainable development at home. Its consequences are being felt today with increasing balance of trade moving toward India's favor. Unless Nepal's political direction does not become clear, Nepal's development would continue to suffer. Restoration of confidence in political leadership and order for creating peaceful atmosphere are preconditions.

The poverty index provided by the government maintains that now only about 25 percent people of the country is below the poverty line. In his book *In Defence of Democracy*, Ram Sharan Mahat, who himself played a key role in his various capacities, Vice Chairman of Planning Commission, Minister, and Member of Parliament, has strongly argued the impressive economic records during the "turbulent years" (1991/2004). In his view, in the midst of political instability, the country had recorded about 5 percent growth with substantial improvement in agriculture, roads, education, employment, health, literacy, etc.[28] Regarding poverty, Mahat writes:

> ... people across all income groups, regions and ecological belts have better access to education, health and economic services. People own perception about their welfare and well being has undergone positive change. The economy has also undergone structural changes, with an increased role of private sector in production, employment and income. The share of traditional agriculture in national production has declined, while that of non-agricultural sources has made noticeable gains.

[27] See Eugene Bramer Mihaly, *Foreign Aid and Politics in Nepal: A Case Study* (London: Oxford University Press, 1965), p. 78.

[28] See Ram Sharan Mahat, *In Defence of Democracy: Dynamics and Fault Lines of Nepal's Political Economy* (Delhi: Adroit Publishers, 2005), pp. 164–165.

Remittance income has emerged as an important factor in raising rural income and reducing poverty.[29]

Nevertheless, some fault lines have been identified admitting that "a large section of population, particularly the historically neglected and discriminated Dalits, indigenous communities, and women have not benefited from the fruits of development in an equitable manner. Economic disparities, instead of declining, have accentuated" during the period under review.

One strong argument put forward by Mahat is that democracy does not hinder development. On the contrary, the traditional authoritarian regime of the Nepali variety had failed to provide an impressive performance record notwithstanding a very strong commitment by King Mahendra in 1960 and later by King Birendra. Sometimes, in a country like Nepal, statistics alone do not provide the essence of progress. Taking education as an indicator today, the numbers of schools, colleges, and universities show that the country is moving ahead quite rapidly. Time factor and level of consciousness or other variables might have made such a growth possible. About 400,000 students appeared in the School Leaving Certificate examination in 2010. There are more than 8,000 private schools in the country as of 2010, in addition to public schools funded by the government.

However, it is debatable what in fact constitutes the indicators of growth that naturally helps improve the living standard of people. Has the new development so far achieved during the period since the planning process began upgraded the living standard of poorest of the poor or has it only created a class of nouveau riche? Has the increase in numbers of school-going children or mushrooming of schools and colleges transformed the social and economic conditions? These questions are related to quality education and other aspects of manpower development.

Going by the indicators, Nepal's sluggish development did never catch up with other countries of South Asia. Now Bangladesh, which has a high density of population, has surpassed Nepal in GDP growth.

---

[29] Mahat, ibid., p. 178.

Bangladesh has been able to control population despite facing heavy odds of an Islamic country. Its rural development scheme revolutionized by the Grameen Bank and other agencies has made impressive gains over the years, although, given the recurrent political crisis faced by the country, its progress is only relatively better. In contrast, Nepal did not make much progress despite the 30-year-long authoritarian monarchical rule where no parties could work as obstructionist elements despite King Mahendra's accusation that they were bent on destroying the unity and integrity of the country. His proclamation in the 1960 December coup that terminated the parliamentary democracy and dismissed the elected government impressed on the people that the parties were the main culprit for Nepal's woes. So he had promised to open a spring of development for achieving targets within 10 years, what other countries had taken a century.

However, after 10 years, realizing the failure of his regime, he once again said that the 1970s would be the decade of development. Nepal's authoritarian model could neither be democratic nor did it show its economic miracles as promised by the ambitious king. The policy of diversification of trade that aimed at reducing economic dependency on India only helped to flood Nepal with consumer goods from third countries. Although this policy served well the interests of few, it did not create economic opportunities based on social justice. Poverty level continued to remain the same for a long time and balance of trade remained as usual. As this program was the precursor for liberalization of economy or what was generally known as market economy with emphasis on "deregulation," "decontrol," and privatization, no substantive change was evident during the 1985–1990 period.

As it has been said:

> ... the data of multilateral institutions such as World Bank and International Monetary Fund (IMF) reveal that Nepal experienced less than 5 percent economic growth rare even in the 'golden era of liberalization'. The neo-liberal policy makers and politicians were often mesmerized even with that sluggish growth rate, when in essence; they needed to be more concerned with the structure and quality of economic growth.[30]

[30] See Bhim Prasad Bhurtel, "Revisiting Economic Policy," *The Kathmandu Post*, Kathmandu, April 17, 2010.

Elaborating further, a Nepali commentator presents a good critique of the so-called liberal economy and writes:

> The widening of the vertical and horizontal disparities in economy is creating two types of Nepal societies that are polarized in terms of income and poverty. Nepal has become more divided in terms of access to health, education and political economic resources. The gulf between the poor and rich has widened even further during the last decades when neo-liberal and free-market assaulted the common mass. Out of US$ 5.4 billion GDP in 2003/4, US$ 2.88 billion was shared by the richest 20 percent of the population and only US$ 0.286 billion was shared by the poorest 20 percent.... The share of income of the richest 20 percent soared to nearly 54 percent from 39.67 percent in 1994/95.

Thus, in sum, it was "ruthless growth" that could benefit only a "handful rich traders, few assembling industrialists and the powerful elites." Such a policy that was enforced with a bang did not extend democracy nor did it empower people. Similarly, since it was a dependent economy shored by remittance, INGOs, foreign financial institutions like the World Bank and The Asian Development, or by other donors, it did not reduce the high rate of unemployment and underemployment. But its positive side was that it increased national income.[31]

Such negative side of development has been balanced by the infrastructures of roads, educational institutions, media development, and diversification of economic activities at both rural and urban areas. It has been said that compared to the long period (1951–1993) during which only 9,000 kilometers of road was constructed, the period between 1993 and 2004, 8,000 kilometers of road was constructed. Roads have changed not only productive relation patterns but also helped generate economic activities.

Nevertheless, it has been argued that poverty did not come down proportionately for all the people in different regions. Second, "income inequality increased simultaneously with the decrease in poverty incidence for the period 1995/96 and 2003/04." As it has been stated: "what is worrisome is that the declining of poverty is accompanied by rising

---

[31] Ibid.

income and expenditure inequalities."[32] It means that the policy of liberalization or of inclusive growth has not seeped through the layers of poor people. So, "as long as significant segment of disadvantaged group of people are not included in the mainstream development process, there is possibility that the entire chain of prosperity will be broken."[33]

Crisis of legitimacy of power in recent times is also intricately related to the faulty economic policies and their concomitant impacts on generating the vicious circle of unemployment. The 2010 turmoil in Thailand (Red-shirt movement) was more to do with the failure of inclusive economic growth than only as a pro-Thaksin (former Prime Minister Thaksin Snehawatra) mobilization of peasantry and laborers. The Thai turmoil seemed to be a great eye-opener for Nepali party leaders and others as well. In order to relate it to the Nepali context, the following passage is worth examining:

> To understand this, and also to begin to comprehend the extent of general dissatis-faction with the economic regime, it is useful to examine the relationship between economic growth and employment (which determines the material conditions of the bulk of the Thai population, even the peasantry). Thailand, in common with many developing countries, is generally a labour surplus economy engaged in an uneven and unbalanced process of industrialization. Yet aggregate gross domestic product (GDP) growth rates have run far ahead of aggregate employment growth, even when the measure of employment includes all form of self-employment, casual work and even part-timework.[34]

My purpose here is to relate legitimacy as an inclusive process to which no believers in democracy can ignore. Although it is not a new approach as it had been time and again postulated by both political thinkers and, later, social scientists, democracy was not taken as an inclusive process in the world. Seymour Martin Lipset, a pioneering social scientist, did elaborate on the correlation between "the existence

[32] See Bishwambher Pyakuryal, "Political Economy of Inclusive Growth," *Kathmandu Post*, March 31, 2010.

[33] Ibid.

[34] See Jayati Ghosh, "Thailand in Crisis," *The Asian Age*, New Delhi, April 20, 2010.

of democracy and such variables as per capita wealth, industrialization, urbanization, and the level of education."[35] Since most of such preconditions were enunciated on the basis of their experiences in democracies in the West, some features such as per capita wealth can be relevant to us also. But most of these early authors did not know the agriculture as the important aspect of reducing poverty and hence did not even mention it in their writings. Other alternative strategies of development are no less important for developing democracy in poor countries like Nepal. Thus, land reform, job opportunities, and sustainable increase in income level of general people, and education are some of the key variables for us.

By the middle of 2010, Nepal's per capita income has been estimated as US$568 by the Central Bureau of Statistics. It is said that during the 2000–2001, the per capita Gross National Income (GNI) of a Nepali was US$259 only, but it has doubled to US$568 in 2009–2010. How could such a frog jump be possible is not revealed fully. However, Nepal hits the bottom among the low income group members of South Asia. The dismal growth rate has been recorded in the post-2006 movement period and the reasons were not far to seek. Recession across the world and protectionist policies adopted by the developed countries, frequent strikes and disturbances, and their impacts on the overall economic and political sectors are some of the principal reasons attributed to the slow growth. Moreover, the highly politicized and partisan labor unions that often go berserk for getting their demands fulfilled or for other political activities have hit the industrial sector hard.

Direct foreign investment is decreasing due to frequent labor disturbances, disorderly political situation, crisis of governance, and corruption. Nepal's corruption is on the rise every year. A Transparency International (2010) study has shown Nepal as one of the most corrupt (146th position out of 178) countries in the world. In South Asia, Bhutan has been identified as the least corrupt in the region. The level of corruption is becoming higher every year, more so in the post-2006 change.

[35] S. M. Lipset, "Some Social Requisites for Democracy: Economic Development and Political Legitimacy," *American Political Science Review*, 53, 1: 1959, pp. 69–105. As mentioned in Robert Pinkney, *Democracy in the Third World* (New Delhi: Viva Books, second edn, 2008).

The country's political volatility and crisis of governance in addition to numerous other factors have become the cause of declining foreign investment. Among the main conditions necessary for attraction of foreign investment, these four have been identified as important. They are: market and prospects of profit, credibility and status of partners within the country, political stability and conditions of security, and the meaningful roles of those who are in different positions of the government.[36] Since Nepal faces many of such conditions, the overall economic development in terms of capital formation, infrastructure building is almost stagnant. So the nonproductive sectors of the economy, such as remittances, money earned from tourism, may increase revenue for maintaining the day-to-day functioning of the government and other related areas but they can hardly create infrastructure and reduce social disparities existing in the country.

Extreme consumerist trends and lack of strong regulatory policy measures are no less responsible for complicating the economic situation in the country. Unlimited imports of luxurious cars, liquidity crunch due to investment in real estate and housing, imports of petroleum products to meet the greater needs of middle class, and the sick enterprises (corporations) run on government subsidies have turned out to be the obstacles to development. The gap between the increase of population (2.5 percent) and the rate of economic growth (3.5–5 percent) has not helped reduce poverty level of general people. The agricultural sector, which still provides employment to 65 percent of the population, is neglected. The land system continues to be ignored despite populist slogans of political parties that they would take measures for distribution of lands to the tillers. Unused lands exist as the old mindset to hold lands for reaping benefits continue. And all those, regardless of parties and ideologies (Leftist, Centrist, and Rightists), along with the rest, have not made a break with the past and, hence, the uncontrollable trend of land-holding. Taking various aspects into account, it has been found that

---

[36] Krishnahari Baskota, "Baideshik Lagani Akarshit Garne Upayaharu" [Means for Attracting Foreign Investment], *Nagarik Daily*, October 27, 2010.

disequilibrium between increase in per capita income and poverty reduction exists. Poverty, in fact, has increased in recent years.[37] Crisis of governance and decline of the state is also the important factor for tardy development. The pathetic condition of the country could be observed in early 2010s when, disgusted with the failure of the state or crisis of governance, the leading business leaders went to the extent of threatening the prime minister to hand over the key of their industries to him if the anarchic situation did not come under control within a month. As peace and development are the sine qua non of overall progress, people reflect their feeling when they get an opportunity to demonstrate.

Although a lot of infrastructural development has taken place along with the greater awareness of people, crisis has also developed in alarming proportions. It was believed that the end of Maoist insurgency and end of monarchy would set the trends of peace and development, assuring the people that their sacrifices would not go in vain, but such assurances are proved wrong. So, as Panday observes:

> ... few will deny that societal disintegration has reached a historical threshold, a point where Nepal is teetering between the prevailing savagery of its ruling elites and the simmering class rupture at its core. It is a classic case of a chaotic clash between classes.[38]

Now clashes have assumed various forms—ethnic, tribal, regional, communal, sectarian, caste, etc.—that subsume core principles of democracy. So, Nepal's present/future woes would be cured only by taking bold initiatives by leaders of political parties who should rise above petty partisan and personal interests. So far such gestures are not forthcoming as of now, dimming all hopes of making new Nepal.

[37] See the views of Pitambar Sharma, Bishwambhar Pyakuryal, Keshav Prasad Acharya, Dependra Bahadur Chhetri, Hari Roka, and Bhim Prasad Bhurtel in *Mulyankan Monthly*, June–July 2010.

[38] Writing the foreword to a book by Nanda R. Shrestha, *In the Name of Development: A Reflection on Nepal* (Kathmandu: Educational Enterprise, 1998), Devendra Raj Panday wrote these sentences in 1998, i.e., 12 years ago and in the wake of the ongoing Maoist insurgency which ended in 2006.

Social disparity has been widened by the prevailing educational conditions of the country. Consequently, it has divided the people into privileged and underprivileged sections, thus, enabling only the former to get benefits from quality education. The emergence of the nouveau riche in which category the new political elites also belong has further made the Nepali state vulnerable. Such polarization into classes which in course of time start making a distinction between the "creamy layers" and the deprived populace belonging to all social categories. It means more fissures within each community transcending caste, ethnic and other ties which were holding these communities together for centuries. Here, Marxian economic determinism may work to inspire these deprived people. The implosion of neoliberalism in 2008 has resurrected the interest in Marx.

Is Nepal still "semi-colonial" and "semi-feudal country" as described by the Nepali Left parties? Apparently yes it is, because of the excessive dependency on foreign donors and international financial institutions. Seventy percent of Nepal's budgetary allocations are determined by these donors let alone its trade relations with India. Many people have preferred to put Nepal into the "center–periphery" framework as India is the center and Nepal is a periphery. However, such a description seems to be simplistic in that it has ignored the existing international order where each country is needed to interact. It can also be called "interdependent relationship" even while accepting the dominant role of some economic powers at the center. Even China–US relations are based on such close partnership given the trade relations between the two countries.

Similarly, the semi-feudal nature of the Nepali state and society needs to be contextualized as many remnants of the old Shah and Rana systems do not exist despite the continuation of the old feudal orientations and culture that have been successful to make inroads into the Nepali state and elite structure. Yet, as Chaitanya Mishra says, it is not appropriate to call Nepal as a "semi-colonial" and "semi-feudal" because of the changed national and international contexts. He writes:

I have, on the other hand, for quite some time argued that Nepal's economy acquired a decidedly capitalist tendency as early as the mid-1880s, and that is much closer now to the capitalist pole rather than to the pre-capitalist, feudal or semi-feudal one.[39]

Whatever the description, Nepal's transformation into an egalitarian state is being obstructed by the elites whose middle class, defined more by the today's consumerist aptitude and continued feudal influence, work as anti-progress. Although the same elites were also instrumental in forging coalition with the Maoists against the monarchy, their inability to keep pace with the new demands for democratization was also evident. Nevertheless, compared to many countries in South Asia and in other regions, Nepalis in general are not averse to change. Such a contradictory situation continues to exist because of weak foundations of political parties. Moreover, the emergence of UCPN (Maoist) as a force, which was legitimized by the CA elections of 2008 and later by its capacity to mobilize people belonging to different strata, especially the lower class, drove other parties to panic. The Maoist leaders were/are themselves responsible for creating such a hiatus between them and other parties. As a result, politics is increasingly becoming polarized as if the Maoist party is the messiah of poor people; the rest including the NC and CPN–UML are the parties of the status quo. The coalition formed against the Maoist party following its ouster from power in 2009 had almost ripped CPN–UML for being too subservient to the NC despite being the communist party with a Marxist Leninist brand. Many are of the opinion that CPN–UML was/is fast losing its credibility as a Left party as it neither fully embraces the agenda of socioeconomic change nor has it prepared itself to fully transform into a liberal democratic party, albeit with a bias for egalitarianism. On the one hand, its claim that it has been working as a moderating force between the two extremes—the NC's penchant for being status quoist and the extremist Maoists—seems to be untenable because of increasing bonhomie with the NC for power. The Maoist political rhetoric, on the other hand, suggests that they are still hesitant to be fully transformed into competitive pluralist democracy.

[39] See Chaitanya Mishra, *Essays on the Sociology of Nepal* (Kathmandu: Fine Print Inc., 2007), p. 19, and *Punjibad ra Nepal* (Capitalism and Nepal) (Kathmandu: Mulyankan 2062 VS), pp. 184–185.

Nepal is also greatly affected by the powerful impacts of globalization creating its own nexus within the country. On the one hand, the fractured ideology rules the roost, despite the triumph of liberal democracy by name; on the other hand, a remarkable dynamism seems to be propelling the society and politics. In the name of Marx, Lenin, and Mao, movements have been launched by firing the imagination of poor and other deprived sections of society, but Marx and Mao are soon forgotten for short-term gains and greed. Yet, such a duality of approach is not new in the Nepali context as other countries, including China, have also been affected by such duality. It has been rightly said:

> There is no Marxism left in China, though there are bits of Leninism. The revolutionary proletariats, in the shape of leaders who are often the prince's children of an earlier generation of leading cadres, dictate policies that bear little resemblance to any known form of socialism.[40]

Since development is very much related to some sort of an ideology, countries without sufficient liberal ideological background and movements often tend to be a part of "post-ideological age." However, to cite Patten again, "post-ideological for some, may be—but not for those of us stubbornly attached to the belief that economic and political liberalism are always eventually found to be joined at the hip."[41]

Parties and Crisis of Governance

Nepal's main problem of development is the crisis of governance. And all forms of governments—monarchical authoritarian, elected, minority or majority, coalition, and single party—have been affected by the viruses of governance crisis. During the royal rule for 30 years and later during the period of elected government (1990–2005), no distinct change was noticed in elite attitude and political culture. The outstanding issues that

---

[40] Chris Patten, *What Next?: Surviving the Twenty-First Century* (Victoria, Australia: Penguin Books, 2008), p. 401.
[41] Ibid.

were urgently needed to be addressed by the new elites received only passing references in speeches and documents. But when the Maoists started capitalizing the issue of discrimination, more specifically the issues of ethnic, Dalit, gender, and region, the Deuba government (then the undivided NC) started forming commissions for them. Yet, no substantive policies and programs were enforced to develop the processes with which the various social and regional groups could be included.

Since governance is also a process, institutional behavior, elite accountability, and procedures are preconditions of it. In Nepal, there has been no institutional growth in political, administrative, police, and army as all of them have had been greatly afflicted by authoritarian traditional political culture prevalent in the country for the last 240 years. It was basically the *hukumi tantra* or peremptory command having no coherence and procedures. What was more significant was that there was no distinction between civil and military administration because all top-ranking military posts were automatically occupied by the family members. The people were only silent spectators whose influence in resources and power was almost nonexistent. However, the Brahmans and other upper-caste members had some advisory roles with which they could be closer to the rulers.

The changes brought about by the 1990 movement for the restoration of democracy could not also set definite trends in the art of governance. Leaders of political parties who came to power or sat in the opposition did not help develop institutions, ensure accountability, and transparency. Educational institutions were in shambles, cronyism, favoritism, and nepotism continued to triumph, a criterion of achievement was never encouraged, and universally accepted norm of democratic governance and administration not followed. The splits of parties became a routine affair, leaders and workers displayed utter normlessness in governance. As result, rampant corruption in governance along with the vulgar ostentatious lifestyles of people's representatives was evident. The feudal political culture was not replaced by a new sense of direction and feeling of responsibility. Democracy, thus, turned out to be a facade dashing all hopes of being inclusive and substantive. Although the 1990 Constitution embraced people of Nepal as sovereign and laid down certain guiding principles for ending socioeconomic disparities and for social justice, no policies were implemented toward mitigating the existing social, economic, and political gaps. On the contrary, the disparity gap widened even after the introduction of multiparty system in 1990. The awareness created by democratic exercises as well as by the Maoist insurgency is not channeled for democratic consolidation. Even in the economic sector, the statistics show that during a decade of multiparty rule, Nepal's decade-long development record has surpassed the pace of development of the 30-year-long monarchical rule. Yet, these development efforts have not helped transform Nepal's economic conditions significantly.

On the contrary, widespread gloom has descended on the country because politics continues to be fraught with uncertainties. Its principal causes are: lack of culture of accountability, dominance of "pretentious ideology" or ambivalent ideological positions of parties, lack of performance, overdependence on external support psychologically, politically and economically, and failure of leaders to make a smooth democratic transition. On top of them is the lack of minimum value consensus needed for charting a course of development.

The Maoist–other parties row developed following Maoist supremo Prachanda's speech that he had delivered in a camp (Shaktikhor), albeit confidentially, that much numbers were not genuine as the party wanted to swell the numbers who were, under the Peace Agreement, entitled to be looked after by the state. Prachanda's speech was interpreted as a high degree of duplicity and drove other parties not to trust the Maoists for the latter's hidden agendas. Its fallout explicitly revealed following the Maoist decision to remove the COAS for his alleged defiance of government line. Such a precipitated action prompted other parties to back the COAS asking him not to resign. They also deserted the Maoists urging the president to reject the move of the prime minister. Finding himself in an awkward position, Prime Minister Prachanda resigned on grounds of violation of civilian supremacy by the president.

The Unified Maoist Party is the first party in the CA, which also works as the Parliament that can elect any party leader as prime minister if he/she can garner the support of 301 members. The Maoists have lost the technical majority but remains the single largest party with double the seats of both the NC and the CPN–UML. It is, thus, natural that the UN Secretary General wanted to impress on the political leaders to work toward a national government. Political parties that are scared of the Maoists have interpreted the UN version as preference to the Maoists.

The reactions of the NC and the CPN–UML or any other party in government also show the crisis of legitimacy both internally and externally. A person who has been defeated from two separate parliamentary constituencies from his own home district and also from the capital, Kathmandu, became the prime minister. Madhav K. Nepal had been brought into the CA by the Maoist leaders themselves for chairing the main Constitutional Committee in the CA. It was also a strategy on the side of the Maoists to show a gesture to the former general secretary of the UML. Later, the Maoists repented that it was their great mistake to make Mr Nepal the chairman after getting him admitted into the CA. A member of the UML facilitated his entry by resigning his membership on the assurance that he would get a plump post (diplomatic), which he got later on.

It was not only the question of the prime minister; many other ministers who held important portfolios, like foreign affairs and defense were defeated, in the CA election. So the question of actual legitimacy arose within and outside the country. Madhav Kumar Nepal who resigned his post of party general secretary after the elections had said publicly that he would not accept any post after his defeat.

Moreover, expectation that the new non-Maoist coalition government would manage the Maoists by bringing them into government has been belied. On the contrary, all parties became increasingly belligerent vis-à-vis the UCPN (Maoist). And more perceptual and psychological considerations seemed to have created standoff between the Maoist and the anti-Maoist parties. First, the Maoist leaders' own utterances that went against the spirit of multiparty system and political pluralism scared other non-Maoist parties. They believed that the Maoists were really bent on creating their own model of people's democracy despite their occasional assurances they gave to others that they would not deviate from their commitment to multiparty system. Many of its moves also made the other parties believe that its agenda of "civilian control" was nothing more than the capture of the state power. Such trust deficit was/is evident even today with all other parties trying to malign the Maoists for not changing its original line of thinking. Its commitment to disband the YCL, a youth wing of the party, to restore property seized during the insurgency and to end the culture of impunity, etc., has not been met.

Yet, in retrospect, it can be argued that the process of transformation of the CPN–UML had taken longer than that of the UCPN (Maoist) with a small difference between them. The CPN–UML was only momentarily involved in the "campaign of liquidation of class enemies" in the early 1970s and changed its violent line subsequently. The Communist Party of Nepal (Marxist Leninist) (CPN [ML]), which became the CPN–UML after the merger of the Marxist Leninst (ML) party and the CPN (Marxist) on the eve of the 1991 election, accepted Jantako Bahudaliya Janbad (people's multiparty democracy) under the leadership of Madan Bhandari. However, the CPN–UML continues to be a communist party with all traditional symbols, rhetoric, and names of Western leaders like Marx-Engels and Lenin. Its ambivalent approaches to numerous issues have often been proved as sources of embarrassment to it. Now the CPN–UML derides the Maoists for not being temperamentally suited to the spirit of liberal democracy even after becoming a first party in the 2008 CA election and running the government under its leadership for nine months. The second difference between the processes of transformation of the two is that the UML had no problem of accommodation of its combatants, nor did it decide to join multiparty democracy as a consequence of agreements as did the Maoists and other leaders of parties. The CPN (Maoist) party came after spending 10 long years in guerrilla warfare and obviously needed some guarantees to its ex-combatants for integration, rehabilitation, and monitoring. The UN was, thus, invited to play the role of facilitator unless the peace process came to a logical conclusion.

Nepal's peace process, which is inextricably connected to the consolidation of democracy, has suffered due to overindulgence of political forces for short-term gains. The crisis of legitimacy of the present government and the Maoists' determined bid to capitalize the issue of "civilian control," which by implication is related to the supremacy of government not that of the ceremonial head of state, has also cast a dark shadow on the peace and constitutional processes. Other parties that petitioned to the president to reject the decision of the prime minister to remove the COAS are not prepared to accept the Maoist move taken in the name of correction. In their opinion, the president was right in not accepting the decision of the prime minister who had lost the support of majority parties in his own government. The UN wanted to bridge this gap in order not to derail the peace process and the agenda of constitution making.

Let me briefly summarize the status of Nepal internally and externally. The Nepali state is becoming weaker by every passing day, though it has not crumbled as many tend to suggest. Nevertheless, development is hard-hit due to 15–16 hours of power cut; closure of industries because of the uninterrupted strikes, threats, and extortion; crisis of governance; lack of strong and committed leadership to hold together; misunderstanding of vital issues raised for restructuring of the state; and failure of leaders of parties to sit together in finding a way out for settling down the pertinent issues and problems facing the country. Above all, failure of parties to agree on setting parameters for writing the constitution is likely to reverse the process of democratization. Vanishing democratic culture which was supposed to be possessed by the middle class has created democratic crisis. Old generation members of middle class have failed to inculcate democratic culture despite making the movements successful. Now the new middle class is more dangerous compared to any threat emanating from the downtrodden. Consumerist culture, penchant for ostentatious lifestyle, easy money flow due to NGOs and INGOs, or because of rampant corruption and criminalization of politics and culture of violence has overshadowed the prospect of democratic sustainability.

The Nepali state is in deep trouble for the first time in its modern history. The challenges are both internal and external. In a state of flux, political forces seem to have lost their direction at a time when their capacity to steer the course of development needed to be reflected. Instead of forging a new consensus for heralding a smooth transition to stable democracy, political forces seem to have learned no lessons from the past mistakes. High degree of irresponsibility displayed by the leaders of parties is likely to take the country to catastrophe. Quarrels of political leaders for petty interests in the post-CA election or the failure of the Nepali state and governance, as a result, have many negative pointers for the future. Since democracy is both a culture and process, both are becoming increasingly elusive in Nepal. Coming as they do from different ideological backgrounds, leaders of parties have not yet been able to comprehend the consequences if they fail to provide a stable constitutional order in the new republican Nepal. The country's progress is at a standstill due to messy political situation created by the failures of political parties. It is not only the Nepali state which is in greatest risk today, lack of governance has also added woes to the people whose minimum aspiration is limited to peace and stability.

Democracy's Future

Democracy in Nepal remains a powerful rallying force behind political upheavals that have occurred since 1950. Apparently, such upheavals were the pacesetters of history. Yet, examining them deeply, they at the same time also turned out to be regressive. Both national and external factors were responsible for undoing the evolutionary process. In the past, monarchy was singled out as a culprit for democratic retardation. Now, with the monarchy gone, who do we curse for yet another democratic setback? Obviously the political parties could be blamed for being reckless, undemocratic, unresponsive to the wishes of the people, and above all, their failure to address the burgeoning problems with courage, determination, and vision. All these qualities may not necessarily be found in most leaders, nor should we be idealistic and unrealistic in our thinking. However, leaders should know the context and time of their roles.

The impact of the fractured ideological position of parties, shifting support base due to trends of fusion of various ideological persuasions, if any, and lack of leaders and well-knit organizations based on democratic values and norms can be taken as some of the causes responsible for democratic underdevelopment. Moreover, as discussed in other chapters, culture of violence and waves of ethnic, regional, and other parochial trends can be counted as negatives for democracy. Such issues become powerful when the leaders or the government become weak. If the major leaders of parties are really committed to face them, taking them as threats to democracy, many problems would be settled.

Although it is difficult to deal with Nepali politics from a class perspective because of the thin divisions between class and caste or urban–rural composition of people, our narrative would be incomplete if we do not examine the emergence of a new class or a petty bourgeoisie whose overall life cycles are determined by consumerist culture. Temptations are high for earning money by any means, as money earned by both fair and foul means is needed for ostentatious lifestyle. Even if Nepal's rural politics does not take a class form, boundary lines between rural and urban are fast eroding in recent years. The trends of globalization are so powerful that it becomes difficult for an ordinary citizen to insulate oneself from them. The private and public school divide and the presence of what we call the *bhuin phutta barga* (upstart class), whose orientations and culture are beyond the imagination of ordinary Nepalis, are not likely to be real defenders of democratic development. Since people belonging to this category have become rich overnight due to money earned easily or by fluke, the structure of relations among different groups has undergone dramatic changes. Moreover, since politics and money power are increasingly interlinked, politicians, security agencies, bureaucracy, teachers, students, and traders are all together in the game.

The decline of democracy in Nepal is particularly precipitated by the so-called middle class whose greed for money, if not power, has also seeped down to the rural level. It seems that no party workers would be inclined to spend their prime of youth in jail as young men/women used to sacrifice in the past for the cause of freedom. Whoever is in politics, in various forms and roles, it is because of their hope that their interests would be served by their association with certain parties or groups. However, caution has to be taken that the poor and other oppressed and marginalized sections of society might have joined politics for better future in case their parties' government came to power. The new generation of middle-class politicians and others are, thus, motivated more for "recognition" with return of wealth.

The middle class or even the people at the bottom are not likely to protect democracy if their orientations go against the spirit of democratic culture. The people who have had been raising the banner of democracy for so long are likely to be the "culprits." In an article published in *Newsweek* on March 22, 2010, an interesting analysis has been made by Joshua Kurlantzick:

> ... many of the same middle-class men and women who once helped push dictators out of power are now seeing just how difficult it can be to establish democracy, and are pining for the days of autocracy. Why has this happened? In many cases because the early leaders of the young democracies that emerged in the 1990s failed to recognize that free societies require strong institutions, a loyal opposition to the ruling party, and a willingness to compromise. Instead, they saw democracy just as garnering semi-regular votes; after they won, they then used all tools of power to dominate their countries and to hand out benefits to their allies or tribe.[42]

Such understanding of democracy that fails to deliver would make people disillusioned and hence the reverse trend begins to unfold. Thus, the middle class, which was considered the fortress of democracy, is no more valid.

Nepal's situation is slightly different due to the intermixing roles of the middle and the common people in shaping today's Nepali politics. The composition of the CA and greater demand for further representation and empowerment of people belonging to the lower strata would erase the boundary between the two layers. Nevertheless, from economic point of view, the gap between the privileged and underprivileged class would remain. The continued caste domination, which takes time to change, and class based on wealth would also remain. Greater dependence of political parties on business houses, private school owners that have also developed their economic clout, and international donors or

---

[42] See Joshua Kurlantzick, "A Global Decline in Political Freedom Is Partly the Fault of the Middle Class," *Newsweek*, March 22, 2010, p. 30.

NGOs and INGOs have contributed to the making of a "new class," however small its size may be.

Thus, class in terms of Marxian stratification may not be comparable with other countries but the gaps do exist in any society and class as a concept and reality will continue to figure in social studies. The Maoist revolution in China had clearly modified such a Marxian formulation when Mao made peasantry as the base for developing his theory of revolution. So it is not the industrial workers or "proletariat" but the peasants and other suppressed people who were taken as the vanguards of revolution. How the Maoist strategy of reaching out to the Dalits, women, hill groups, and Tarai ethnic and caste groups, and the entire poverty-ridden people worked effectively for its armed insurgency could be an example of the patterns of change in the country. It is due to this Maoist background and compulsion that other parties too were under pressure to make the CA and their own organizations more inclusive. Concerning the women participation in the Maoist insurgency and its likely impacts on the emancipation of women in the future, one Nepali scholar has, thus, remarked:

> The issue of gender is highlighted more by the Maoists than by other parties. It is certain that the human rights of women would be more prominently raised in the future in Nepal. All the exploited, subordinated, subjugated and marginalized women can no longer be included under the patriarchal social structure because the women have participated as rebels in the Maoist movement for taking revenge or for compensation to all kinds of exploitation, and for emancipation from the subjugation and suppression.[43]

Much of our discourse so far developed through various chapters of this book has identified the three major villains of democracy: monarchy, parties, and the external powers. The monarch's role was also facilitated by the weak leaders of political parties who were perennially haunted by the shadow of monarchy. Monarchy took it as an opportunity to extend

---

[43] Indra Adhikari, "Women in Conflict: The Gender Perspective in Maoist Insurgency" in Lok Raj Baral, ed., *Nepal: Facets of Maoist Insurgency* (Delhi: Adroit, 2006), p. 82.

NEPAL—NATION-STATE IN THE WILDERNESS

its scope once it knew the weaknesses of parties. However, such a game proved fatal when the politics of compromise was castigated by the ambitious King. It is a paradoxical situation that the same parties that had championed the case of monarchy had to abandon it subsequently for their own existence. Ironically, however, the abolition of monarchy has not improved the image of political leaders. On the contrary, popular disenchantment with the parties had increased because of the failures of leaders steer the course of future development. So, given the interparty conflict, democracy's future is becoming uncertain.

External players who often helped parties to restore democracy also play negative roles showing their own preference to parties and leaders. Their interventionist roles become active when parties leaders themselves become weak both psychologically and organizationally. Their temptation to be close to India and China, for example, has encouraged these powers to be more interventionist for influencing the internal politics of Nepal. It is particularly significant when China and India are emerging as competitive powers whose future activities need to be appropriately balanced by Nepal. However, this needs both acumen and status of leaders.

5

Nepal and the World

Managing Geopolitics

This chapter tries to reflect on the emerging trends in global politics and their short-, medium-, and long-term impacts on Nepal. The triangular relations between Nepal, China, and India along with the larger interests of other powers also need to be dealt with to situate Nepal in such multiple dimensions. It is particularly important in the present context when Nepal's own internal upheavals are not settled. Whatever goodwill and sympathy Nepal has earned by serving the peace keeping operations of the UN and by developing friendly relations with as many countries of the world as possible is also becoming controversial. Bilateral relations with neighbors that used to reap benefits in competitive sense are also now seen with suspicion. Monarchy that had provided a semblance of stability has been abolished but no alternative forces that fill up the vacuum have yet emerged despite the existence of political parties of all hues and orientations. Since most of them are in fervent and follow divergent approaches to vital issues confronting the country, they lack direction and confidence. The post-CA election scenario of Nepali politics suggests that both internally and externally Nepal's image has shrunk a great deal. The principal reason of this is the loss of credibility of political leaders who now have come to the center stage but have failed to comprehend the emerging complexity of national, regional, and global politics.

The two major casualties of Maoist–other political parties' conflict are the peace process and the making of a new constitution by the CA. The root of conflict and mistrust between them could be traced to the Fifth Amendment to the Interim Constitution, 2007, with an alternative to *sahamati* or politics of understanding. According to this arrangement, a government could be formed either by consensus among political parties or by simple majority (based on the first-past-the-post system). The emergence of the CPN (Maoist), now Unified CPN (Maoist), as the first party in the CA election apparently made the two parties—the NC and the CPN–UML—paranoid as all their calculations proved wrong by the election verdict. Although the UCPN (Maoist) also failed to get absolute majority, its emergence as the first party that displaced the other former two from their first and second positions was a major gain. The post–Jan Andolan Nepali politics is also characterized by the dramatic increase of the impact of the Tarai politics, which, for decades, was monopolized by the NC as well as by the CPN–UML after the 1990s. It is appropriate to say that these two principal parties had been able to keep the Tarai leaders in their fold until the Madhesh identity politics sprang abruptly immediately after the 2006 movement.

How Nepal's immediate neighbors, China and India, and other countries like the US, the EU, and Japan see the morphosed Nepali politics needs to be examined. Many in Nepal are of the view that India is, in fact, perceived as one of the "players" in Nepali politics not only because of geographical proximity and other factors but also due to embedded psychology that it really matters. Most political leaders in recent years have shown by their action and mindset that without courting India, the prospect of power is remote. Hence, they divert all their energy to appease Indian establishment so that the southern neighbor could put them into power. Such a mindset of Nepali political elites is not shaped by their understanding of the emergent geopolitical dynamics; rather, they are driven by their own desire and complex.

However, in the given context, geopolitics is discussed in both regional and international level so that the interplay of forces could be observed. The "vignettes of Nepal" are so alluring that Nepalis and foreigners alike are enchanted with the country as a whole. Now enter the big world players with different motives making Nepal as one of the strategic centers for power gravitation. In the past, they appeared as distant watchers and did not become so assertive as they are today. Yet, their assertiveness, except in case of India and China, is believed to have been seen through "Indian prism," because of the changing power balance in Asia and the world.

Regionally, during the Cold War, the South Asian countries either preferred to be nonaligned between the two superpowers, the US- and the USSR-led blocs, but some like Pakistan joined the Western alliance system led by the US. Since the Cold War is over along with the bipolar international order, the scope of this chapter is accordingly limited to regional geopolitics, but, nonetheless, trying to conjoin it with the emerging trends in international politics. Nepal's geopolitical context can only be connected to its two traditional neighbors—India and China—but it has "become evident that the geopolitical environment is determined not only by the established but also by emerging powers."[1]

The role played by geopolitics in bringing Nepal closer to Indian orbit has also added newer dimensions to relations. Conflicting orientations of political elites and lack of deeper understanding and confidence have dented the mutual trust and confidence. In the context of Nepal, geopolitics entails numerous domains such as security, economy, demography, sociocultural aspects, politics, and people. Given such vast array of areas related to India and Nepal, and to a lesser extent to China, the very idea of nation-state gets blurred. It becomes difficult to delineate the boundary if one goes strictly by the very concept of nation-state. The consequences of geopolitics include the blurred economic relations, dependent foreign policy and national security, influence on shaping domestic politics, and chances of national disintegration. When political elites fail to probe into the deepened interstate relations (with India) and become less objective and more jingoistic, crises creep into the country. The pre-1950 rulers seemed to be more adept at handling foreign policy

---

[1] Cristobal Rovira Kaltwasser, "Moving Beyond the Washington Consensus: The Resurgence of the Left in Latin America," *International Politics and Society*, 3, 2010, p. 56.

with the neighbors on the basis of realistic approach. It paid them dividends when they could successfully protect their own political interest, i.e., perpetuation in power in the name of national independence and pride. At the same time, their understanding of the emergent geopolitical trends with which they could put up good bargain for maintaining independence also worked as a protective shield for oligarchy.

Although China and Nepal had historical links in different ways, such contacts were pushed to the background with the rise of the British power in India. China itself was a declining power in the early 20th century until it roared as a lion after the successful communist revolution in 1949. For Nepal, the integration of Tibet in 1950 and the fear and anxiety created by communism made both India and Nepal paranoid. The Qing dynasty of China had "originally brought Tibet under loose Chinese influence" in the early decades of the 18th century, though its grip was loosened until the Qing intervened again and established a form of tributary rule. In 1910, Chinese (Qing) "reasserted control." When the Chinese power waned after the revolution in 1911, Tibet could enjoy some sort of freedom.

However, the pre-1950 Nepali rulers had never faced the geopolitical pulls and pressures as the governments of the post-revolution (1950) period. The presence of the People's Republic of China in Tibet in 1950 brought the two contending Asian powers, communist China and democratic India, closer to Nepal. Tibet that worked as a buffer in the past was now the Tibetan Autonomous Region of China. But the rupture developed with China not providing the "promised autonomy" drove the Tibetans to revolt against the Chinese rule in 1959. The Chinese crushed the uprising but the Dalai Lama and his close associates managed to escape to India and took refuge there. These developments soon changed the Sino–Indian cordiality into hostility with spillover effects on Nepal's relations with these two neighbors. Accepting it as fait accompli, most countries, including the Dalai Lama, accept the Chinese sovereignty but urge China to grant more autonomy with Tibetan identity. In this context, one British scholar has thus commented:

> The Chinese strategy towards Tibet has comprised a range of different approaches.
> It has pursued a strategy of repression and forced assimilation, which has included

. refusing to Dalai Lama, restricting the role of Buddhist priests, and forbidding
Tibetan students and government workers from visiting monasteries or participating in religious ceremonies ... In addition China has encouraged large-scale Han
migration to Tibet in an effort to alert the balance of the population and thereby
weaken the position of the Tibetans, who for the most part live in the rural areas
and in segregated urban ghettos, whereas the Han, who comprise over half the
population of Lhasa, are concentrated in the urban areas.[2]

The three Himalayan states (Bhutan, Nepal, and Sikkim) and India were
prompted by the turn of new events to rethink their strategic relations
so as to stem any threat to be posed by China. The new alliances formed
between India and other adjoining states in 1949–1950 clubbed them
together despite separate (bilateral) arrangements by India with each
kingdom. The Treaty of Peace and Friendship of 1950 concluded between India and Nepal, thus, came in the wake of the then emergent
developments. As its detailed narrative has already been presented in
Chapter 3, it is repeated here against the new geopolitical or strategic
background.

Initial paranoia of India and Nepal was soon reconciled, leading to the
policy of adjustment to the revolutionary change in China and its presence in Tibet. As a consequence, India recognized Tibet as the autonomous region of China and pledged to follow one China policy when most
of the Western countries led by the US recognized "Nationalist China"
(Formosa) as legitimate China. So in the name of China, Formosa, by
proxy, represented China in different world forums including the UN
Security Council, though the People's Republic of China continued to
treat Formosa as a renegade part of China. Such a proxy ended following President Nixon's visit to China and signing of the Shanghai
Communiqué in 1972. But India and Nepal had consistently supported
the People's Republic of China, notwithstanding the US material and
political support to the Nationalist China.

On the part of India and Nepal, their recognition of the People's
Republic of China's legitimacy, obviously to the chagrin of the US, was

[2] Martin Jacques, *When China Rules the World: The Rise of the Middle Kingdom
and the End of the Western World* (London: Penguin Books, 2009), pp. 252–253.

based on principle and realism. How could Nepal, a next-door neighbor and whose overall orientations were not at variance with India or with other nonaligned countries, join the Western bandwagon against China? Moreover, China's new strategic formulations of the 1950s had encouraged other powers to be assured of its role.

The five principles of peaceful coexistence (*panchshila*) enunciated by Indian Prime Minister Nehru, Chinese Premier Chou En-lai, and Indonesian President Sukarno in Bandung in 1955 were also the guiding principles for establishing Nepal's diplomatic relation with China. As these principles laid emphasis on mutual respect for each other's internal integrity and sovereignty, nonaggression, noninterference in each other's internal affairs, for any reasons—of an economic, political, or ideological character, equality, mutual benefit, and peaceful coexistence—all the three countries, China, India, and Nepal, affirmed them in conducting their foreign policies though the two Asian giants failed to adhere to these principles following the Tibetan uprising in 1959 and with the Dalai Lama and his followers taking shelter in India.

Chinese scholars, working inside the country, often echo the policies of the government. In the present context too, principles are always affirmed despite their actual application in real politick. A Chinese scholar has, thus, stated the characteristics of a new "strategic culture" of China:

> The strategic culture, in its new diplomacy and new security concept, is embodied in four credos: pursuing partnership and not leadership; friendship, not confrontation; commitment to equal and mutual security and common prosperity; putting economics over politics; and recognizing the diversity of the world, emphasizing co-existence in peace, and pursuing cooperation in a multilateral framework.[3]

Nepal's recognition of the People's Republic of China in 1955 also indicated a major departure from its past policy without undermining the structure of relations with India. Nehru, who appreciated Nepal's

---

[3] See Xuecheng Liu, "China's Strategic Culture and Its Political Dynamics" in V. P. Malik and Jorg Schultz, eds, *The Rise of China: Perspectives from Asia and Europe* (New Delhi: Pentagon Press, 2008), p. 2.

independence and sovereignty and territorial integrity, had expressed the burgeoning geopolitical trends and Nepal's imperative to develop relations with China.[4] Nevertheless, India's wariness was evident in Nehru's communications with the Nepali leaders that Nepal might play "China card" or undermine special security relations with India. Situated between the two big powers, Nepal's problem of maintaining a harmonious balance between China and India increased in course of time as the latter's trust deficit reflected in events and trends. Strained Sino–Indian relations that had developed following the flight of the Dalai Lama from Tibet in 1959 taking asylum in India and border incursions reported from both sides had repercussions on Nepal too. In the post-1950 Indo–Nepal relations, the Nepali leaders who became critical of India's alleged interference or of roles or behaviors were branded as anti-Indian. Even Matrika Prasad Koirala did not accept Jawaharlal Nehru's views on continuing the same old British-India's policy toward Nepal. The letters exchanged between the two prime ministers suggest two approaches of India: India's continued British-India policy along with the elements of change. The other concern was about stability and democracy but not with the doses of radicalism as B. P. Koirala wanted to pursue. M. P. Koirala who was known as a pro-Indian has revealed that he had tried to withstand the pressure of India on many issues to which the latter did not appreciate.[5] How India saw Nepal with suspicion could be observed in the letters exchanged between the Indian Prime Minister, Nehru and M. P. Koirala in the early 1950s. It is worth quoting Nehru in connection with Indian attitude toward Nepal. Nehru wrote to Koirala:

> Another matter, to which I drew your attention, was the new contacts that Nepal was developing with other foreign countries without any reference to us. This

---

[4] The long list of letters put in the Appendix of the book suggest how India's policy toward Nepal continues to be the same despite a lot of changes that have taken place in the South Asian region and in the world. See in detail, M. P. Koirala, *A Role in a Revolution* (Kathmandu: Jagadamba Prakashan, 2008).

[5] Ibid. See also Avtar Singh Bhasin, *Nepal-India, Nepal-China Relations Documents 1947-June 2005*, Volume 1 (New Delhi: Geetika Publishers, 2005).

seemed to me contrary to our agreements and to the policy which the Nepalese Government had assured us would be followed in regard to foreign affairs and foreign contacts.[6]

During the period of the first-ever elected government headed by B. P. Koirala (1959–1960), Nepal–India relations were not as cordial as many had presumed. Yet, people, who always saw the NC leaders as pro-Indian could find fault with what the government did. How B. P. Koirala skirted Nehru's statement that he gave in connection with the developing strained relations of India with China following the flight of the Dalai Lama from Tibet in 1959 was interesting. Disclosing the content of the letter exchanged with the 1950 Treaty and reaffirming India's position vis-à-vis the mutual security arrangement of both the countries, Nehru declared that "any aggression against Bhutan and Nepal would be regarded as an aggression on India."[7] This statement came as a response to China's incursion into the Nepali territory in Mustang area killing two Nepali guards. As the statement was made unilaterally and since both Nepal and China were now neighbors, such Indian declaration was embarrassing for the elected government, which was already under pressure of opposition inside parliament and outside. Responding to Nehru, B. P. Koirala said:

Nepal is a fully sovereign independent nation. It decides its external and home policy according to its own judgment and its own liking without ever referring to any outside authorities. Our Treaty of Peace and Friendship with India affirms this. I take Mr. Nehru's statement as an expression of friendship that in case of aggression against Nepal, India would send help if such help was ever sought. It would never be taken as suggesting that India could take unilateral action. Is there apprehension of danger from any quarter? The answer is definitely no. We are at peace with everybody and we do not apprehend any danger from any quarter.[8]

[6] M. P. Koirala, *A Role in a Revolution* (Kathmandu: Jagadamba Prakashan, 2008), p. 255.

[7] See *The Statesman*, Calcutta, November 28, 1959.

[8] As cited in Rishikesh Shaha, *Modern Nepal*, Vol. II (Delhi: Manohar, 1990), p. 197.

Quickly responding to B. P. Koirala's remarks, Nehru said that these were the "expressions of friendship" which the Nepali prime minister had correctly interpreted.[9]

In retrospect, the two contradictory situations seemed to have been developed in defining new geopolitical realities. First is the policy of recognition of and adjustment to the new security environment produced as a result of the rise of communist China and its presence in Tibet; and second, problem of hyperactive geopolitics and its impacts on trilateral relations. Such strained relations could be taken both positively and negatively by Nepal. Its positive part was instant satisfaction of rulers and a few elites that India had been humbled by the Chinese allowing the then beleaguered rulers of Nepal to heave sigh of relief following the Chinese statement in 1962 that China would come to rescue Nepal if any foolhardy attempt was made to invade Nepal from any quarter (India). As a result, India too had to follow a policy of adjustment with the royal regime in Nepal. It started pumping massive economic assistance into Nepal with a view of neutralizing the advancing Chinese influence in the Himalayan country. Avoiding repetition, it can be said that the major test of Nepal's foreign policy could be observed in two events—in and during the Bangladesh War of Liberation in 1970–1971. The first period (1959–1962) dragged Nepal directly into the Sino–Indian conflict without being involved in it. India did not ask for joint action presumably considering the grave implications and dangers to the very existence of Nepal.

Yet, the Indian rulers did not hide their wariness over Nepal's maneuverability between China and India. Calculative and shrewd as he was, King Mahendra decided to chart his own political course in both domestic and foreign policies. Such policies were geared to fan nationalist sentiment and project him as real champion of independence and national sovereignty. His decision to terminate multiparty democracy,

---

[9] See *Kalpana* (Kathmandu), November 29, 1959. In details, see Jagadish Sharma, *Nepal: Struggle for Existence* (Kathmandu: Gorkhapatra Sansthan, 1986), pp. 132–134.

dismissing it as divisive foreign import, and his determined bid to be independent of India paid off handsomely for consolidating his regime as well as to produce China as a countervailing force to India. By using this strategy, Nepal, rejecting Indian objection, concluded a treaty with China to establish a road link of 104 kilometers between the Chinese border, Kodari, and Kathmandu. Although Nepal and China had historical links, it was a major decision taken at a time when both the immediate neighbors were almost close to war. Mahendra retorted saying that since communism did not travel by mule, how could it travel by automobile (taxi)?[10]

Many people interpreted Nepal's move as a strategy that aimed at undermining the traditional India–Nepal relations based on multiplicity of factors, most importantly security and economic. Nevertheless, guided by a new thinking on improving India–Nepal relations, rapprochement was developed by sending a new ambassador to Nepal by the new prime minister, Lal Bahadur Shashtri, in 1964. Sriman Narayan, who was perceived as a Palace favorite due to his docile behavior and art of conducting diplomacy with the traditional monarch, succeeded in cultivating King Mahendra to a certain degree for fulfilling Indian interest.[11] Since the NC dissidents, then living in India, had already suspended their anti-regime armed movement in 1962, it was imperative for India to improve relations with Nepal. Its positive result could be seen in an Understanding on Import of Arms by Nepal which was signed by the two sides in January 1965 in New Delhi. According to it, it was done with the objective of "strengthening the security and independence of Nepal." It was also agreed that India would provide "all training facilities required for the Nepalese armed forces personnel in the training establishments in India." Moreover, it was important that the three governments—India

[10] His Majesty King Mahendra Bir Bikram Shah Deva, *Proclamations, Speeches and Messages* Vol. 2, (Kathmandu: HMG, 1976), p. 3.

[11] See Sriman Naryan, *India and Nepal: An Exercise in Open Diplomacy* (Bombay: Popular Prakashan, 1970). See also, Ramakant, *Nepal, China and India* (New Delhi: Abhinav, 1976).

along with the US and the UK—were also to be involved for "supplementing assistance from India to understand that if there are any shortfalls in the supply of arms and equipment by the Government of India, these two Governments will also fill the gaps to the extent of their ability."[12]

Such bonhomie soon turned into diplomatic confrontation in 1969 following India's assertion of "special relationship" with Nepal as determined by the 1950 Treaty. Nepal was more provoked by Indian External Affairs Minister Dinesh Singh's speech that he made in Kathmandu highlighting the "integral part of overall relationship between the two countries." He said: "… any substantial change in these arrangements would mean compelling India to seal the open border, and withdraw of special trade and economic benefits offered to Nepal under the prevailing relationship."[13]

Giving an interview to the official daily the *Rising Nepal* on June 24, 1969, Prime Minister Kirtinidhi Bista replied to India stating:

The Treaty of Peace and Friendship was signed between the two countries in 1950, three years after India became independent. Since then, in India, there have been several military developments of important character. Such developments have taken place in India's relations with the Soviet Union and the United States, on the one hand, and with Pakistan and China, on the other. Nepal was not informed of these developments, and India, therefore, has herself led Nepal assume that exchange of information in such cases is not necessary.

Referring to the Indian military group, the prime minister went on to say:

The Indian personnel in the check-posts were posted because the Nepalese were not available. Since the Nepalese are trained now with India's own assistance, His Majesty's Government feels that they can be withdrawn. The Indian military

---

[12] See the text of the Understanding signed by the Royal Nepalese Ambassador Y. N. Khanal and Y. D. Gundevia, Foreign Secretary to the GoI, in S. D. Muni, *India and Nepal: A Changing Relationship* (New Delhi: Konark, 1972), pp. 196–198.

[13] S. D. Muni, *India and Nepal: A Changing Relationship* (Delhi: Konark, 1992), p. 46. See also Sangeeta Thapliyal, *The Mutual Security: The Case of India-Nepal* (New Delhi: Lancer, 1998), p. 98.

Group came to reorganize the Royal Nepalese Army. The task of organization is complete, and we appreciate their services. But the purpose for which they came being complete, they should be withdrawn. To connect their presence with the Treaty or with any overall relations is not correct. Such an attempt provides grounds for misinterpretation of India's intention towards Nepal by interested parties.

Regarding the arms assistance (refer to 1965 Understanding), Bista said that

while the negotiations for the Amendment of the Agreement were going on, it was suggested verbally by India that the Government of India would advise His Majesty's Government to cancel the Agreement instead of amending it. His Majesty's Government have [has] accordingly written to India, and so far as Nepal is concerned, the Agreement does not stand any more.[14]

The interview also defined special relationship between India and Nepal admitting that such relations are "extensive" with the open border and intimacy that have existed through the ages. Since these relations have benefited both sides, it was not correct to say that Nepal alone had been the beneficiary. "But," as the prime minister said:

... to our way of thinking, it is not possible that Nepal should compromise its sovereignty for India's so-called security. *The theory of special relations for Nepal outside geographical, social, and economic realities is out of step with modern developments in our relations. It is possible to make sovereignty and mutual security compatible with trust and confidence between two peoples that have governed our relations through times immemorial*[15] (emphasis added).

It seemed that the interview was well formulated with language of firmness and expression of realities guiding India–Nepal relations. It was also noteworthy of Indian diplomatic maturity while reacting to Nepal's demand for withdrawal of military group from Nepal's northern border. Yet, the panchayat members and other anti-Indian elements took

[14] See Avtar Singh Bhasin, *Nepal-India, Nepal-China Relations Documents 1947-June 2005*, Volume 1 (New Delhi: Geetika Publishers, 2005), pp. 522–523. See also for editorial and other comments, *The Rising Nepal*, Kathmandu, June 25 and 29, 1969.

[15] Ibid.

Bista's interview as a cue for showing *rashtrabad*, which has had been the phenomenon of Nepali politics. They spit fire against India by holding demonstrations, giving speeches, passing resolutions, and organizing seminars.

Not surprisingly, the Chinese too took umbrage against India and applauded Bista's interview that tried to redefine special relationship outside the security framework.[16] Using derogatory language, the Chinese fully supported Nepal's stand interpreting it as a total rejection of the "special relations" that imply security aspect as well. Given the then strained Sino–Indian relations, the Chinese anti-India tirade was understandable.

Active geopolitics was more clearly observed before, during, and after the Bangladesh War of Liberation. How a landlocked country sandwiched between the two big and hostile neighbors was dictated by circumstances for departing from its previous position was seen during the India–Pakistan War in 1970. As the war was precipitated by the influx of refugees from the erstwhile East Pakistan (now Bangladesh) and India's own interest in making a truncated Pakistan, cutting off its eastern wing, its importance was enhanced from both geopolitical and regional power points of view. Since Chinese big support was already in the news and since the US was also behind its ally, Pakistan, India supported by the then Soviet Union, the involvement of big powers was itself indicative how South Asian region was being turned into a big arena of power play. Nepal who had all along been taking developments in East Pakistan as the internal affair of Pakistan continued to stick to it unless a new picture of the emergence of a new republic of Bangladesh emerged. Supporting the crushing of the Bangladesh liberation movement by the West Pakistani military regime led by Yahya Khan, the government daily the *Rising Nepal* wrote, "anywhere and at any time the states have treated and continue to treat secessionist cases with heavy laws."[17]

The impacts of the prospective birth of a new republic and the emergence of India as a regional power made Nepal rethink on its original position on the issue of Bangladesh. A dramatic policy shift could be

[16] Ibid.

[17] Reported in *Tribune* (Chandigarh), April 6, 1971. See also, *The Times of India* (New Delhi), and *The Statesman*, Calcutta, September 9, 1970.

observed during the UN General Assembly session that was going to pass a resolution urging India to declare an immediate ceasefire and withdrawal of both Indian and Pakistani armies to their previous positions. To the surprise of many, King Mahendra instructed the Nepali representative to the UN to abstain from voting, which was going to censor India. So the Nepali representative not only abstained but also expressed the view that what was to be taken into account was the "limitations of Nepal as a small country surrounded by bigger and more powerful neighbours and incapable either of defending itself alone from external attack or of imposing her will on others by means of the use or threat of force."[18]

Nepal's last, hour decision to abstain from the resolution was an overture to India. Nepal took such a decision despite Chinese support to Pakistan. It was also a realization of Nepal's severe limitations when the two neighbors turn into belligerents. India's previous image that it was a weak power vis-à-vis China, and China's image that it could forestall India in order to keep the territorial integrity of Pakistan intact, proved wrong contrary to the Chinese declaration that it would open another war front on the India–China border in Sikkim. Such bullish declaration that had given initial hope to General Yahya Khan could not be materialized as India supported by the Soviet Union might have decided to devise counter measures in case the Chinese joined the war against India. Sisson and Rose state that "China behaved exactly as Pakistan and India expected during the 1971 war."[19] For, India by then had known

---

[18] General Assembly Official Record (GAOR), Session 26, December 7, 1970. See also Lok Raj Baral, *Oppositional Politics in Nepal* (New Delhi: Abhinav, 1977), Chapter V.

[19] Some Pakistani extremists like Zulfikar Ali Bhutto seemed to have misread the Chinese policy in 1971. On being asked to spell out the Chinese position by Bhutto, Premier Zhou Enlai was reported to have replied that "war was unlikely, but if it occurred Chinese military forces would not intervene directly in support of Pakistan, although China would support Pakistan politically and provide material assistance." See Richard Sisson and Leo E. Rose, *War and Secession: Pakistan, India, and Creation of Bangladesh* (New Delhi: Vistar Publications, 1990), pp. 251–252 and notes 36, 37, 38, and 39.

that China would not intervene militarily despite its close security relations with Pakistan. It was an eye-opener for Nepal also, suggesting that it cannot always play the China card as some Nepali zealots think so. Yet, China would not mind to be assertive if its own security is threatened by any power by proxy or by direct involvement.

Chinese diplomacy seems to work in different forms—verbal campaigns against its potential foes, mild messages that convey its concern, direct language of threat that it would not hesitate to take punitive action in case its interests are threatened, and military action, the last resort in case other options fail.[20] During the height of Cultural Revolution, China showed its displeasure with the Nepali Government. In 1967, a small group of Nepali students affiliated to the NC pulled down the Mao's portrait at the Ramailo Mela (fair) in Kathmandu city, demanding that instead of putting Mao's photo at the Chinese stall, the king's photo should be hung. It might be recalled that during those days, the Chinese embassy used to distribute Mao's batches, photos, and red books on a massive scale freely for propaganda. Reacting to this incident, the Chinese ambassador threatened to break the skull of the Bagmati zonal commissioner presuming that on his prompting the students might have opposed the Chinese leader's photo.

In 1989, when India unilaterally decided to terminate the Treaty of Trade and the Treaty of Transit, Nepal–India relations reached the lowest ebb as had reached in 1970. It was expected by the Nepali regime that China would be able to provide alternative petroleum products in order to reduce the economic burden felt by the Nepali people following India's decision to stop essential supplies. Nepal's landlocked situation itself makes it dependant on India in many respects as the economic lifeline of Nepal lies in India. All goods in transit come via Indian ports using Indian means of transport. Even in normal times, when the goods stop to flow into Nepal, much of Nepal's economic activity is affected. Moreover, Indian security perception gets easily mixed up with economic and social relations as well. Unilateral decision to terminate the trade

---

[20] Sisson and Rose, ibid.

and transit treaties by India also came as a reaction to Nepal's decision to import Chinese arms without consulting India. Taking it as a breach of the spirit of the 1950 Treaty, the Indian Government interpreted Nepal's decision as prejudicial to former's security interest. How such a strong Indian reaction to Nepal's move turned out to be beneficial to the opponents of the royal regime could be seen in overwhelming support lent by the Indian political parties to the restoration of multiparty system in 1990.[21] China did not react against Nepal's movement supported openly by the Indian parties and also by the Western powers, human rights organizations, media, and intellectuals. However, such a quiet diplomacy professed by the Chinese is now changed after gathering confidence of a potential world power.

New Geopolitical Context: Rise of China and India

It has been already proclaimed that the 21st century will be a century of Asia. It is called the age of "Asian renaissance" as it is characterized by high rate of economic growth (China and India) and developed economies of Japan, Korea, Taiwan, and other countries of the Asia-Pacific region. It is not only economic growth that matters, the increasing regional and international status being achieved by China and India owing to their overall military capability is taken seriously. Thus, "economically and politically, Asia appears poised to determine the new world order. With the world's fastest growing markets, fastest-rising military expenditures and most serious hotspots (including the epicenter of international terrorism), Asia hold the key to the future of global order."[22] Whether or not such a scenario is likely to emerge needs to be seen in future. China's economic picture and military capability cannot be compared with India

---

[21] In detail, see Lok Raj Baral, *Nepal: Problems of Governance* (Delhi: Konark, 1993).

[22] Brahma Chellaney, *Asian Juggernaut: The Rise of China, India and Japan* (New Delhi: HarperCollins, 2006), p. 1.

despite the latter also being on the power loop. India's economic growth is more than 8 percent next to China, but its population and other staggering problems such as divisive social and political structures, internal and cross-country terrorism are likely to come as obstacles to India's march to greatness.

It has been said that "a new world order, the future of which remains unclear, is being driven by China's emergence as a global power."[23] Its size, population, rate of economic growth, social cohesion and its impact on maintaining political stability, its military capability, and its gradual reach to the various continents have all the potentials of a superpower. Such a phenomenal rise of China has disturbed the Western powers led by the US. In 2010, according to the World Bank, Goldman Sachs, and others, including Chinese authorities themselves, China has overtaken Japan as number two in economy and is expected to surpass the US by around 2025.[24]

Comparing Chinese rapid economic growth and its rising assertive role in the world, the *Times of India* wrote an editorial stating:

> The Indian economy was 80 per cent of the size of China's in 1990, but only 25 per cent now. What's imponderable is how this growing disproportion could affect Chinese strategic calculations. As of now there are signs that Beijing is growing more and more assertive not only on the world stage, but also in its immediate neighbourhood ... It's quite possible that as Beijing's confidence grows, it will become less and less amenable to settling the boundary dispute with India. On the contrary it could increasingly use its alliance with Islamabad to pressure India, making the prospect of India-Pakistan peace recede. If so, this could shape up as New Delhi's greatest foreign policy challenge.[25]

[23] Martin Jacques, *When China Rules the World: The Rise of the Middle Kingdom and the End of the Western World* (London: Penguin Books, 2009), p. 318.

[24] China's chief currency regulator, Yi Gang, claimed its second position next to the US economy adding that "China is still a developing country." "If China can keep up a clip of 5–6 percent a year in the 2020s, it will have maintained rapid growth for 50 years, which Yi said, would be unprecedented in human history." See *Republica*, Kathmandu, August 1, 2010.

[25] Editorial, *The Times of India*, New Delhi, August 2, 2010.

Since the end of the Cold War, the Soviet Union does no longer hold the status of a superpower. Since the end of communism in today's Russia together with the separation of 15 republics from Russia as well as the domestic economic and political turbulence seemed to limit its capacity as a world power. Although it is too early to predict any definite trends of world politics at this stage because of China's own contradictions of one-party rule and liberal economy it has followed, China's relative capacity to manage such two contradictory approaches has been supported by its own cultural heritage. China's double-digit growth rate, which remains more or less stable over the years, and its market worthiness across the world is being seen with both curiosity and feeling of insecurity. Most Western powers, except the US, have already started showing their decline in relative sense, but "China's arrival on the world market ushered in a new kind of global awareness of China: it marked the foothills of China's emergence as a global power."[26]

Presenting a different scenario in the context of changing power balance, no definite prediction can be made yet. "After all, Europe is rich but wimpy. China is rich nationally but still dirt poor on a per capita basis and, therefore, will be compelled to remain focused inwardly and regionally."[27]

What about India? The Chinese do not recognize India as its global competitor. India, in Chinese eyes, is a regional power with all potentials of being a great power in the time to come. Yet, it depends on India's internal situation, which is obscured by divisiveness, linkages between external and internal threats, and above all, Pakistan's own nuclear status that is primarily India-centric. As it has been said, India "has not yet achieved the economic and political profile that China enjoys regionally and globally."[28]

[26] Ibid., p. 319.

[27] Michael Mandelbaum, *The Frugal Superpower: America's Global Leadership in a Cash-strapped Era* (Johns Hopkins University, 2010) as cited in Thomas Friedman, "Superbroke, Superfrugal, Superpower?" *Republica*, Kathmandu, September 6, 2010.

[28] Harsh V. Pant, "China Rising" in Ira Pandey, ed., *India China: Neighbours Strangers* (New Delhi: HarperCollins, 2009), p. 96.

However, it must be admitted that both China and India are moving ahead notwithstanding India's overarching problems or even crises in some cases. If China's political future remains uncertain despite some of the positive elements for continuing the one-party system, India is also expected to manage its crisis as it has been doing since it got independence in 1947. For China, the present system seems to be beneficial for staying its course; for India, democracy by contrast is functional for making it vibrant and economically developmental despite its relatively less faster growth than that of China. China's political future is, however, full of dangers as state-friendly market economy is also prone to political challenges or even instability. Although China has learned lessons from the failures of the Soviet system after 70 years of its debut, there is no guarantee to the stability of the present situation, marked by economic and political contradictions. Nevertheless, China does not meet the qualifications of the traditional idea of the nation-state (Westphalian) system because of its own characteristics of "a civilization-state." As it has been stated:

> Most of what China is today—its social relations and customs, its ways of being, its sense of superiority, its belief in the state, its commitment to unity—are products of Chinese civilization rather than its recent incarnation as a nation-state. On the surface it may seem like a nation-state, but its geological formation is that of a civilization-state.[29]

Yet, China combines the elements of its old values and culture with that of modern state system in order to be integral to the global system. Internally, China's political culture still seems to be guided by its past, but as a member of the world community, it needs to be imbibed with modern system that comprised all the determinants of power and status. So China's emergence as a world power will as much be supported by its internal cohesion and stability as by its enhanced international image. Its polity, elite cohesiveness, order, military, and other capabilities are

[29] Martin Jacques, *When China Rules the World: The Rise of the Middle Kingdom and the End of the Western World* (London: Penguin Books, 2009), p. 417.

significant aspects for good image projection. China seems to be emerging with these combined elements.

India, by contrast, is multiethnic, multilingual, and a multireligious country. Its political system is plural and democratic where elections are held regularly for electing power elites. Parties take their turn in elections and form governments if they manage to garner majority in central and state parliaments. The era of one-party dominant system was over long ago giving rise to the phase of coalition politics. India's is a parliamentary system whose head of government is an elected prime minister, and the president is a nominal head with both symbolic and actual functions to be discharged on the advice of the council of ministers. However, parliamentary executive has undergone a change due to the emergence of coalition politics as determined by a variety of political parties with whose support the largest party in parliament heads the government. As a result, governmental effectiveness is occasionally compromised due to pulls and pressures of coalition partners. But, given the diversity of the country and the multiplicity of national and regional parties and groups, India seems to have managed the coalition politics well.

India is indeed a surprise to the world because of both economic growth and democratic sustainability. Highlighting this aspect, British Prime Minister David Cameron said:

> From the British perspective, it's clear why India matters. Most obviously, there is the dynamism of your economy…. But your economy isn't the only reason India matters to Britain. There's also your democracy with its three million elected representatives—a beacon to our world. There is your tradition of tolerance, with dozens of faiths and hundreds of languages living side by side—a lesson to our world.[30]

The regional geopolitics has now been extended to the global politics in many respects. The triangular relations also form a part of it as the countries of the other regions also interact, compete, and work as countervailing actors to each other. For, no countries of the world can take

---

[30] David Cameron, "A Stronger, Wider, Deeper Relationship," *The Hindu*, New Delhi, July 30, 2010.

China and India lightly. On the contrary, the world has started looking east for economic and strategic reasons. Baldev Raj Nayar's book, *The Geopolitics of Globalization*, is also relevant to the South Asian region. Against bilateral, regional, and global contexts, Nepal is now so situated that it will draw a lot of attention to its location and will have prospects of being either a balancer of forces or of being a zone of conflict. Its crisis of governability, political uncertainty, weak economy, vanishing norms of democracy, increase in the culture of violence, political instability, declining role of parties and their leaders, excessive penetration of external forces to influence developments in Nepal, and lack of national confidence to manage such external pulls and pressures have all the elements of a "failed state." Concerned with the stability and peace in Tibet's vicinity, China seems to read into the worsening domestic conditions of Nepal. The emergence of various types of movements—Madhese, hill ethnic, and religious—and the lackadaisical approach of political leaders to settle them has given rise to Chinese sensitivity. Moreover, China's assertive postures have come to the open when it started recording unprecedented economic growth and other success stories such as holding Olympic Games smoothly, its capacity to reach out to other continents, and its international political clout perceived as a potential world power.

Both China and India seem to be equally worried about Nepal's unpredictable developments and its failure to chart its course of development. The visit of the Nepali home minister to New Delhi and Beijing, taking with him the head of Nepal Police, was only to convince the two sides that security of both the countries cannot be threatened from the Nepali soil. The Chinese who generally used to remain quiet earlier on the domestic developments of Nepal have now started voicing their concern over the possible repercussions on the South Asian region. During the indefinite strike organized by the Maoists in May 2010, China came out with a statement showing its concern over the consequences for the region.[31] In each bilateral visit, including those of the defense-related

[31] See also Geja Sharma Wagle, "Failed State Syndrome," *The Kathmandu Post*, Kathmandu, August 4, 2010.

personnel, security concerns are shown as if Nepal was increasingly turning into a zone of conflict. Their reach is not only confined to civilian authorities and political parties, but also to security establishments, thus, giving the impression that both China and India have lost their confidence in the government and, hence, the temptation to cultivating relations with other formal and nonformal sectors.

Indian contacts transcend all areas, given its extensive and close links with Nepal. Links between the Indian Army and the NA can be traced to the 19th century. After the Treaty of Sugauli, the British, appreciating the fighting instinct of the Nepalis, started recruiting them into its army. Such a relationship continued even after India became independent in 1947. The tripartite agreement reached between India, Nepal, and Britain made provisions for recruitment of Nepalis into the Indian and British armies. Now the British Government is downsizing the Nepali troops following the gradual loss of empire. But India continues to maintain the old connection and has not taken any step in reducing the size of Nepali recruits into its army. The occasional distrust, twists, and turns evidenced in Nepal–India relations have not created any adverse impacts on recruitment issue. On the contrary, much solidarity between the Indian and Nepali armies continues even today. The alleged concern shown by the Indian Army chief over the issue of dismissal of the then NA chief by the Maoist-led government in 2009 and other formal and informal contacts between the two armies prove their age-old ties.

However, similar kind of relationship between the Nepali and Chinese armies is not yet possible, though there has been a significant departure in recent years as the NA personnel are also trained in China, Britain, and the US. Moreover, the US involvement in Nepali civilian and security establishments was/is was unprecedentedly high during and after the Maoist insurgency. Such involvement was particularly noticed following the terrorist attack on the US on September 9, 2001. Whether the US could have taken as much interest in eliminating the Maoist threat to Nepali as it did in the post-9/11 period needs to be further probed. In this context, it has been said that "it is difficult to say if the international attention would have been drawn to Nepalese Maoists at all, even after the November 2001 if September 11 had not occurred."[32] Linking the Maoist insurgency with terrorism, the Western powers, especially the US, the UK, and some other European countries, and India supported the Nepali Government to suppress the Maoists. The US involvement was much visible with most dignitaries visiting military barracks, giving statements against the Maoists, and assuring economic and military assistance.

It seemed that Nepal had suddenly turned into a playground for international players though the objectives of them were at least similar insofar as their overt declarations were concerned. It was not only India and the US or other Western powers, but China also joined the chorus to assure Nepal for assistance against the Maoists. However, China did not put the "terrorist tag" to the Maoists but preferred to call them "revolutionaries." The US arm supplies included I-16 AZ rifles, helicopters, twin-engine STOL plane, and other ammunitions and nonlethal weapons. But supplies and assistance were stopped after King Gyanendra usurped all powers departing from the established constitutional processes. India too followed suit as the king did not care for the advice not to derail political process as well as to sideline political parties.

Although external pressure has often been exerted on the political elites of Nepal, however, it is not a new thing. It happened for the right cause insofar as it remained an advice. But the manner in which political leaders regardless of parties started succumbing to external factors for taking decision in the post-2006 movement is shameful. The fault lies with leaders who, instead of becoming popular on the strength of the people, count on foreign power, particularly India, for being in power.

China is now a strategic competitor for India, the EU, the US, and the East Asian countries, both militarily and economically. Containing China policy would not however be realistic in view of various dimensions of a potential world power. Stating the US policy of containment as ill-judged, an American scholar says: "The US policy on China is

---

[32] S. D. Muni, *Maoist Insurgency in Nepal: The Challenges and the Response* (Delhi: Rupa & Co., 2003), p. 49.

misguided. Wealthy China would not be a status quo power but an aggressive state determined to achieve regional hegemony." China in the present context is being perceived both as a regional and global hegemon, unlikely to be checked, while it seems to be satisfied with its regional role with global significance.[33]

Each country—India, China, and Nepal—has both weaknesses and strengths. Chinese authoritarian regime might have certain advantages for quickening the pace of development. But the fragility of the regime is also evident when it reacts to a minor event with more stringent measures than necessary. Its suppression of dissent and methods of dealing with ethnic groups, including those who have been demanding the identity of their provincial languages, Cantonese for example, are likely to pose greater challenges in the future. Social and political uncertainties loom large if the present impacts of globalization continue. Although China has managed to retain some sort of state control over the enterprises despite being it an integral part of the world economy, "the Chinese state still views private capitalists as a political threat and that is why it does not let them grow beyond a threshold."[34] In the projections of the World Bank and Goldman Sachs as well as by other agencies, both China and India are "not simply undergoing rapid economic growth, but undergoing a transformation into capitalist states." But Prem Shankar Jha still doubts saying:

> ... the future will not be assured for either country until it succeeds in harmonizing their interests.... China lacks the political institutions that can perform this task,

---

[33] See John J. Mearsheimer, *The Tragedy of Great Powers Politics* (New York: W. W. Norton, 2001), as cited in Baldev Raj Nayar, *The Geo-Politics of Globalization: The Consequences for Development* (New Delhi: Oxford University Press, 2005), p. 212.

[34] Ashutosh Varshney, "Checks and Balances: An Analysis of the Strengths and Weaknesses of China and India as Competitors," *India Today*, August 9, 2010, p. 55. For a more comparative economic perspective, see Pranab Bardhan, *Awakening Giants, Feet of Clay: Assessing The Economic Rise of China and India* (Princeton: Princeton University Press).

while India, which has them, has allowed many of them to atrophy through neglect or get corrupted till they have all but ceased to function.[35]

Yet, the Morgan Stanley report has predicted that India will overtake China by 2015 if India continued its reforms. India's growth is projected as hastening between 2011 and 2015, and China's as slowing. Key to this transformation will be India's young working population, reforms agenda, and deeper embrace of globalization. It is said India will add 136 million to its workforce by 2020, compared to China's ageing 23 million.[36]

Impacts on Nepal

The rise of two powers—China and India—and the declining capacity of the Nepali state to catch up with such trends have compounded the crises of Nepal. What would be the future of Nepal in the context of emerging powers in its neighborhood? Will it be able to withstand its own caveats at a time when both its bordering neighbors are on the rise? What can be the Nepal's strengths for coping with the overarching crises it is encountering in the post-2006 movement? How is it going to set its foreign policy agendas by way of mitigating the flaws that have crept into the structures of state? Do politicians alone have the onus of miserable conditions that Nepal is passing through today? Will Nepal be able to handle the geopolitical crisis if the two neighbors turn hostile to the extent of going to war as they had done in the early 1960s? What economic miracles are expected to respond to the emergent economies of neighbors?

In addition to the above-mentioned questions, Nepal's internal political context is both serious and challenging for the present. Domestically, Nepal is full of uncertainties. Leaders of parties have lost their direction

---

[35] Prem Shankar Jha, *India & China: The Battle between Soft and Hard Power* (New Delhi: Penguin, 2010), pp. 346–347.

[36] See "Racing the Dragon," *The Times of India*, New Delhi, August 19, 2010.

for making change sustainable. It is just like a rudderless ship, full of risks of being met with an accident. Foreign policy, which is supposed to articulate vital national interest, is now an abandoned area. All casual functions are discharged in absence of well-developed institution headed by a foreign minister having minimum idea of foreign policy. A sound foreign policy based on ground realities should be the major concern of today's Nepal, but post-1990, political parties are not serious about projecting Nepal's international image. In the past, the king had personalized the state and its policies making both the regime interest and national interest the same despite the legitimacy crisis of regime. Today, the question of personalization does not arise because of the end of such regimes. Now the people of Nepal are sovereign both in symbol and substance. Yet, the failures of parties to continue their past understanding until the new constitution is in place have made people frustrated. The change from Maoist insurgency to multiparty democracy had indeed been a source of inspiration to people, but such hope is also lost owing to the ambivalent Maoist position on the issue of liberal democracy. The conflicting statements stemming from the Maoist quarters have made politics not only volatile but also uncertain. More dangerous developments are related to the possibility of frittering away of the fundamental gains such as constituent assembly, republican order, peace, and institutional consolidation. Nevertheless, since the Maoists have limited options but to continue the peace process and democratic development, good sense may prevail for smooth change.

Compared to politics, the developmental picture is not so much disappointing as it has been made out by macro-economists. Tremendous changes are taking place across the country in spite of lack of effective governance and direction of change. Roads being built, diversification of economic activities of people, spread of communication networks and education institutions, manpower employment in other countries, and remittance economy that has contributed much to revenue of the state, are some of the bright aspects. Moreover, that Nepalis are now better qualified to deal with different areas such as social sectors (health, education) cannot be dismissed cursorily. It does not mean the emergent trends need not be raised and discussed. What are the problems, issues, and trends that have become dominant in today's Nepal? The following areas can be put forth for deeper examination with strategies for managing them.

Ethnic Sub-nationalism and Interstate Relations

Ethnicity occupied the agenda of the Maoist party during the 10-year-long insurgency. The CPN (M) (now UCPN [Maosit]) had been able to mobilize various hill ethnic groups, Dalits, and other deprived sections of society, to make a strong guerilla force. Its campaign of socio-economic and political transformation worked well. As a result, the Maoists could put a stiff resistance to the security forces of the state, though there had been a controversy over the actual support lent by the RNA to the civilian authority. The Maoists, therefore, needed new recruits from various deprived sections of the society, such as ethnic groups, Dalits, and women. It could provide as much background to addressing the issue of "inclusion" as to the ethnicization of Nepali politics. The Maoists planned to carve out nine autonomous regions for dispersing power and resources along ethnic lines giving rise to regionalism (Madhesh) and ethnicization of politics.

The Madhese movement that erupted in the immediate aftermath of the 2006 Jan Andolan and much-hyped demand of ethnic-based federal provinces were new to the leaders of Nepali parties. Knowingly or unknowingly, most of them succumbed to these demands without any serious studies of each issue. As a result, each group—ethnic, regional, Dalits, and gender—turned out to be the most effective constituencies for the parties to broaden their support base in the respective areas. What is more important today is that political ideology is relegated to the background because of the greater politicization of ethnicity and regionalism and greater ethnicization of politics from the grassroots to the central level.

It must, however, be fair enough to state that no hill ethnic and caste groups or the Muslims seem to have cross-border linkages for influencing geopolitics. But the Madhesh has greater intercourse with the northern states of India due to proximity and other socioeconomic factors. Nepal and India have 1,751 kilometer–long open border, allowing people to move freely without any visa and passport. Political parties of Nepal are not serious about the regulation of the Nepal–India border in the new context. Instead, they preferred to be ultranationalists for political survival. But such deviation costs them, the country, and the people.

India's relationship with the people of Tarai always has always figured in bilateral relations. The opening of the Indian Consulate in Birganj is specifically planned for catering to the services of the people of Tarai, although other bilateral matters also come within its scope. High expectation of the Madheses from India was/is high, thus, making them oblige to what India does for them. Suspicion of the Nepali elites, mostly from the hills, that the Madheses are prone to creating a new separate state of Madhesh has been nullified by the Madheses. It has now been proved that the Tarai cannot be separated from the rest of the country due to its high bargaining position vis-à-vis the state. The post-Madhese movement has drastically changed the context, impressing on the hill elites that all regions, groups and communities, and gender should be treated equally by the state. So a new Madhese identity has been established for empowerment and for sharing power and resources in all spheres of the country. As stated earlier, India's own role will have to be modified in view of the emerging consciousness of making Nepal strong without, however, being anti-Indian. India's interest will, therefore, be served more by keeping Nepal's territorial integrity intact rather than make effort to creating a new separate. The demographic structure of Tarai and increasing realism on the part of the general Nepalis that mutual relations need to be cooperative and cordial may be conducive for bilateral relations. Changes taking place in neighboring states of India are also likely to be positive for Nepal–India relations.

Open border is also the demand of the Chinese as they want to be treated equally as done to the Indians. The people of both the countries living near the Nepal–China border can use each other's territories locally, but it is not a general rule. The Chinese are particularly sensitive to the crossing of the border by the Tibetans who use it illegally for making Nepal a conduit to India where the Dalai Lama lives. Tibetans are active in Kathmandu and hold demonstrations in front of the UN office in order to protest against the Chinese role in Tibet. China is not happy with such anti-Tibet activities carried out from Nepal. Chinese hypersensitivity could be seen when the Dalai Lama wanted to visit Lumbini, the birth place of Buddha, as a pilgrim. He allegedly sought permission of the Nepali Government for the visit to which the Chinese reacted strongly, warning Nepal of its consequences. The visit has never taken place as no Nepali Government wants to antagonize the Chinese by allowing the Dalai Lama even for a day, whereas other Western countries, the US, Japan, Australia, and Taiwan, plus a host of others, do not bother with the Chinese protests. India, where the Dalai Lama and his followers have been living as refugees, seems to have overcome the Chinese concerns by giving categorical statements that India would not permit the monks to carry on any anti-Chinese activity from the Indian soil. Such asymmetrical deals suggest Nepal's limitations in foreign policy.

Externality of Internal Politics

The scope for geopolitical maneuverability as was evident in the 1960s can no longer be applied today. Various reasons can be attributed to it. First, the new elites of Nepal who conduct foreign policy are not conversant with the geopolitical dynamics, nor are they serious about developing formal and informal institutions for conducting serious studies on various aspects of international politics. Such a drought in studies is as much related to the power elites' inability to govern as the overall decline of institutions such as university and other informal institutions. Consultancy works that are carried out with the help of foreign donors do not meet the requirements sought by the country since their own priority and objectives are limited. Moreover, no donors would like to publish research articles or books based on sound theory and methodology as they prefer products suitable for their mission. Even some policy studies recommended by some NGOs and INGOs can hardly be implemented in absence of qualified leadership and institutions.

Second, dealing with powerful neighbors needs to be supported by an objective approach, not based on abnormal elite behaviors as were/are being observed over the years. The manner in which India was dragged into the controversy of the COAS and the Maoist leadership in 2009, and the developments that followed leading to the resignation of Prime Minister Pushpa Kamal Dahal Prachanda, suggested the delicate nature of India–Nepal relations. This incident that helped the general due to the weight thrown by all the other non-Maoist parties and the alleged Indian advice that the army should not be disturbed on any pretext cannot always work. The Chinese would be active if they perceive that other countries are also interfering in Nepal; how China started courting the Maoists since the fall of the Maoist-led government is a case in point. The Maoists becoming anti-India has also given a leeway to the Chinese, thus, prompting the Maoist leader Prachanda to arrive at some sort of a "strategic understanding" between India, China, and Nepal on resolving the internal political impasse. Flurry of visits to China by the Maoist guerrilla leaders seemed to have made suspicious of its fallout. The Maoist overtures for creating trust and confidence failed to convince India that the Maoist party has transformed itself into a civilian party. Despite the peace agreement concluded in 2006, the integration of ex-Maoist combatants is not yet complete. India and other parties are not prepared to hand over the leadership of the government to the Maoist party before the demobilization of the People's Liberation Army.

In the wake of forming a new government after Madhav Kumar Nepal–led coalition government resigned for what the prime minister said government of *rashtriya sahamati* (national unity government), neither the NC candidate, Ram Chandra Poudel, nor the Maoist leader, Prachanda, could gain a majority of 301 in a House of 601 despite 13 rounds of voting as per the Constitution. According to Article 38 of the Constitution, only two methods can be adopted: consensus or majority. When the first option becomes inoperative, the second option (majority) is adopted to form a government. The deadlock continued due to the trust deficit between the Maoists and the other parties that want to end the issue of management of guerrillas and fulfillment of some other demands put forth by non-Maoist parties. Eventually, the Maoist party has agreed to integrate 6,500 combatants into the NA, while other combatants would be given freedom to lead independent life or will be rehabilitated in different ways as decided by the four parties' agreement of November 2011. On the contrary, the Maoists want to manage only after the constitution is made or all should be integrated into the army. India and the Western powers echo such approach of the non-Maoist parties, thus, establishing active links between domestic politics and external players.

India and the US in particular are more actively involved than other powers for impressing the parties to take the process to a logical conclusion. What was more surprising was that, perhaps knowing that the Maoists were likely to get the support of the votes of the Tarai (Madhesh parties), Shyam Saran, special envoy of Indian prime minister, Manmohan Singh, arrived in Kathmandu for a three-day visit during which he first met the members of parliament from the Tarai and then started meeting leaders of parties, the president, the prime minister, and the COAS. As he had reached a day before the election of the prime minister (contested by the Maoist leader, Prachanda, and the NC leader, Poudel), he desisted the Madhese leaders from casting their vote to the Maoist candidate, the former prime minister, Prachanda. It seemed that India did not want to give a second chance to Prachanda as his party was yet to be fully transformed into a civilian party. In addition, India which reeled under the Maoist insurgency in about 230 districts of the country is not confident of the Maoist role in Nepal. In its calculation, the manner in which Prachanda spit anti-Indian sentiments after quitting the government as well as the alleged Maoist tilt toward China, Shyam Saran wanted to impress on the Maoists that they should wait for heading the government until the peace process came to a conclusion and the constitution was prepared. He also advised the Maoists to join the national unity government to be headed by a non-Maoist party leader. India assured the Maoists that it has no objection to the Maoist party heading the government after the integration of army and transformation of the party fully into the multiparty politics.

The dinner hosted by the Indian ambassador where Syam Saran and the top Madhese leaders were specially invited led to a hat trick for restraining them from ensuring the victory of Prachanda. Let it be known that the Madhese leaders were closer to the Maoists insofar as the issues were concerned and had almost decided to support Prachanda in the fourth round of voting. But the Saran visit foiled the prospect of Maoist victory. Chiding both the Indian establishment for its "patronizing behavior," a commentator wrote that "the case itself is a symptom of a much deeper malaise: flawed Indian policy, and a Nepali political culture with a shockingly high dependence on external patronage."[37] It has also been said that New Delhi has "alienated many actors, and generated enormous resentment" with all political leaders—Prachanda, J. N. Khanal, and Upendra (a Madhese leader)—blaming India for denying the opportunity to head the government or for splitting the party (the MJF, for example). Such a blame game is not a new phenomenon in Nepali politics. Politicians themselves scramble for maximizing Indian favor believing that it can be the shortcut to power and privileges. To cite Jha again:

> Individual politicians across the spectrum are deeply enmeshed in this network. They solicit funds regularly, ask for "advice" try to use Delhi or a wing of the embassy to undercut their own rivals within their parties, and in return promise to play with the larger Indian game.[38]

Questions have often been raised over the Indian interference in Nepal's internal affairs. Shyam Saran's visit as a special envoy of Prime Minister Manmohan Singh similarly stirred the political atmosphere at a time when the election to the post of the prime minister was being held next day. It can be argued that sending a special envoy to play the role of a facilitator for ending the political impasse is not wrong. Such practices are found in countries having close relations. Moreover, immediately after his arrival in Kathmandu, Saran disclosed that he had been sent by the prime minister to ascertain the views of political leaders who had been bogged down in not finding a way out for electing a prime minister through the procedures of the Interim Constitution. He also said that he had no political preference for any party or leader as any party could head the government. But as any other political non-Maoist party, India was also concerned about management of ex-combatants and arms

---

[37] Prashant Jha, "Patronizing Behavior," *Nepali Times*, August 13–19, 2010.
[38] Ibid.

through an understanding to be reached between the Maoists and the other parties. How could a party with guerrillas and arms claim as having been fully transformed into a civilian party? All such suggestions and concerns shown by India therefore did not amount to interference until certain parties were advised not to ensure the victory of Prachanda in the fourth round of election. Unless the Maoists abided by the agreements they had signed before, India, taking a cue from the past Maoist leaders' anti-Indian tirade and impatience for establishing its dominance in all branches of government including the army, did not trust the Maoists. This perception continued to prompt both Indian and other parties to make a common cause vis-à-vis the Maoist chance of coming to power again. Much electoral humiliation occurred when Prachanda failed not only to mobilize the votes of the four-party Madhese Front but also of his own party, though his party members took the election casually by not reaching the venue in time. It was believed that Saran's advice on the Madhese leaders made them abstain from voting, which prevented the victory of Prachanda. Since then, Prachanda started calling it a "proxy war" with India.

India's own rationale cannot also be dismissed casually since the much unsettled political situation precipitated by myopic politicians might be construed as a fertile ground for enhanced activities of other powers. In addition, the networks established by the national, regional, and international terrorist groups have become a common agenda of many. Nepal, which has porous international borders and does not meet the standard of security inside the country, is put as a zone of security risks for India. The Kathmandu airport in particular is singled out as a security threat to India as terrorists and different categories of criminals have had used it as a conduit for their activities. The hijacking of IC-814 in 1999 and smuggling of fake Indian currencies into Nepal by the Pakistani agents are also reported.

Above all, India considers Nepal as the sphere of influence or a security backyard. Even a thoroughbred democrat and idealist like Nehru did not fail to spell out India's security interest echoing the same old British-Indian policy, despite his firm commitment to respect Nepal's national independence, sovereignty, and territorial integrity. Since the

Treaty of Sugauli (1815–1816), Nepal and India agreed to work together with renewed affirmations and modifications but at the same time retaining the core of a "special relationship." Thus, irrespective of any leader or party in power in India, the substance of Nepal–India relations will remain the same.

The unraveling developments in Nepal of various dimensions and intensity and the declining role of the Nepali state to cope with such developments have given grounds to external powers. How would China respond to such developments perceived by it as having been overwhelmingly influenced by India and the West led by the US is likely to be more challenging for Nepal than ever before. Given the arrogance of power that may be reflected in their dealing with lesser powers, it can be assumed that both China and India are likely to be more competitive in the future making Nepal a focal arena. India thinks that "Beijing could be tempted to use India's soft underbelly" in order to, what Prime Minister Manmohan Singh remarked, "keep India in low-level equilibrium."[39]

China has not accepted Arunachal Pradesh and some parts of Kashmir as Indian territories. Its close strategic links with Pakistan and the latter's own interest to make China a countervailing force to India have emboldened China to be intransigent for not compromising on disputed areas. The Karakoram Highway is likely to be strategically and economically significant for China. It is assumed that the Karakoram route to the sea-lanes in the Gulf would be cheaper than the long route through the Indian and the Pacific Ocean for supply fuel. Chinese penetration in the disputed areas of Kashmir has increased where both China and Pakistan share common objective of displacing India from there as well as to prepare grounds for setting foot in the region stretching to the Mediterranean. Such convergence of Chinese and Pakistani interests may spoil the prospect of better India–Pakistan relations. Nor is it likely to help develop SAARC as a viable regional organization.

---

[39] Frustrated by the "continuing pinpricks" of relations, Prime Minister Singh expressed his views with a group of journalists on September 6, 2010. See *The Times of India*, New Delhi, September 7, 2010.

Convergence and Divergence of Interests

The convergence of global and regional-level interests of India and the US and its allies has widened the scope of geopolitics. Now Nepal has to interact with more powers. It has been acknowledged that environment and climate change has emerged as a discipline on the international scene. Climate change has posed a great threat to all the countries of the world. The rising sea level, melting of snow in the Himalayas, and its impacts on ecology of the region (drought conditions, floods and earthquakes, etc.), which are caused by global warming, have made each country nervous. Solution to such problems does not seem to be at hand unless all the industrialized countries or countries with huge population pay serious attention to stemming it. Conferences are held, commitments are made, but effective action-oriented programmers and follow-up actions are not on the horizon. Climate change now includes as varied areas such as listed above as the security implications. In South Asia, if the rivers flowing from Tibet to Nepal and India dry up causing drought conditions in the entire South Asian region or if China decides unilaterally to use all its water potentials, its effect on the river systems of the region will be tremendous.

It is believed that on some situations, both India and the US, even other Western powers and Japan, have started seeing Nepali developments through the Indian prism. It can be especially relevant in the context of deteriorating domestic politics and its anticipated impacts on regional geopolitics where China, India, and other Western powers, especially the US, may lock their horns in the name of "contain China policy," though such Cold War mindset of containing each other by using all kinds of resources—military strength, including nuclear capability; economic tentacles spread for winning over allies; political clout to be strengthened on ideological grounds; cultural intercourse to be conducted between and among small, medium, and big powers; and other intervening variables employed—does not work when cooperation in economic and other fields needs to be maintained. For, today's interdependence, more prominently dictated by the trends of globalization, cannot cancel each other notwithstanding political competition for enhancing as well as

217

maintaining status quo. China and the US or China and India or other countries need to follow cooperative policies. The global economic crisis faced by the US in particular and the relative capacity displayed by China and India have also dismissed some established theses that free market economy enunciated and implemented by the West could no longer stem such crises, thus, prompting them to adopt certain policy shift. It had been reported that Marx's *Capitalism* and other related books dominated the US market during the global economic crisis, 2008–2009, in order to comprehend the intricacies of world economy. If the state forfeits its role completely, then crisis may recur. Since China and India in particular could manage the crisis reasonably well, it was also a lesson for many Western countries to review the policies imposed by them on other countries.

China's emergence as another superpower is contingent on many qualifications and resources. As it has been said: "It is too early to say about the bipolar world gravitating on the US and China." Projections on the scope of other emerging powers such as India suggest that trends of multicolor world are likely to be a reality. If the US and China become the centers of power in the perceived "bipolar system," such system "is not forever. Sooner or later the game begin all over again when one of the two dominant powers succumbs to imperial overstretch."[40]

Nepal has been able to survive as a nation-state through its modern history. But the major test lies ahead. In the past, Nepal had managed the British power and later India and China by using conventional strategies and tactics that were buttressed by domestic peace and stability. As the rulers could be comfortable despite economic hardship, destitute, oppression, and suppression, they could pay all their attention to foreign front. Now the internal situation is as much related to political stability as to development, peace, and stability.

Nepal's economy, which is becoming increasingly dependent on India in recent years, has also not felt the heat of the world economic crisis. Yet, Nepali products such as carpets and garments, which were the most important export items, failed to enter the Western markets due to

[40] Nitin Desai, "When Two's Company?" *The Times of India*, January 4, 2010.

lack of interest shown by these countries. As a result, economic dependence on India increased. The closure of industries due to frequent strike, power shortage, smuggling, plus a host of other factors added to the woes of the landlocked country. Similarly, since Nepal has not much to export to China, Chinese consumer goods continued flooding the Nepali market. Thus, heavy trade deficit persists making Nepal more dependent on others.

A settled political environment, effective governance, development, and peace are the ingredients of a sound foreign policy. Nepal's present state of economic situation does not fit into the emerging economies because of the continued internal disturbances heightened by inter-party squabbling. It is said: "When economic interest converges, political mistrust is normalized and when political interest converges, economic diplomacy works."[41] However, a sound foreign policy itself constitutes good economic relations. Increased economic trade between China and India, which is as of 2010 tuned to US$60 billion per annum (more than Indian trade with SAARC countries combined) and Nepal's increasing balance of trade have created caveats. Both strategic and economic interests of China seem to work in tandem in Tibetan areas closer to the Nepali border, "[a]nd Chinese decision to move south-westward through the Tibetan plateau is highly strategic." China's high dam projects in Tibet, the construction of 25,000 kilometers of highways in Tibet, a spectacular 4,000 kilometer railway line linking Beijing to Lhasa, a 1,000 kilometer oil pipeline,[42] and other activities will have tremendous impacts on China's role in South Asia. As China shares its border with Nepal and concentrates its developmental activities in Nepal with a view to extending them to other parts, they would definitely enhance its strategic objectives. Although the Chinese know the limitations of Nepal very well and even were reported to have suggested Nepali political leaders

[41] Bishwambhar Pyakuryal, "Economic Diplomacy," *Republica*, Kathmandu, August 11, 2010.

[42] See Alok Bohara, "Win-Win-Win: A Trilateral Agreement with India and China May Be the Only Way to Move Forward Together," *Nepali* Times, August 13, 2010.

visiting China that Nepal should have good relations with India without being unfriendly to China.[43] China's large global and regional-level interests would not also be fulfilled by unnecessarily becoming unfriendly to India. China can become a world power only when it continues bilateral trade with other countries without provoking its international competitors like the US, the EU, and India by showing its aggressive postures. Yet, psychology of power makes a country arrogant that in turn may also give grounds to hostilities.

The continued strained India–Pakistan relations on the one hand and not so congenial security environment along the China–India border on the other have made their relations more complex. In addition, the Pakistani question of survival aggravated by terrorism and Pakistan's limited capacity to respond to it is making the latter increasingly dependent on other powers. The spillover effects of responses to terrorism in the region has also been felt by Nepal, with India showing its own concerns over terrorist activities to be carried out from Nepal. So both the US and India are in common on this issue and have warned Nepal that its border and airports might be used by the terrorists against India. Since Nepal's own capacity to cope with internal and external security threats is low, it is very difficult to satisfy the demands of other countries.

Concluding Observations

The security relations between Nepal and India are not likely to be fundamentally different in the future. Nepal's attraction is being increased due to its strategic location where each big and powerful country wants to set its foot. So the foreign policy pursued in the past would not suffice to manage active power players, nor will Nepal's conventional wisdom

---

[43] Such expressions of the Chinese came from time to time. The latest one was reported in *Himal Khabar Patrika*, March 14–28, 2005, where the Chinese Ambassador to Nepal, Sun Heiping, was reported to have said: "You can change your neighbours but you cannot change your neighbouring countries. The geographic location of Nepal, which shares border with Tibet Autonomous Region of China is very much crucial for stability and prosperity in Tibet."

and strategy be relevant to the changed context. Nepal's only option is to be more realistic in comprehending the emerging dimensions of regional and world politics as well as to adopt strong policy measures for internal development. Economically backward Nepal will only be a liability for India and China whose own developmental performances are strikingly different from others.

Nepal's domestic stability, peace and development, and the maturity in thinking about the country and the people only assure its neighbors. Empowerment of people making them owner of the developmental processes and democracy would generate national confidence. But confidence should not be driven by empty slogans of nationalism. It must be understood that *rashtriyata* is not necessarily anti-Indianism; it goes much beyond it. If the people are permanently reeling under poverty and start losing their confidence in Nepal's intrinsic strength, abstract slogans of nationalism do not help them. The issue of 1950 Treaty often figures in Nepali politics as it has been taken as the singular cause for Nepal's underdevelopment.

The abrogation of the 1950 Treaty may give temporary satisfaction to some elites and leaders, but it will also 'open Pandora's box.' If the post-abrogation phase continues the old pattern of bilateral relations (open border, opportunities to be provided to the nationals of both the countries), then no-treaty regime can be possible. On the contrary, if India prefers to treat Nepal at par with other countries and seal the border or use other strategies to deal with Nepal on a variety of areas including trade and transit and other preferences that have had been provided to Nepal, it leads to catastrophe.

Any new decisions to be taken cannot be unilateral in the given context, because only coordinated and cooperative policies to be pursued by both the countries would help them. In my opinion, instead of raising the issue of the 1950 Treaty every now and then, Nepal should now concentrate its energy on developing the country and institutionalizing democracy, making people confident of their future. Since domestic context of security has wider ramifications for bilateral, regional, and internal security, chances of the regime's survival depend on socioeconomic and political empowerment of citizens. So internal development

221

has indeed become an independent variable for making Nepal strong and independent.

It also needs to be noted that Nepal's landlocked position and close economic interdependence (dependence) does not allow Nepal to be fully independent of policy decisions. Nor does it allow playing one neighbor against the other. Trust and confidence to be generated between Nepal and other countries, especially neighbors, alone can complement to the efforts of development.

Nepal, being placed in the strategic zone of the region, particularly between China and India, needs to play a more moderate and balancing role between the two neighbors. The location of Nepal, which is physically integral to the Gangetic plain, the heartland of India, makes India more concerned about its security. Some concerns shown by India on Nepal's internal development are related to its own vital interest. Such concerns that focus on Nepal's peace, progress and stability, and democracy cannot be construed as interference.

Similarly, China's major concern is Tibet to which the Nepali side needs to be serious. Now with the enhanced regional and global power position of India and China, strategic dimensions are likely to be more complex for Nepal. How China is increasingly showing its concerns over Nepal's internal and external developments has been vociferously raised by visiting Chinese dignitaries and its representatives in Nepal.

It is also witnessed that perceptions rather than substance make the elites of Nepal and India unnecessarily hypersensitive. The psyche that India is the key factor for bringing about changes either in the government or in regime makes Nepali politicians both jittery and grateful depending on the conditions in which they react. Lack of culture of empathy, thus, gives rise to distrust on both sides. The Indian side should not also be prejudiced against certain parties and individuals or governments taking into account the changed internal political dynamics of Nepal. If political parties are fragmented and weak, it would be difficult to deal with small groups and individuals. But political parties of Nepal too, regardless of their backgrounds and orientation, should try to be more mature and objective in dealing with neighbors and other powers. Casualness with which relations are conducted would be only suicidal for the country.

It seems that difficult days are ahead for Nepali policymakers. Internal situation is in a mess with the major parties responsible for bringing about a radical change quarreling for no substantive reasons. Economic, regional, ethnic, and governance crises are looming large indicating no concerted effort to resolve them. If Nepal fails to maintain a minimum level of development, keeping its own house in order by consolidating representative institutions, its aspirations to be an independent and sovereign nation would also be undermined. Above all, minimum levels of consensus among the major political forces, internal development, peace, and stability are the prerequisites for a sound foreign policy. A policy based on objective analysis and pragmatism alone would be able to deal with neighbors and other powers, now active in Nepal.

Nepal's economic relations with China and India are contingent on political preconditions. But meeting such preconditions needs a sound national foreign policy buttressed by economic self-sufficiency. Ironically, however, political instability, failure in economic and foreign policies, and other indicators have only provided an alarming picture for the country. But slogans of empty nationalism (*rashtrabad*) and high degree of irresponsibility shown by political elites and the ripples they create for mistrust and enmity[44] are the greatest stumbling blocks for peace, stability, and development.

Where does Nepal stand today nationally and internationally is a difficult question to answer. Its neighbors, China and India, are not assured of the fluid situation of Nepal with major parties paying short shrift to foreign and strategic policies. The unpredictable political scenario has cast a shadow on firm and sound relations. China seems to be anxious to set a foothold through some political and social organizations. China's

---

[44] Babu Ram Bhattarai, the leader of the UCPN (Maoist), by way of criticizing the so-called *rashtrabadi*, has stated that unless internal feudalism and external oppression end, there is no scope for making Nepal independent both eco-nomically and politically. See Babu Ram Bhattarai, "Pragatisheel Rashtra-badko Antarbastu" [Internal Element of Progressive Nationalism], *Nagarik Daily*, Kathmandu, August 11, 2010.

burgeoning relations with the UCPN (Maoist) has become transparent with the frequency of visits of senior Maoist leaders in recent years. Isolated from other parties, India and other powers, the Maoists found China as a powerful external ally, while for China, making the largest party of Nepal as its ally, was a political gain. Are Nepali elites inviting more active (interventionist) roles of these powers in the future by turning Nepal into a pariah state or do they continue to maintain the country's independence and sovereignty with prudence and dexterity?

Anti-Indian sentiment is on the rise in Nepal following India's insistence on traditional policy toward Nepal. Its preference of the non-Maoist parties for running the government and the Maoist's strong reaction against it have strained India–Maoist relations. Since no political problems are likely to be solved without the Maoists, India, on its side, cannot also ignore the Maoist party for long. Improved relations between them alone would slacken the Maoist's anti-Indian campaign. Restoring a balance between China and India is also a problem for the Maoist party as its dependence on China would not enhance its prospect of power. Even if India's future will have a reduced role in Nepal in view of the emergence of China as a countervailing power, Nepalis cannot berate the significance of India, itself an emerging power. However, going by the interviews of the senior Maoist leaders, including Prachanda, China has suggested them during their visit to China in the last week of October, 2010, that, being the largest party, the UCPN (Maoist) should develop relations with India. Taking it a cue, Prachanda stated in an exclusive interview with a daily that he would soon undertake a rapport-building visit to Delhi after the extended party meeting in Gorkha.[45] Subsequently, it was felt that both India and the Maoist leaders wanted to improve relations and have undertaken certain positive steps toward this direction.

India's conventional approach to improving bilateral relations may not work in the given context. The upcoming generation of Nepalis, including the young Madheses, may not necessarily see Nepal–India relations as their elders used to do. Their own horizon, social contacts,

---

[45] *Kantipur*, October 31, 2010.

economic opportunities, and numerous other factors may change their perceptions. Similarly, the changing political dynamics and elite orientation may not remain the same. So the Indian mindset needs to be changed for a better understanding of the emerging trends in bilateral relations. If India does not like Chinese or the strong presence of other countries in the Tarai, China too wants reciprocity from Nepal by discouraging other powers not to be close to Nepal–Tibet borders. In the past, India had prevailed on Nepal for not permitting the Chinese to undertake construction works in the Tarai. But how long Nepal would be able to resist the Chinese pressure for treating them at par with India? This question is as much related to Nepal as India and China. A broad strategic understanding between Nepal, India, and China on Nepal may be a prescription for removing fears and distrust overshadowing triangular relations. India baiting from the side of Nepali politicians and India's old mindset that Nepal should always remain a pliant state may not work in the changing regional and global context.

Nepal's relations with the other powers are marginally confined to the US, the EU, and the UK. Other development partners, except Japan, also belong to the west and, hence, there has been a general frustration with the drifting political situation in Nepal. Since they had accepted Nepal's conflict transformation and smooth transition from monarchy to democracy as exemplary developments worth emulating in other countries of the world, these achievements are both symbolic and substantive, and are likely to be frittered away if political leaders of Nepal, so much smart for waging frequent movements with triumphs, allow them to peter out.

Nepal and the UN are not at ease due to controversy raised by the Nepali government leaders about the role of the UNMIN or by the remarks made by the UN Secretary General, Ban Ki-moon, who vouched for a national unity government for timely promulgation of the constitution and for deciding the fate of Maoist combatants. Ban Ki-moon said: "The government of national unity remains desirable for timely promulgation of the statute and for the successful integration of and rehabilitation of Maoist fighters." He added that Nepal's peace process would collapse because of the "deepening differences between major political parties."[46] Ban Ki-moon was assailed by the ruling political parties for his warning that Nepal's peace process could collapse if the differences of parties continued. Surprisingly, the Nepali Government leaders took it as interference in internal affairs urging the Secretary General to express opinion on ground realties. The UNMIN was criticized for its alleged favor of the CPN (Maoist) whose former combatants of 19,000 are in the camps. The UNMIN is assigned the task of monitoring the combatants including their verification for determining eligibility. More than 4,000 were disqualified for not meeting the age bar of 18 years.

The UN, unlike Nepal's bilateral relations with other countries, cannot be prejudicial to the interest of a member country. Nepal has also been taking pride for being a member of the UN since 1955.

Moreover, the doctrine of interference has undergone a major transformation on the issue of human rights violations and democracy. The former Secretary General, Kofi Annan, had expounded that the UN could interfere in case of violation of human rights. Since the UN is committed to maintaining peace and order across the world, its genuine concern over the stalled peace process in Nepal should be taken in positive light.[47] For Nepal, the UN membership was both a symbol and substance of independence and territorial integrity. Nepal has become one the beneficiaries in terms of developmental aid, peace-keeping missions, etc. Thousands of Nepali security personnel—army and police—have served the UN through the peace-keeping operations and have been able to create good impression. Then how did the question of interference arise when the Secretary General, of course on the advice of the UNMIN, "encouraged" the political forces to move ahead as per the spirit of the Interim Constitution and peace agreements signed by the same parties' leaders for making a smooth transition to peace and stability.

Nepal has lost its internal and external credibility ever since the CA election 2008. Internally, failure of parties to make a new democratic

[16] *Kathmandu Post*, November 1, 2009

[47] For comments and criticism of the government's reaction, see Lok Raj Baral, "What Interference?" *Kathmandu Post*, November 11, 2009.

constitution in time was not a good example worth emulating by others. The peace process that earned international and national acclamation is now in peril with parties taking divergent approaches to it. Interpretations are marked by high degree of opportunism and myopia. The army that was put under the monitoring of the UNMIN did not like to abide by the UNMIN's code of conduct, and at the behest of government had started taking its own decision. Frustrated by the political leaders who have forgotten the main agenda of constitution making and the peace process, the UN Secretary General Ban Ki-moon indicated that it is likely that he may withdraw the UNMIN if Nepali parties failed to renew it with the same mandate as it was given in 2007. Since the mandate oversees the activities of both the NA and the ex-combatants, the truncated mandate excluding the NA from its jurisdiction may not be acceptable to the UN.[48] Now with the UNMIN gone, a special committee has taken over the task of the UNMIN to which all powers including the UN have endorsed.

[48] The anguish and frustration shown by the UN Secretary General has been published by *Republica* (Kathmandu) on September 4, 2010. He stated that he "was not in favour of repeated extensions of the mission's mandate in an atmosphere of persistent and unfounded criticism that complicates its ability to function."

See also the UNMIN Representative Karin Landgreen's Report to the UN Security Council presented on September 7, 2007. See the text in *Kathmandu Post*, September 9, 2010.

6

What Next?

"We live in a world which no longer questions itself, which lives from one day to another managing successive crises and struggling to brace itself for new ones, without knowing where it is going and without trying to plan the itinerary."[1]

Nepal has passed through various types of upheavals. Some of them are of fundamental nature and epoch-making, others are repetitive. The end of monarchy, termination of 10-year-long Maoist insurgency, and its peaceful transformation into multiparty system, making the CPN (Maoist) as the largest party in the CA, enabling it to form a government, were also significant. The ease with which the Nepalis accepted such changes is no less meaningful. Nevertheless, the fundamental questions have also arisen along with such changes. The present chapter will, therefore, provide a synoptic picture of the past in order to show the future perspective of Nepal.

A few searching questions being asked today are: Has Nepal reached a dead end? Has the Nepali state failed or is it a "failing state"? Can democracy be institutionalized and sustainable? Do such questions and inquiries bear truth or are simply the outbursts of agonizing conditions prevalent in the country? Arguments for and against can be made in the historical context but it becomes rather hasty to see the end of the Nepali

[1] Zygmunt Bauman, *In Search of Politics* (Stanford: Stanford University, 1999).

state. If certain preconditions do not exist in a state, though these conditions can be substantiated in absolute terms, then they are put into the category of failed states. Erosion of state authority resulting in anarchical conditions, lack of extractive capability for meeting financing the functionaries of state, lack of stability, absence of peace, lack of regulative capacity and accountability of elites, crisis of governance, etc., can be listed as some indicators. Since there is no clear universal definition of a "failed state," its interpretations also vary. Yet, the term has been used "in the sense of a state that has been rendered ineffective" in multiple senses. Nepal's situation in particular is more problematic because both the strengths and weaknesses exist. Politically, Nepal is fraught with uncertainties and dangers. Its incoherent political development based on what I prefer to call "jump theory of politics," fractured political culture, and its negative impacts on giving shape to the consequences of "revolution"—popular sovereignty to be established through a constitution made by the CA, establishment of peace and order, political stability, drastic reduction of social disparity, which is still embedded in Nepali society, and guarantee to the security of the country, both internally and externally, are some of the pressing problems for Nepal.

Nepal faces three crises today. First, ideologically, the Nepali political class has not yet reached a "minimum consensus" on the nature of future political order. Ideologically, there has been a major difference between the largest party, the UCPN (Maoist), and the other parties including those who want to be identified as Left variants. The Maoist leaders seem to use liberal democratic ideology as a strategy that can be changed into their own models if situation allows them to do so. For them, accepting multiparty liberal democracy is like "makeshift ideology" that is accepted out of compulsion. Their realization in the mid-course of people's war (insurgency) that the rigid Maoist approach to Nepali politics would land them nowhere prompted them to adopt a new line, which took them to the multiparty system. In the Chunwang meeting in western Nepal, the Maoists changed from "Prachanda path" that had adopted the orthodox Maoist line of People's Democracy into Republican Democracy (*loktantrakmak ganatantra*). The same meeting also decided to develop working relations with those with whom the Maoists had been treating as enemies (with the parliamentary parties) to participate in peaceful movements in the country. Such Maoist decisions and flexibility of other parties to move toward the CA and other people-oriented agendas set by the Maoists brought them closer to forge the 12-point understanding in 2005.

Although the Maoists have covered a long distance toward competitive system and people's republic, the party continues to be plagued by ambivalent approach to the course it has adopted in order to contextualize itself into the ongoing national and international developments. In all its closed-door meetings and deliberations, some hard-core leaders still think that the Chunwang decision was wrong. Nullifying all the major achievements made after the Chunwang meeting, they think the former decision led the party to the "encirclement of the rightist, imperialists and also of the reformist Trotskyites" that eventually makes the party submissive (*atma samarpan gareko*) before the expansionist and right reformist.[2] All such contradictory approaches and dilemmas have damaged the Maoists. The simmering conflicts within the party, which sometimes explode openly, have debilitated the party besides encouraging the trends of political backlash by anti-change forces. According to the Maoists, a new inner contradiction has begun with the "petit bourgeoisie" despite the end of feudalism represented by monarchy. It is also interesting to observe the Maoist contradictory line when it talks of opening a front in which the royalists ("*rashtrabadi* and patriotic") are included, while stigmatizing the NC and the CPN–UML as retrogressive forces. The Maoist effort to club together the royalists and themselves is basically to offset the Indian influence or what they call "Indian expansionism" in Nepal.

However, Nepal's Left politics has invariably landed in multiparty system after undergoing both trial and tribulation. The Jhapali (Naxalite type) movement ended soon after the realization of its leaders that it was not irrelevant to the Nepali context. Although the ML Party took

---

[2] For an analysis, see Pradeep Gyawali, "Maobadi Bhitrako Bibad ra Tyaska Pravab" [Controversies within the Maoists and Their Impacts], *Kantipur*, September 17, 2010.

some time to transform it into multiparty politics, its participation in the 1990 pro-multiparty movement fully made it a systemic party, as was the NC. Initiated by Madan Bhandari, the party adopted *Janatako Bahudaliya Janbad* (multiparty people's democracy) as its ideology and became a part of the system jointly carved out by the NC and itself in 1990, but it continues to keep its identity as an ML party.

Although no development would be sacrosanct, it will be difficult for the Maoist leaders to reverse their previous decision. Personality clash that has hit the effectiveness of the Left movement in the country may once again be repeated, making the Maoist party weaker in the future. How the party leadership would prove its efficacy either in the government or in opposition would be the sole criterion of evaluation by the people. But under no circumstances the Left trend in Nepali politics can be undermined. They have been able to reap benefits from the failures of parliamentary parties. Their meteoric progress fed by revolutionary slogans and desire for change attracted the downtrodden, marginalized, and oppressed sections of the society. In addition, even middle-class people who wanted peace and stability thought that the Maoists were the best alternative to other parties whose image was tarnished. Hoping for peace and stability and transcending old ideological and party lines, people made the Maoist the largest party in the CA. How the Maoists will preserve this capital and move ahead with its pro-people agenda within the framework of pluralist democracy needs to be seen.

Such transformation took place after signing the 12-point understanding with the SPA, formed before for the mounting opposition to the royal absolutism. But it must be admitted that the Maoists had all along been demanding election to the CA as a benchmark for finding a negotiated settlement with the regime regardless of its nature. Since no royal governments including elected ones were capable of accepting this basic demand, the Maoists had no options but to continue the struggle. The issue of republic, which was another demand, could have been given up if the royal governments of different hues could have taken courage to accept it. Subsequently, the royal coup of 2005 changed the context, enabling the SPA and the Maoists to work together against the monarchy. Its consequences were both unexpected and historical watershed in both forms if not fully in substance. Structurally, Nepal changed into republic and the agendas that are already decided are likely to federalize the political structure. Other agencies of the state—army, police, armed police, bureaucracy—remained unchanged except the shift of loyalty to the elected government.

But the traditional ethos of Nepali elites, despite being instrumental in bringing about a revolution, remains unchanged. Such a paradoxical situation has made Nepali politics more intractable with powerful trends of political backlash. Entrenched traditional values and the failure of parties and leaders to orient themselves in the new changed context as well as values on the one hand and a growing popular disenchantment with the behaviors and performances of parties and leaders on the other has dimmed the scope of sustainable democratic evolution. The parliamentary process adopted by the Interim Constitution (2007), mixed election system, political heterogeneity precipitated by fractured mandate, and split-prone parties have further added to the woes of democratic stability. As a result, the same old game of horse trading has begun in order to be in the government by any means. Even the indulgence of the UCPN (Maoist) in vote-purchasing activities is disclosed. A telephonic dialogue between a Chinese official and Krishna Bahadur Mahara, the politburo member and head of foreign department of the party, has come to light. It has been stated that the Chinese had asked Mahara how much money the party needed for enabling Prachanda, prime ministerial candidate and chairman of the party, to win the post of prime minister. Mahara's reply was 500 million, one million each for 50 members.[3] Such a talk had taken place just on the eve of seventh round of voting held for electing a prime minister. Due to lack of trust and confidence, all the non-Maoist

---

[3] Krishna Bahadur Mahara's first reaction to the audiotape was negative, saying that it was fabricated by the television channel—Nepal One—beamed from New Delhi on September 2, 2010. Later, he indirectly confirmed saying that "whether it is true or not is not an important matter, even if it is correct, it is a plot." See *Republica* and *Nagarik Daily*, Kathmandu, September 4, 2010. For his acceptance of the audiotaped conversation, September 13, 2010.

parties either remained neutral by not taking part in the election or voted for and against the two candidates of the NC and the UCPN (Maoist) according to their choice. However, both failed to garner the required simple majority in absence of other parties. The Maoists who have had been all along denouncing the dirty game played by "parliamentary parties" were now repeating the same for "capturing power." However, the Maoist supremo withdrew his candidature after seven rounds in order to put pressure on the NC candidate to withdraw and prepare grounds for consensus. Fearing that the Maoist and the CPN–UML might be able to mobilize the required votes for electing a prime minister, the NC continued to contest, while the Madhese parties abstained from voting.

Failure of electing a prime minister even after 17 rounds indicated that the parliamentary system with the first-past-the-post system did not work in Nepal. The Speaker of the Parliament, Subash Nembang, said that it was the failure of both the system and process. Such scenarios point to the fact that democratic commitment of leaders of principal parties was only a sham and pretentious since their own greed for power and privileges made them myopic and blind. Fatigued with such state of affairs, many people feel that democracy is still a distant possibility in Nepal. If the government formation process remains elusive, which is likely to be a regular feature in the given conditions of political parties, how could the people expect affective governance? Since governance is related to delivery capacity, which is yet another legitimacy besides constitutional–legal legitimacy, the nonfunctioning organ cannot meet the requirements of a legitimate government. But the post-movement situation demonstrated that democracy for which the unprecedented movement was launched is turned into a chimera.

The second crisis is related to the role of parties. Seen through the prism of multiparty system, all including the UCPN (Maoist) are committed to it. All parties, including the Maoist, are in the Parliament despite Maoist objection to the word "parliament." In order to satisfy the ego of the Maoists, both the words "byabasthapika" and "sansad" have been used with a hyphen between the two. It is now legislature-parliament. Nevertheless, the UCPN (Maoist) is also a part of the Parliamentary Constitution (Interim) and the party is very much systemic. It is the largest party in the Parliament and the leader of the UCPN (Maoist) is the leader of opposition who enjoys all the privileges and perks of opposition leader with ministerial rank. It is also an irony that the same party's indulgence in parliamentary horse trading (buying and winning over members) has been revealed during the abortive attempts to get elected to the post of prime minister in 2010.

Problems of parties have stalled the democratic process as well as the development of the country. But one cannot understand on what basic reasons these parties are at loggerheads. All of them have accepted the agreements reached before and all have committed to abide by the spirit of the Constitution unless a new constitution is made by the CA. All the major parties—the UCPN (Maoist), the NC, and the CPN–UML—in particular accuse each other for being too Rightist (the NC and to some extent, the CPN–UML, and the extreme Left [Maoist]). Each sees the other as a retrogressive party on the ground that some parties like the CPN–UML and the NC (D) changed their positions to be close to the Palace. The NC leader Deuba in particular was accused of splitting the party in order to head the government after making a decision to dissolve the Parliament. Subsequently, Deuba was thrown into the ditch by the king for what he said "incompetence" to hold fresh election. Violating all constitutional requirements and changing prime ministers frequently, King Gyanendra showed his unlimited ambition. Finally, by way of pacifying Deuba, the king again appointed him prime minister, whereupon the latter declared that the "Gorkhali king has done justice" to him.

The NC has occupied the forefront in all three major changes in Nepal—1951, 1990, and 2006. In 1990, it departed from the B. P. Koirala line that rejected any kind of joint front with the communists, in general maintaining that if it worked with them, the NC's democratic identity would be lost. But his colleague, Ganesh Man Singh, who became supreme leader after B. P.'s death in 1982, changed this line in 1990 in order to make the movement for the restoration of party system a success. Girija Prasad Koirala, in 2005, joined hands with the Maoists and with other communist groups against the monarchical absolutism. All the major parties, including the Maoist, accepted his leadership and also made him prime minister after the success of the movement. Even when the NC and the Maoist parted their company after the CA election, Koirala as a rallying figure continued in politics.

The NC's core ideological position has also undergone a change from time to time despite its commitment to multiparty system. It abandoned the agenda of the CA in 1958 accepting the Constitution awarded by the "sovereign King." The party once again affirmed its faith in the CA following the royal coup of 1960. Following the pressure politics, the party used ideology as a convenient strategy changing it from time to time. In 1967, the party in exile had passed a resolution of the CA, but reversed it a year later to "cooperate with the king for further development of the constitution [partyless]." The CA agenda was resurrected in 2005 when the SPA led by the NC decided to forge an understanding with the Maoists (then waging insurgency) against monarchy. It joined the Maoists to abolish monarchy realizing that the traditional institution perennially obstructed democratic development. Many people argue that B. P. Koirala, who had offered "national reconciliation with the king" till his death in 1982, would have adhered to it by rejecting any kind of working relationship with the communists as he had done after his release from jail in 1968. B. P. Koirala who could well comprehend the context and timing of political situation would also have changed his earlier view that he formulated by adopting the strategy of "politics is the art of possible." Harassed by the imposition of emergency in India by Indira Gandhi and losing all hopes for immediate return of democracy in Nepal, he had decided to return from India in 1975. B. P. Koirala was a monarchist by ideology and temperament, wanting monarchy to be supportive of democracy as it was still considered a symbol of unity and stability. In his view, if monarchy proved to be detrimental to democracy and "didn't need the people, then the people would also do not need it."[4] Thus, B. P.'s support to monarchy was conditional and contextual. As a dynamic leader, his attitude toward monarchy would have been changed if he had lived longer under the absolute rule of the king as Gyanendra did following the Palace massacre of 2001.

[4] B. P. Koirala, "Rajtantra" [Monarchy], *Tarun Bulletin No. 3–4* (Varanasi), September, 1971.

Girija Prasad Koirala's role to transform the NC into a republican party as well as to make it inclusionary was also dictated by circumstances. If the NC would have failed to lead the anti-king movement after the second coup staged by King Gyanendra in 2005, other forces, obviously the Maoist would have done it alone or in concert with other parties. But, the NC's leadership was necessary for international legitimacy. The transformed political scenario that establishes the Left trend in the country was also a compelling reason to be flexible for embracing all such agendas concerning social justice and democratization. Now the NC has worked as a moderating force along with its commitment to republican democracy based on what it has declared "a policy of socialism with social justice." The Twelfth Party Conference (*Mahadhibeshan*) held in September 2010 has once again emphasized the socioeconomic transformation of the country. It has been stated that the NC would not depart from socialism but it cannot embrace fully the old concept of state controlled economic system.[5]

Despite all ups and downs, the NC has continued to preserve its identity as a liberal democratic party. Sometimes it had to compromise with the king, and sometimes it struggled against it for democracy. Its opportunistic coalitions formed with disparate parties and groups had sapped the image of the party, though it withheld its total support to the absolute monarchs causing friction between them. Now the NC is forced to be progressive as well as democratic for its identity and survival. The 12-party convention has tried to democratize the party but how the new leadership would be able to maintain organizational unity and meet the challenges thrown upon it by the new situation and forces is yet to be seen.

Another big party is the CPN–UML, which appeared to be more anxious to be close to the Palace when the opportunity arose. Sometimes, it accepted the leadership of former *panchas* to head the coalition government, and at other times it joined the royal regime saying that "regression

[5] See the economic policy adopted by the Twelfth Party Conference of the NC in *Karobar Daily*, September 21, 2010.

is half-improved," but finally it met the same fate as other collaborators had faced. The party joined the opposition camp following the last assault of the king on parliamentary politics. Popularly known as the second royal coup (2005), this move of Gynendra eventually proved suicidal for monarchy itself when all the political forces rallied against it by deciding to launch a movement first, for stripping the king of all his powers, and then hold the CA election to make a new democratic constitution. Later, the CA itself formalized the end of monarchy after all parties, regardless of their previous ideological orientations, went in favor of republic. A tiny section of the NC, however, lamented that the party could not have gone too far for abolition of monarchy as the NC, from its very birth in the late 1940s, had been a strong believer in constitutional monarchy. Surprisingly, however, even the former ideologues of the party-less regime, except for a few, unanimously endorsed the CA declaration. Some dissentients argued that only a nationwide referendum could settle such issues as republic and secularism.

There has been a tendency to accuse leaders of other parties for all sins committed by them in the past and today. It has been claimed by the NC leaders that it is the only democratic party because the Maoist, in their opinion, can soon turn into one-party dictatorship. However, all principal parties worked together for the Maoist agendas such as republic, CA election, inclusive democracy, and federalism.[6] Yet, the Maoists perceive the NC as a conservative party that dithers on being progressive. The NC's dilemma is that it falters in taking timely decisions as had happened to the agenda of the republic and the CA and such other issues that are concerned with social justice. It also accuses the Maoist for being too close to the former royalists in the name of *rashtrabad* as if other parties (the NC, the CPN–UML, and the Madhese parties) lack that credential. But the top Maoist leaders who spent their time in India

---

[6] For an analytical view of the three political parties—the UCPN (Maoist), the NC, and the CPN–UML—see Krishna Murari Bhandari, "Kangress Bhitra Kangress Khoi?" [Where Is Congress within Congress?], *Annapurna Post*, Kathmandu, September 15, 2010.

during the insurgency and who accepted the Indian Government's facilitation to forge the 12-point understanding or later for making the change process a success suddenly turned anti-Indian. Such volte-face is often observed in the post-2006 Nepal. Sometimes the Maoist leaders are inveterate critics of India for its "interference," and at times they seem to be anxious to be close to India for favor.

But, to rubbish other parties as pro-Indian does not make sense as all tend to become pro- and anti-Indian depending on the kind of favor or disfavor they get. Thus, the real sense of *rashtrabad* is missing, because this agenda is so encompassing and inclusive that empty slogans and abstract rhetoric do not constitute nationalism. Empowerment of people, increase of consciousness, development, and confidence to be built in the minds of people alone make *rashtriyata* strong. So, scratching each other's back and accusing others as foreign agents, obsessed with mutual threat perceptions, and distrust give us dim prospect of democracy, development, peace, and stability. The Joint Madhese Forum, formed in the wake of prime ministerial election, obviously for influencing the result in favor of Madhesh (Tarai), is a loose combination of four Madhesh parties—MJF, Madhesh Janadhikar Forum (Democratic), T–MLP, and Nepal Sadbhawana Party. These four parties, it might be recalled, had been discouraged by India not to ensure the victory of Prachanda as prime minister until the Maoist did transform itself into a civilian party. It meant that the Maoist should fully separate itself from the former combatants, living in camps, and also wind up the YCL as a militant organization in addition to the return of property confiscated during the insurgency. This could be possible only through the peace process as determined by various agreements reached before. Monitoring, integration, and rehabilitation were the three broad outlines with which the process should have been completed.

All parties are divisive on personal grounds. Splits and rejoining is common for furthering one's own prospect for power and status. The voting pattern during the election held to choose a prime minister has shown that most of them could be the wild cards had a single party lacked few votes for winning the election. Due to the peculiar composition of the Parliament, the first major role could be played by the big three parties—the Maoist, the NC, and the CPN–UML. Both the CPN–UML and the Madhese parties became the deciding factors. Either the CPN–UML or the Maoist could produce the magic number or the CPN–UML, the NC, and the Madhesh parties were in a position to get a prime minister. The Maoist, the Madhese combination, plus the other smaller parties too could give a chance to Prachanda. At one stage, the Madhese parties stated that the Maoists were closer to them on agenda basis, but they could not gather courage to support the Maoist party during the prime minister's election due to the reasons spelled out before.

The foregoing narrative leads us to oversee the future of political parties. As of 2010, no single party seems to occupy a dominant position despite being the first, second, and third in the CA election. Can the UCPN (Maoist) retain its present status in the future? How can it implement its radical social and economic agendas in order to be different from other parties, especially the NC and the CPN–UML? How can it control its erosion when it fails to convince the people that it can alone deliver to them? A series of strategic and tactical failures of the party after its ouster from power in 2009 have impressed the conscious people that the leaders are still too immature to navigate in the turbulent political weather of Nepal. Its comparison to an eagle by Prachanda, putting other parties into the category of chicken, needs to be tested. What kind of political system the political parties would like to adopt and what electoral methods will determine the role of parties? Yet, popularity will only propel any political party into power. However, such popularity needs to be tested only through fair and free elections.

It seems that Nepali political parties are in zero-sum game where one party's failure is another party's gain. The Maoist in particular is likely to see this game giving grounds to the moderation of the NC or to the CPN–UML, despite the latter's problem to prosper between the Maoist and the NC. A moderate section of Nepali society may prefer to a non-communist NC emerging as a strong force but it depends on its own organizational unity, vision, and determination to chart the course of democratic process. The CPN–UML identity is also changing—from a communist party into a moderate democratic party despite its suffix and prefix of "Marxist Leninist."

Finally, the internal crisis, which is the result of ideological ambiguity, split personality, and fractured party syndrome, has contributed to inviting unprecedented external involvement in Nepal. Flurry of official and nonofficial foreign delegations and vociferous concerns shown by them, especially India and China, show that Nepal's difficult days are ahead. Both the neighbors lack confidence in the capacity of Nepal to preserve their vital security interests. Lack of policy articulation, which can be possible only when a stable and effective government is in place, has made the country captive of reckless politicians. Since a sound foreign policy and diplomacy is a reliable tool of national security of a country like Nepal, politicians have hardly given any thought to this area.

Economically, Nepal, sandwiched between India and China, whose economic growth rates are high, is being left behind. Instead of making a bridge between the prospering economies of China and India, developing skill of getting comparative advantage is becoming low due to murky political situation. Some of the indicators produced in Table 6.1 would provide us with glimpses of economy. It does not mean that no positive developments have taken place in Nepal. Tourism and remittances continue to be the major sources of revenue despite the overall decline in trade and industry sectors.

Table 6.1
Remittance Flows in Nepal 1995–1996, 2003–2004, 2008–2009

Description	1995–1996	2003–2004	2008–2009
Households receiving remittances (%)	23.4	31.9	30.0
Average remittance per recipient household (nominal NPR)	15,160	34,698	105,400
Share of remittances from Nepal (%)	44.7	23.5	10.6
From India (%)	32.9	23.2	17.2
From other countries (%)	22.4	53.3	72.2
Share of remittance income in recipient households (%)	26.6	35.4	66.0
Per capita remittance (nominal NPR)	625	2,100	7,894
Total remittances received in Nepal (nominal NPR billion)	12.9	46.3	213.0

Source: Central Bureau of Statistics (Kathmandu: National Planning Commission, 1995–2009).

What the overall impact of the remittance economy on improving the living standard of Nepalis is needs to be studied. Generally, the remittance economy seems to have improved the conditions of those who work as labor force abroad. However, compared to other countries, remittance from India is decreasing as the income variations in India and other countries (Korea, Gulf, Malaysia, and others) also determine the income of laborers.

The tourism sector has become more lucrative for Nepali economy. Tourist arrivals have increased following the end of the Maoist insurgency. With a target of bringing one million tourists in the country, 2011 was declared as the year of tourism. Percentage of tourist arrivals in Nepal suggests that Nepal will continue as one of the attractive destinations for tourists. Trekking, pilgrimage, honeymooners' destination, sightseeing, and rafting have contributed to this flourishing trade. The number of tourist arrival by air increased by 12.8 percent to 411,584 in 2009–2010 from that of 364,830 in 200–2009. In the review year, the share of tourist arrival from India and the third countries by air recorded a growth of 22.1 percent and 77.9 percent, respectively. In the previous year, such shares were 24.1 percent and 75.9 percent, respectively.

The number of tourist arrival from third world countries had decreased by 0.5 percent in the previous year. In the review year, the number of tourist arrival from India increased by 3.8 percent to 91,117, as against a decline of 2.3 percent in the previous year.

But, even to keep this sector alive, political stability, peace, and environment needs to be guaranteed. Climate change, which is increasingly turning unpredictable and devastating causes landslides, floods, displacement, drought conditions, and thus, enhances the prospect of poverty. Agriculture, which still engages more than 70 percent population of the country despite its relative decline in contributing to national economy, also needs to be developed through a variety of policy measures and their implementation. The agriculture and nonagriculture sectors are estimated to grow at 1.1 percent and 5.1 percent, respectively, in 2009–2010. The growth rates were 3.0 percent and 4.7 percent, respectively, in the previous year.

The security situation of the country is not fully improved as the sporadic killings, kidnappings, and other criminal activities continue. Crime has also increased due to trends of rural–urban migrations with the cities and towns and other centers increasingly becoming the sites of criminal activities. The Tarai region, in particular, has become the safe haven for criminals by misusing the open India–Nepal border. There has also been a tendency on the part of politicians to work in tandem with criminal and other bizarre groups for money and muscle power. Moreover, the volatility of Tarai politics and over-politicized trade unionism has also contributed to disorder and violence. Consequently, the industries located in the Tarai are generally closed, affecting the industrial growth of the country.

If the Tarai is marred by criminal and other violent activities, the hills are afflicted by frequent strikes and closures of highways. The hill ethnic groups that have sprung up in the name of promoting the rights of ethnic groups or for carving out autonomous regions resort to strikes, threats, and extortion. So, taking advantage of weak governance and divisive politics, such groups often cripple the country's regular activities, impressing on us that Nepal has nothing more to offer than anarchism. Although these trends cannot become permanent features of the Nepali society and state, they are likely to die down only after the state and political elites start paying adequate attention to address the genuine grievances or adopt coercive measures to stem such unruly trends. It can be said that many problems remain unattended because of the failure of political leaders. If the identified stakeholders are engaged seriously by the leaders, no nagging problems remain unresolved. But the crisis of governance and the failure of political elites to cope with challenges put before the country have added complexity.

One of the reasons for the sudden spurt of violence or of demands that have sprung from various quarters is due to political drift precipitated by ambiguous ideology and marked deviation of major parties from the set goals. Schizophrenic leaders give rise to systemic breakdowns losing direction. The constitution-making process, a common goal for the Nepali people, has suffered when the political parties' gave premium to government making through simple majority that could hardly be possible at a time when the principal parties have divergent lines and strategies. The politics of denial has been activated for not allowing any party to form a government. Since no single party can form a government without the support of other main parties, a broad coalition is imperative and hence, the replication of the old game played shamelessly in the name of parliamentary system.

Many are of the view that the foregoing trends are inherent characteristics of a transitional stage of development and hence there is no cause of alarm. But any transition has definite ideology, direction, and leadership role. Given the present Nepali context, if such transition becomes too long to accomplish its set goals, its chance of being unsuccessful is also pretty high. Political heterogeneity and spurious ideological and normative commitment may, in all probability, not make the transition a success. It will be more so if the regional and international power players become more tempted to intervene when they see that their vital interests are threatened by wrangling political forces. Managing such roles of external players need clear national and foreign policies making them as tools of diplomacy.

The Left–Right Divide: Myth or Reality?

Has Nepali politics suffered from the Left–Right divide? Is Nepal turning into a communist state with more than 60 percent domination of the "Left" parties in today's CA? These questions are pertinent in the changing national, regional, and global politics. If one goes by the figures and trends, the meteoric rise of "communists" is evident. The middle class that has now been enlarged due to a variety of reasons—education, migration, globalization, remittances, and other opportunities made available within the country—is also flexible enough to adopt people-oriented agendas, thus, defying the very classical view of Leftism. If a person holds his liberal political ideology with all the attributes of modern democracy—formalized opposition, accountability of government to the people, regular free and fair election, free press, pluralism but embraces radical socioeconomic agendas for people at large—why does not he become a progressive democrat? Some call it "the Left turn of the Middle Class" if one likes to use "Left" instead of calling democrat.

Any political party that fails to embrace socioeconomic agendas that aim at eradicating poverty, promoting social justice, making inclusive democracy possible by empowering the weaker sections of society has the least chance of survival. In a country like Nepal, people's choice falls on those parties that bring people closer to them. On the contrary, if the "Left" themselves become regressive in their orientation and action, betraying the spirit of egalitarian people-centric policies and future agendas, then they forfeit the credential of democrats.

However, the terms "Left" and "Right" have become common in political narrative. It is used for convenience, not for substance, as the term "Left" is so abused that if a person or a party wants to be different from others are called as progressives or Leftists. But the origin of these two terms "Left" and "Right" have a certain meaning for role or ideological differentiation. Originated from the French Revolutionary Parliament where "radical" representatives sat to the left of the presiding officer's chair, "the conservatives" sat to the right, then they were called as Left and Right. In the given French context, the Leftists were associated with demands for popular sovereignty, democratic control over political, social, and economic life. On the one hand, the Left has been identified with radicalization of democratic movements for transforming social institutions in a manner that improves the human condition. The conservatives, on the other hand, warn of the "perverse" unintended consequences of social change, thus, praising the "prescriptive" wisdom for evolutionary approaches to the institutional and cultural practices.[7]

During the intensified debates over liberalism and socialism, the Left–Right divide got primacy in socioeconomic and political policies. Those who saw the least role of the state in production, exchange and distribution of wealth, and adopted laissez-faire policies, sharply contrasted with the socialists, though the latter were not recognized as genuine "Leftists" or communists as the Leftist. The working-class concept and the idea of universal suffrage and secularism all belonged to the domain of the

---

[7] See Joseph M. Schwartz, "Left" in Joel Krieger, ed., *The Oxford Companion to Politics of the World* (New York: Oxford University Press, 2001, second edn), pp. 493–494.

Left, as those who could not mark a departure from the past did not accept the sudden break with the old practices and tradition. Edmund Burke in his book *On the Reflection on Revolution* has presented himself as inveterate critic of French Revolution that not only radicalized the French society and politics but also set in train trends of political instability. By contrast, England became more stable and peaceful. It adopted an incremental approach to democratic evolution, which, in French perception, was conservative and traditional. In Britain, changes first took place at the top—parliament—where the feudal aristocrats forced the monarchy to change its character. Yet, in Britain too, the origin of Labour Party from within parliament accepted some elements of "Left" but not to the extent of making Britain a republic. It upheld the view that even within the constitutional monarchical framework where monarchy "has been sold to democracy," many social and economic reforms could be introduced without breaking with the past.

The Third Way policy adopted in the name of new labor suggests that the dogma also changes if they become irrelevant to the time and context. Tony Blair's Labour Party won the three elections on the basis of its renewal campaign that made a substantial departure from its past ideological position as a socialist party. It realized that socialism also needs to be updated and has to be contextual for survival. The Third Way, which was the idea of Anthony Giddens, political sociologist and the "guru" of Blair, gave a new twist to democratic socialism by advocating both the elements of social welfare programs and the role of the state-regulated economic concepts and practices. Thus, the New Labor seemed to move slightly to the Center in order to be different from the classical socialistic theories and practices.

The modern Right "contends that economic redistribution and state regulation promote inefficiency and restriction of liberty." So, "for Left, liberty and equality are synergistic, for Right they stand in tension."[8] But the British Conservative Party had to make compromises with the Liberal after it failed to win a comfortable majority in the 2010 parliamentary election.

---

[8] Ibid.

The Nepali political divide is at best compromising, at worse deceptive. Both the schools of thought, if one goes by such a division—Left and Right—have made compromises while forming coalition governments from time to time. The so-called extreme Right—the traditional monarchists who served the partyless regime since its birth—could head the coalition governments in the 1990s. The "revolutionaries" of both the CPN–UML and the NC accepted their former adversaries as leaders. Acclaimed as the leader of the movement, G. P. Koirala became the unanimous choice to head the post–Jan Andolan Interim Government until the CA election. Subsequently, when the CA election did not go in its favor and with the Maoists not accepting G. P. as unanimous candidate for the first republican president, the Maoists and the NC leaders parted their company. Consequently, the NC decided to sit in the opposition, while other parties regardless of ideology, joined the Maoist-led government. Thus, ideology in Nepali politics is used as a strategy for power. Sometimes it is used in a thinly veiled manner, other times they are blatantly transparent.

Nevertheless, the NC that has had occupied a centrist position ever since its birth in the late 1940s is often accused by the "Left" of being a party of status quo. Its policy of national reconciliation offered by B. P. Koirala to the king has had been parroted by his followers as a mantra. Guided by the then ground reality, he wanted to cultivate the king (the power center) because of the weakened position of the NC. The king was perceived as the symbol of unity and stability whose cooperation was essential for nationalism and democracy. Bishweshwar Prasad Koirala also said that his "neck was tied to that of the king" stressing the point that only the king and democratic party could be natural ally vis-à-vis the "communists" sui generis. Surprisingly, B. P. Koirala had developed his own perception of the "communists" in Nepal and, hence, could not be reliable ally for him during his lifetime. Ironically, however, B. P.'s understanding of the Nepali monarchy was flawed as he was time and again betrayed by the Palace when the latter got its upper hand. Its betrayal was witnessed during the referendum of 1979–1980, held for testing the popularity of nonparty regime.

The NC has had been misunderstood in its historical trajectories and also for occasional volte-face it demonstrated as a "Rightist" party. So it was painted in different colors by the so-called Leftists. In reality, however, some "Left" parties have surpassed the NC in order to be close to the Palace. To be fair, the NC made a lot of compromises for adjustment out of compulsions, but it did not support unconditionally the role of absolute monarchy. Its lowest points were in 1968 and 1980 when the party decided to offer its cooperation to the King by making a departure from the agenda of the CA and while asking for removing the condition of membership of one of the class and professional organizations of the partyless regime in 1980. Since such undertaking was tantamount to accepting a "partyless" regime, the NC leaders boycotted the first panchayat general elections held on the basis of adult franchise.

The "Left" parties that identify with the foreign leaders—Lenin and Mao—are neither Leninist nor Maoist. All these parties are the principal players in a multiparty parliamentary system. In practice, the CPN–UML is different from the NC in one respect—the name. Now the UCPN (Maoist) seems to be on the same track as others, thus, erasing the classical division of the Left and Right. From ideological point of view, all the major parties are in common—republic based on popular sovereignty, inclusiveness, federalism for distribution of power and resources and liberty and equality. The Maoists pretend that they are different from others because they do not subscribe to pluralism as it has been adopted in the Western liberal democracy.

The Left and Right division gets blurred due to the loss of support for market economy and global neoliberal dictates. Even a country like the US has to rethink over its full-blown mission of liberalism. Depending on it alone would be risky in the present world where most countries are still poor and incapable of regulating the free market as imposed by the Center. In countries where authoritarian and totalitarian regimes are increasingly turning to the mixture of liberalism and social control, countries with definite liberal proclivities (South Asian countries in particular), the social welfare schemes need to be adopted. Any party irrespective of its identity (Left or Right) has to take a progressive turn (call it Left turn). Politically, Nepal cannot reverse the republican order and all the principles of modern liberal democracy. But at the same time, the regulative power of the state is also felt as a precondition for maintaining social justice and social harmony.

The pattern of electoral politics suggests that ideology plays insignificant role for winning elections. The Maoist victory in the CA election does not vindicate the victory of Maoism with all its attendants in Nepal. Fed up with the NC and the CPN–UML due to their failures to deliver, the voters wanted to favor the new faces and party that had promised a lot for them. How they will vote in the future and how the Maoist party would keep its popularity intact will be significant. To the extent that political parties are deviating from their principal mission, it seems that difficult days are ahead for the Maoists as well. Now people evaluate a party on the basis of performance, not on abstract and empty slogans or populism. The Maoists have yet to be clear about its objective and methods to be adopted for realizing it since other political parties in Nepal and external powers are skeptical about its future role. Reports that circulate in the Nepali media give rise to some questions about its role. The alleged Maoist decision to obstruct the foreign investment and close the projects undertaken by the foreign investors cannot be appreciated. The development of hydropower projects is the only hope for Nepal. But the Maoists want to stop them because they are going to be constructed for export of energy. India is made the obvious target for its alleged interference in dislodging the Maoists from power. However, how could the developmental projects be the victim? A local daily called it "misguided Maoist Stance."

> When it comes to maintaining double standards, probably no other political party in the country can bear the Unified Communist Party of Nepal (Maoist). As a case in point, just take a recent example. One of the party's senior members a few days earlier minced no words in articulating that his party would vociferously protest any export-oriented hydropower project to be launched with foreign investment.

But, this statement, "ironically, stands starkly in contrast to what the party Chairman, Pushpa Kamal Dahal, had told India two years earlier" during his official visit to India. "Dahal had then explicitly shared with

India that Nepal aims to produce 10,000 MW of power in ten years, a major share of which would be exported there."[9]

Taking cognizance of the strong public reactions about the negative approach to hydropower projects, it was clarified that the projects that are being endorsed by the government lacked parliamentary process and transparency. The party vice president stated that the apex body of the party was yet to look into the study report prepared by the other wing and then only the formal view of the party would be made public.[10]

The politics of reaction has slimmed the prospect of consolidation of the republican democracy in Nepal. Parties are tempted more to play to the gallery than to undertake the mission dictated by the mandate of the people. During the 10-year-long insurgency, numerous infrastructural projects were destroyed. Now similar roles cannot be expected from the Maoist side as the people have suffered a lot on different pretexts and experiments with regimes and the so-called ideologies.

What Next?

Our reflective discourse has tried to focus on some of the crises of the post-2006 movement. Some crises were the backlogs of the past and some were/are instant. The agenda of making a new Nepal has, therefore, suffered a setback due to political leaders' lack of commitment, vision,

[9] Some leaders of the UCPN (Maoist) had given statements that the party would stop the 14 hydropower projects to be built by foreign investors among whom 12 are Indians. It meant that the CPN (Maoist) wanted to mix its revengeful politics with country's economic development.

For editorial comment given above, see *Republica*, Kathmandu, September 25, 2010. See also *Karobar Daily*, September 24, 2010.

[10] See Narayan Kazi Shrestha's view, ibid., September 27, 2010. Hari Roka, CA member, has highlighted in detail about the lack of procedures followed by the government while approving the study of 14 projects. In his opinion, most criticisms that the Maoists were against development, etc., were unfounded. See Hari Roka, "Bijuli Utpadanko Kichalo" [Wrangling over Hydropower Generation], *Kantipur*, September 27, 2010.

and determination. So, the replacement of regime—from monarchy to republic—is not felt by the general people. Old feudal–authoritarian values continue with the new elites becoming irrelevant to governance. The Interim Constitution that designed parliamentary process turned out to be a dismal failure prompting the speaker of the Parliament to say that the failure to elect a new prime minister even after several rounds of election was a failure of both the system and process. The continuation of caretaker government indefinitely and all the powers enjoyed by it is not a good omen for Nepal's democratic future.

Thus, the narratives produced in the previous chapters are sufficient bases for locating Nepal's overarching problems. Now, what would be the areas that need to be tackled and with what strategies? First of all, identification of areas that need immediate action plan is essential. Both short-term and long-term strategies can be designed in order to address the following areas:

- Restoration of the authority of Nepali state
- Making a new constitution as per the mandate of people
- End of violence of all forms and intent
- Articulation and vitalization of the agenda of state-restructuring (federalism, democratization of security agencies, bureaucracy, and political parties)
- Common agenda for minimizing social and economic disparities in the country
- Consensus on country's foreign and security policy
- Conceptualization of Nepali *rashtriyata* (nationalism, not ultrana- tionalism) and code to be made for adhering to it by all
- Mobilization of internal and external resources for alleviation of poverty and regional disparity
- Effective governance

Revamping the State

The Nepali state is under strain today but it is not in the collapsing stage. Due to political turmoil and sudden break with the past, paranoia seems to dominate some people that the terminal condition of the state has indeed arrived. Rise of ethnic and regional demands on the one hand and the declining efficacy of the state to respond to such resurgent demands and aspirations on the other make us nervous. So, even for removing such psychology of fear and also to equip with its regulatory functions effectively, the Nepali state needs to be revamped. However, such revamping should not be at the cost of core of democracy. It must establish order on which democratic pillars can be made strong and durable. But how would such a good be possible if popularity of political forces show the trends of decline? In democratic polity, any such revamping agenda should be accompanied by well-knit political organization in both ideological and organizational terms as they alone can harmonize the two processes together.

Many try to relate the revamping agenda to the conflict of various forms and dimensions. The capacity of the Nepali state for the first time was on test during the Maoist insurgency, although it cannot be the sole criterion of judging it. Since the state is also composed of government (elites), the sort of relationship that determines the efficacy of various organs of government needs to be examined. In the given context, the then power structure characterized by a kind of sharing of power between the king and the political parties did not put a brake on the de facto role of the king. It, thus, contrasted with the objective of government that wanted to use the army to deal with the Maoist menace. Baburam Bhattarai himself has confirmed the Maoist's working relationship with the king in his article published immediately after King Birendra's assassination. The conditions put forth by the RNA to the government had also demonstrated the lack of rapport between the elected government and the army. It showed how both the system and leadership should be intertwined in making the state effective.

So state revamping is also an inclusive agenda that entails both normative and organizational parts of government. Normatively, the state fails if its other components such as sovereignty, people, government, and territory start losing their relevance. In the given situation, Nepal's territorial sovereignty has remained intact, despite some controversies raised over borders. The Treaty of Sugauli (1816) and later the return of some lost territories in the western Tarai have determined the present border. Government, which is another element of the state, becomes the prize for all power seekers—monarch and politicians. Now politicians, who come to power through elections and are independent of conducting the affairs of the state, would be blamed as well as applauded for their omissions and commissions. So government today has indeed become an independent variable for shaping the future of the state since the political parties that conduct the affairs of the state matter much in steering the course of events. The manner in which parties falter in their principal mission of making a constitution and holding election for stable and legitimate government has dimmed the hope of general people. If the political elites of present Nepal are not clear about the future agenda of the country, how could the security of state be preserved?

The modern Nepali state, especially in the post-2006 movement, is an amalgam of both liberal and socialist trends. The forces that shape the state come from both liberal and communist backgrounds, although liberal democracy as a core value is common to all. Drawing on these two strands of trends and reinforced by Nepal's own social characteristics of being moderate and synthesizing, the greatest strength of the new Nepali state will be its secularism and democracy with human face. Democracy qua democracy cannot endure if it fails to be emancipator of the downtrodden. Thus, the people living within the delineated boundary should own the state as their common enterprise. So it needs to be both egalitarian and authoritative. Its regulative power, which is enhanced by its coercive side or by voluntarily expressed willingness of its citizens, is the hallmark of the state. For maintaining its image, both symbolic and actual, it needs cohabitation of democratic values and force created for preserving the core values as well as the physical aspects of the state. When all the elements need to work in tandem, the question of making the state absolute does not arise. Political elites and other members of political and civil society can alone shape the character of a new state.

The rapacious character of the traditional authoritarian state was highlighted in the past. The royal regime that lasted for about 30 years (1960–1990) tried to replicate the features of authoritarian state with limited freedoms or what it called "constructive criticism," while the core power structure was supported by force. It was caricatured for being both legitimate and nonparty since the king who was "active and supreme leader of the regime" was above criticism. Now Nepal is a republic with an elected head of state and government. Since the CA is in wilderness about the actual form of government in the future, newer problems fraught with uncertainties have arisen. However, all will depend on the nature of the constitution to be prepared by the CA and the guarantee to making it durable and acceptable.

Making a Constitution

Nepal has experimented with various types of constitutions in the past. But all of them turned out to be failures. In the name of constitution and regime change, people have suffered a lot. The declining economic indicators, particularly observed in productive sectors, and collapsing institutions themselves show how Nepal's uncertainties rule the roost. Although there is no guarantee to political stability through the new constitution to be made by the CA, people still hope that Nepal will be able to overcome many of its daunting problems through the constitutional mechanism. To translate this hope and move ahead with the mission of viable democracy, thinking about the emergent reality needs to be developed. An old-fashioned approach to constitution cannot also salvage the country as the constitutional dynamics needs to be buttressed by other dimensions of national and international politics. If national politics is in order and conducted according to the rules of the game and if all the players abide by such rules, then we can see some scope for both change and regularity of the system. Moreover, one stark reality is that how we reconcile the demand of a strong state with the rising demand for identity politics. The making of a democratic constitution is more challenging at a time when a real Pandora's box has opened; but without taking it in good strides, nothing is likely to be accomplished.

In the given national and international context, the making of a democratic constitution and its immediate implementation becomes a pointer to the future course of Nepali state and polity. Nationally, everything is in ferment trying to take shape but at the same time showing the trends of fragmentation. Even if problems remain within bounds as of today and the political elites fail to make a constitution and regularize the system, it will be difficult to make a prophesy about democracy and the future of the Nepali state. The more we buy time to make a constitution, the more we are likely to be stuck in the quagmire of multiplicity of crises that Nepal had not encountered in the past. Divisive politics, conflict-ridden society, and extreme forms of parochialism that has surfaced in addition to the increasing trends of external pulls and pressures may sidetrack the issue.

The political dynamics which are related to political actors and the making of constitution and its implementation are inseparable. It has/ had been amply reflected in the impasse that stalled the process of con- stitution making. The trust deficit developed after the Maoist exit from power in 2009 has resulted in deadlock for government formation. The major hitch is in handing over power to the largest party criticizing the Maoists for not giving up the hangover of violence. They maintain that they would not give in to the UCPN (Maoist) unless it transforms itself into a civilian party. But it might be recalled that all non-Maoist parties, the NC and the CPN–UML in particular, had agreed to give an equal share with 83 seats each to the Maoist and the CPN–UML in the Interim Parliament. The NC, then the largest party, kept two seats more (85) in a House of 205. The logic behind the NC and other parties' demand for making the Maoist a fully civilian party does not hold much ground as the Maoists were allowed to share the Interim Government along with its participation in the CA election. After it became the first party in the CA, it formed a coalition government with the support of other parties minus the NC. Indeed, all the non-Maoist parties, including the NC, had anointed the Maoists until the controversy arose over the sacking of the chief of the army staff, despite the NC's decision to sit in opposition after the Maoist leaders did not accept the NC President G. P. Koirala as presidential candidate.

Thus, the NC and Maoist row developed not on the issue of the Maoist party being civilian but in power. The Maoist party could have been turned into a civilian party prior to its joining the restored Parliament and the government headed by G. P.Koirala.[11] So the political deadlock created in the name of Maoist conversion into a civilian party (by severing its links with the People's Liberation Army and the YCL) is a lame excuse. Now, instead of ending the deadlock and concentrating on constitution making, the NC ploughed a lonely furrow by fielding a single candidate even after the withdrawal of his rival, Prachanda from the race of prime minister. Since no other party weas supporting the NC on the grounds of reaching a consensus on forming a national unity government, the NC was almost isolated from the rest. At long last, the NC was forced to withdraw its candidate after the 17th round because of the open declaration of its coalition partners, particularly the CPN–UML. Nevertheless, the NC's withdrawal in the name of consensus did not also indicate the end of the problem. It once again demonstrated the great risks of political instability within the parliamentary framework. It has become a mockery of parliamentary system when no prime minister is elected even after completing several rounds. But people still pin high hopes on Nepali politicians who are not as much rigid and orthodox as in many other countries. On the contrary, they are perennially engaged in dialogues so as to reach a negotiated settlement to many outstanding problems they face. Yet, apprehensions arise about the sustainability of parliamentary system. Constitution needs to be framed on a clean slate, putting all the ground realities across the table and not taking any partisan frame of mind. In Nepal, all the parties, national, regional, and individual, see the constitution through their respective prisms and interests. If the NC is rigid on the issue of parliamentary system, the UCPN (Maoist) appeared to be confused as it wanted to make a fusion of both presidential features with parliamentary control. The CPN–UML is also unclear about the type of government, but wants to ensure political stability by electing a prime minister directly by the people. These are not big problems if parties approach them sincerely.

---

[11] For more analysis, see Bishwa Bandhu Thapa, "Pradhanmantriya Pratispardha" [Prime Ministerial Competition], *Annapurna Post*, Kathmandu, September 28, 2010.

It seems that the leaders of political parties have not taken the CA and the Parliament seriously. Their absence from the CA sessions demonstrates how casual they are. A survey conducted by Martin Chautari has exposed their lack of seriousness as if the CA is less important for them. Table 6.2 and Figure 6.1 show the average attendance of some "familiar and influential figures" in the CA. The average attendance of parties also provides us with a glimpse of seriousness of parties.[12]

Their consecutive absence from the CA is also a violation of the Interim Constitution. According to Article 67 of the Constitution, the seat of a member of the CA is said to be deemed vacant "if he/she remains absent from ten consecutive meetings without notification to the Assembly." In the present context, none of the leaders had notified to the CA. Later, a national daily broke the news about their long absence, and then they tried to show their presence in back dates in order to save their membership.

End of Violence

Violence is an integral part of Nepali politics ever since the days of the unification in the 18th century. Nepali history is full of bloodsheds, killings, treachery, perfidy, and conspiracy. All big changes were made successful by violent methods. A party like the NC that came into existence with the Gandhian inspiration adopted violent methods in 1950, 1961, and again in 1971–1975. The two major communist parties—the CPN–UML and the UCPN (Maoist), respectively— had their debut in violence with the former taking weapons for "liquidation of class enemies," the latter going further for waging the 10 years' "liberation war." The 1950 anti-Rana movement ended in compromise with substantive changes to be made for democratizing the new system; the CPN–UML under the leadership of Madan Bhandari was transformed into a systemic party by passing the resolution of *Janatako Bahudaliya Janabad* (people's multiparty system); the Maoist insurgency was transformed into multiparty

---

[12] See Martin Chautari, *Policy Paper*, No. 4, September 2010.

Table 6.2
Trends of Parties' Attendance in the CA

Name	Attendance Rate (percentage)
Sher Bahadur Deuba (NC)	1.98
Pushpa Kamal Dahal "Prachanda" (UCPN [Maoist])	6.93
Bijaya Kumar Gachchedar (Madhesi People's Rights Forum)	9.90
Rajendra Mahato (Nepal Sadbhawana Party)	11.88
Sharatsingh Bhandari (Madhesi People's Rights Forum)	14.74
Krishna Bahadur Mahara (UCPN [Maoist])	14.85
Upendra Yadav (Madhesi People's Rights Forum)	19.80
Madhav Kumar Nepal (CPN–UML)	20.25
Ram Bahadur Thapa 'Badal' (UCPN [Maoist])	20.79
Arju Rana Deuba (NC)	22.77
Renukumari Yadav (Madhesi People's Rights Forum)	24.75
Baburam Bhattarai (UCPN [Maoist]), Jhalanath Khanal (CPN–UML), Pradeep Giri (NC)	27.72
Jaya Prakash Gupta (Madhesi People's Rights Forum)	29.27
Diwakar Golchha (NC)	29.70
Narayanman Bijukchche (Nepal Workers Peasants Party), Top Bahadur Rayamajhi (UCPN [Maoist])	30.69
Binod Kumar Chaudhary (CPN–UML)	31.68
Amik Sherchan (UCPN [Maoist])	33.66
Hitman Shakya (UCPN [Maoist])	35.64
Prakash Sharan Mahat (NC)	36.33
Mahanth Thakur (Tarai Madhese Democratic Party)	38.14
Hisila Yami (UCPN [Maoist])	39.60
Shankar Pokhrel (CPN–UML)	40.59
Lucky Sherpa (CPN–UML)	42.57
Gagan Thapa (NC)	44.55
Pasang Sherpa (CPN–UML)	46.39
Pampha Bhusal (UCPN–M)	47.52
Ram Sharan Mahat (NC), Pari Thapa (CPN–Unified)	48.51
Ram Chandra Paudel (NC)	49.50
Jayapuri Gharti (UCPN [Maoist])	52.48
Sapana Pradhan Malla (CPN–UML)	68.32
Rajendra Kumar Khetan (CPN–ML)	93.81

Source: Martin Chautari, *Policy Paper*, No, 4, Kathmandu, September 2010.

Figure 6.1
Percentage of Attendance of Leaders of Political Parties in the CA

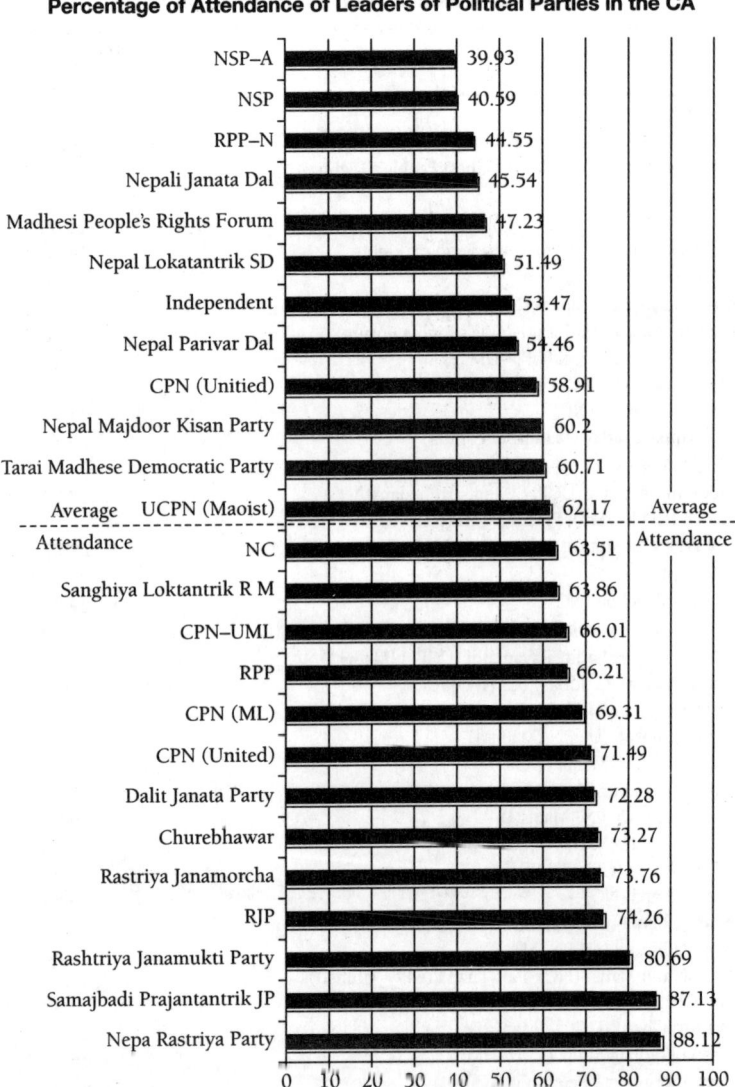

Source: Martin Chautari, *Policy Paper*, No, 4, Kathmandu, September 2010.

system after having succeeded to gain its major objective—the CA and Nepal as a republic. The CA and other demands were endorsed by the NC and the CPN–UML and other SPA members, who subsequently went to the extent of declaring Nepal as a republic. All these major changes suggest that Nepali political development has inherent character of what is called, though in a different context, "caricatured dichotomy" (violence and nonviolence) depending on the conditions in which politics is conducted.

Yet, such mixed orientations have made politics more difficult to inculcate democratic culture. As a result, "the members of the new modernizing elite were distinctively uncomfortable and ill at ease with strange political milieu ... the hard-core oppositionists in the post-1950 period found them in a quandary when it came to determining their strategies."[13] Thus, strategies swung between peaceful and violent means, creating positive and negative effects on stabilizing the system.

Violence that is being referred here is related to the post-2006 politics and its impacts on making society and politics violent and criminal. Taking the Maoist insurgency as a lesson, many groups also sprang up with guns and took to the methods adopted by the Maoists during their war period and even subsequently after they joined the multiparty politics. Killings by both the Maoists and the security agencies in encounters (also in fake) had radicalized the society. Drawing heavily on ethnic, Dalit, and gender basis, the PLA became a formidable force having its wings spread across the country. The poor and oppressed people joined the PLA voluntarily or by force (Maoist conscription). The process of indoctrination for ending the class and caste-based socioeconomic and political relations made them ruthless. Some innocent people lost their lives in encounters, some on being "suspects." Such a countrywide phenomenon could naturally change the attitudes, values, and norms of the new Nepali youth, who were later used by some elders for various purposes—money, politics, revenge, and criminal activities. Born in war, starvation, hatred, and "primitive conditions of livelihood," the youths

---

[13] Lok Raj Baral, *Oppositional Politics in Nepal* (Kathmandu: Himal Books, 2006, second edn), p. 41.

of Nepal were driven by a mission for ending the exploitation. However, they perhaps did not understand that their indoctrinated dream would also turn into a nightmare. The embedded feudal culture and aspirations would not die down soon, nor would their leaders become exemplary in their style and orientation. However, to be fair, radical changes are also underway despite ongoing violent trends in the country.

Democracy and violence embedded in increasing trends of militarization are contradictory. An increase in defense expenditures and militarization of society and people are different aspects, though the trends of militarization of state need to be modest. However, in the given situation, criminalization has crept into violent activities carried out by disparate groups and individuals. I want to make a difference between "militarization" and criminal violence because of the latter trends being ingrained in Nepali society. Criminal violence has negative consequences while militarization becomes a somewhat neutral connotation, despite its use against the pervasive background of "illegitimate actions (which could defy the existing norms, the values of democracy, and the state laws) by certain groups and political parties to gain power and resources."[14] Nevertheless, the militaristic trends of mobilization of youth by various political parties and groups can be put into the discourse of militarization, thus, making a difference between the overt and latent trends of criminalization (see Table 6.3).

What is more alarming is that various caste and kin groups seem to be encouraged to mobilize a defensive force against any potential or real threat to be posed by other caste and ethnic groups. It is also a reaction to the developing trends of ethnicization of politics that cast aspersions on the high-caste groups for being exploitative for centuries. In the Tarai, politics of murder, extortion, abduction, and robbery has become a routine phenomenon. Alarmed at the anti-Pahade hate campaign launched

---

[14] See Anjana Luitel, Bishnu Raj Upreti, and Ashok Rai, "Militarization of the Youth: Hindering State-building in Post-conflict Nepal" in Anjana Luitel, Bishnu Raj Upreti, and Ashok Rai, eds, *The Remake of a State: Post-conflict Challenges and State Building in Nepal* (Kathmandu: NCCR North–South and IINRSC, 2010), p. 196.

Table 6.3

Main Militant Groups Formed by the Political Parties/Groups

Youth Organizations	Mother Organizations	Geographical Influence
Young Communist League	UCPN (Maoist)	All over the country
Youth Force	CPN–UML	All over the country
Madhesi Youth Force	MJF	Eastern, central, and mid-western Terai regions
Chure Bhawar Shanti Sena	Chure Bhawar Ekta Samaj Party	Central and mid-western regions
Security Brigade (Rakshya Bahini)	NSP (Rajendra Mahato)	Central and mid-western regions
Madhesi Commando	NSP	Central and mid-western regions
Terai Madhes Sewa Surakshya Sangh	T–MLP	Mid-western and western regions
All Nepal Democratic Youth Organization	Rastriya Janamorcha Party	Mid-western and western regions
Tharu Sena	Tharuhat Swayatta Parishad	Certain districts of mid-western and western regions (for example, Dang, Kapilbastu and Bardiya)
OBC Regiment	Pichhada Varga Mahasangh	Central Terai region
Limbuwan Volunteers and Limbuwan	Sanghiya Loktantrik Rastriya	Eastern region
Liberation Army	Manch/Limbuwan Rajya Parishad	
Kirat Limbuwan Volunteers	Pallo Kirat Limbuwan Rastriya Manch	Eastern region
Janasurakshya Bal	CPN (Maoists)	Some districts
Madhesi Raksha Bahini	Sadbhawana Party	Some of the Terai districts
Khas Kshetri Unity Society	Khas-Kshetri Unity Society	Some regions

Source: Bishnu Raj Upreti, ed., *The Remake of a State: Post-conflict Challenges and State Building in Nepal* (Kathmandu: NCCR North-South and HNRSC, 2010), p.196.

by the so-called "ultra Madhese" groups, many hill people left their places of residence. It has been stated that, as of 2009, 240 people were killed in 15 Tarai districts in 2009, let alone the sporadic killing of people in other parts of the country. Among the killed people, 27 were killed by the state, 22 by armed groups, 89 by unidentified groups, and one each by the YCL and the Youth Force, the latter two being the young wings of the UCPN (Maoist) and CPN–UML.[15] It has been stated by the government that there are about 109 armed groups, most of them of criminal nature, in the Tarai. Due to open and unregulated India–Nepal border and also collusion between some of such criminal gangs and the security agencies of both the country, surge of criminal activities became possible. India wants to isolate the criminal gangs for effective control. When the criminal and other groups mix up, security threats to the country will also increase. Some reports that circulate in the press both in India and Nepal reveal that some of the gangs have nexus to the politicians.

Tarai continues to be rocked by violence as its seed was first sown during the Maoist insurgency. Even if the Maoists have silenced their guns formally, its effects on spreading gun culture are strong. Analyzing the widespread violence and feeling of insecurity imprinted in the mind of people, some of these features can be put forth: taking arms for political ends, for taking revenge, and for fulfilling selfish interest of others. The meteoric rise of Maoist party after it took arms, particularly following the successful mass movement in 2006 and also due to the emergence of some Tarai parties, the groups with political objective, if any, thought that they too can convert themselves as reckonable political force that could enhance their bargaining clout vis-à-vis the other parties and the state. As a Tarai commentator states that those who have been used by others for selfish ends are of six categories: encouraged by international forces, those used by the police and administration for making money, violence used by the local representatives of parliamentary parties, those who opened organizations for three things—motor cycle, mobile, and *masti* (pleasure)—for unhealthy competition in professions and for being used by others for such activities, those who fled from army and police,

[15] Ibid., p. 199.

262

those who want to destroy the gains made after the 12-point program (2005), and those who have nexus with criminal gangs across the Nepal–India border.[16] The special Security Plan enforced by the government since 2009 has yielded some results, but the trends of extortion, abduction, and murder continue as if culture of violence has come to stay in Nepal. So the muscle, money, and mafia have significantly contributed to prolonging the culture of violence.

It is, however, interesting to know that the Tarai–hill dichotomy created in the Tarai is now being revisited making the cities and towns in the hills as much important for the Tarai people as the Tarai–Madhesh for the hill people. It has been reported that even hundreds of thousands Madheses did not gather courage to visit their villages or places of residence during the Durga Puja (*Dashain*) in 2010 for fear of being killed or harassed by the violent gangs now operating in the Tarai. Kathmandu alone has more than 400,000 permanent residents from Tarai who found it the safest place for them. So are the cases in other cities and towns.

The other militant groups and gangs that operate in various regions and cities work on the pretext of promoting their agendas of creating autonomous federal units in their names such as Limbu, Rai, Sherpa, Magar, Gurung, etc. The Tharu is a distinct community, which neither identifies with the hill ethnic groups nor with the Madheses. The Tharus have also formed their armed groups, overtly or covertly, in order to realize their demand of a separate Tharuhat state. The Muslim and the Dalits seem to be concerned about articulating their grievances in order to develop their accesses to power and resources but have refrained from forming separate militant groups.

Whatever the motivations, these groups were/are the by-product of fluid political situation that defies the very coercive power of the state. Parties and groups that sprang up in the Tarai also fueled the culture of violence. Not that these groups of the hills and the Tarai lack genuine demands but many others seemed to promote them in name of Madhese

[16] See Chandra Kishor, "Taraima Surakchhya Chunauti" [Security Challenges in Tarai], *Kantipur*, October 7, 2010.

interests. Since the government formed by the conglomeration of parties, groups, and individuals failed to take stern measures lest the fresh backlash, the armed gangs and mafia, sometimes in collusion with the police, are reported to be active. Many demands put up by some leading Tarai and hill groups were accepted without weighing their pros and cons. Prime Minister G. P. Koirala had the respectability but no leaders were confident of effective handling of the situation. In absence of effective government action on the one hand and surging regional, ethnic, and other demands on the other, no parties wanted to risk in their constituencies. Moreover, already politicized and militarized by the Maoist, the political landscape has changed drastically.

The remedies for all such ailments and trends are of administrative and political nature. First, the state authority as mentioned before must be restored for effective governance. For this, political parties need to be "national" and then only regional and ethnic, though these two sides cannot be isolated from one another. The reconstructed Nepali state cannot rely only on coercive side since its rule should also be supported by the people of the country. So parties and stakeholders try to engage themselves for making a state, which is both effective and democratic. Its remedies once again boil down to the unity of parties and other stakeholders for forging a common strategy to addressing the politics of violence. A comprehensive security policy and method need to be implemented by the government with a strong mandate and will. For it, a government should be in place first, and then short-, medium-, and long-run policy measures should be formulated. Confidence in leadership and government is a must for establishing order. All the outstanding issues pending in the CA should be sorted out by the combined efforts of all political parties.

The open-border regime existing between Nepal and India is both a boon and curse for both the countries. It is a boon because it has been proved beneficial for the peoples. The open-border regime, which is characterized by several unique features, needs to be properly regulated on the basis of understanding reached between the two governments. The kind of relationship we need in the future should be amicably decided. However, ultranationalism (or is it anti-Indianism?) will not help to undertake joint actions against criminals, terrorists, and other groups bent on thriving on the continuation of existing conditions.

Curbing violence in Nepal is not a one-dimensional problem, for it is related to such areas as socioeconomic transformation, empowerment of the marginalized sections of society, and end of all sorts of disparity gaps existing for centuries in the country. Inasmuch as it is a challenge before the political elites of Nepal, it is also an opportunity to serve the people. The other side is political and administrative that in turn demands effective governance and culture of empathy on the side of those who matter in making such a process accountable and strong. Without inculcating a culture of accountability, integrity, and visionary policymaking, administration alone would not serve the purpose.

Terrorism in its varied forms and orientations has unleashed the culture of terror and threats. Spreading its tentacles across the region and the world, it has become a transnational problem that needs to be curbed with the combined effort of all. Internally, Nepal's own house should be in order, which can be possible only by realizing the gravity of the situation and volatility of country's problem. Here again, national unity and integrity is a must for guaranteeing the future of the country. The demographic onslaught, which is precipitated both by internal population growth and cross-country migration, also needs a solution based on minimum political consensus. People who cross the Indo–Nepal border in large numbers might have contributed to swelling of numbers in the Tarai as the Nepalis do the same in India. The recent controversy over the preparation of voters' list on the basis of citizenship certificate with photo and the reactions of the Madhese leaders against such a move of the Election Commission show that the issue at once assumes political color. The Madhese leaders think that by adopting such a policy for preparing the voter list on citizenship basis, a large number of Madhese people will be deprived of casting their votes.[17]

Although many Madheses might have been deprived of citizenship cards, its remedy is to provide them certificates to those who meet the qualifications prescribed by the Interim Constitution and the laws. But

[17] See *Kantipur* and other dailies, September 29, 2010.

265

the permission to be granted to all those living in the Tarai (without citizenship certificate) is nothing but an absurdity. It seems that the Madhese leaders want to reciprocate the Indian pattern that allows the Nepalis to cast their votes in India without citizenship certificate. Since electoral politics is violence-prone because of tendency of parties to win by any means, the use of muscle, money, and mafia plus violent means may continue unless two things remain unchanged—election method and internalization of democratic political culture.[18]

State Restructuring

One of the controversial issues is state restructuring, especially the agenda of federalism. What would be the basis of units and how are they likely to be functional? Articulation of federalism has drawn more attention than other issues because of the changed context of ethnicization and regionalization. Each ethnic group wants to create autonomous states with the right to self-determination in their respective names. The Limbus of the Eastern Hills, for example, want to make Limbuwan, the Rais want Kirat Pradesh, and the Sherpas, the Gurungs, the Magars, Tharus, all follow such patterns. Only the caste groups—Brahmin, Chhetri, Dalits, and Muslims—and a few others have no such identity, although the Maoist proposal of carving out 14 regions include two regions based on castes. The "one Madhesh Pradesh" demanded by the Madheses includes the territory of the plain—stretching from the eastern to western border. This demand however lacks consensus as the Tharus, the Muslims, and the Dalits of the Tarai do not want such one single Tarai as a unit. Nor do the other hill communities like the Limbu accept it on the grounds that their demand of Limbuwan also includes some parts of the Tarai.

Questions have been raised over the viability and desirability of federal units based on ethnic divisions. Since it is still a hotly debated issue, the CA has to grapple with it by negotiating with various stakeholders

[18] For a detailed view of electoral violence, see Dhruba Kumar, *Electoral Violence and Volatility in Nepal* (Kathmandu: Vajra Books, 2010).

266

and political parties. Republic, federalism, and secularism are the other pillars of the new Nepal according to which the restructuring of state needs to be designed. Since the new regions to be created are likely to be asymmetrical in size and resources, both identity and resource endowment and other capacities have to be taken into consideration while carving out federal units.

It is also a truism that federal units cannot be as much autonomous as are found in some Western countries. Even a balance needs to be struck for division of functions between the Center, region, and local unit. If one goes by the recommendations of the Reconstruction of State Committee, it tends to embrace a centralized federal structure, whereby the Center would be able to cater to the needs of the regional and local units too. It does not mean that such an approach will dilute the capacity of regional units for the spirit of federalism is to make regional and local units less dependent on the Center. Nor are federal functions and devolution of power identical. As federal structure is now a fait accompli, common thinking and common strategy of all parties and stakeholders may lead to a solution.

Restructuring of army, police, bureaucracy, and political parties are also the main agendas of restructuring of state. Democratization of the NA and police force (both civil and military police) and bureaucracy are important aspects of new Nepal. If the NA becomes as yet another autonomous unit by asserting its own right and domain, then the question of democratic sustainability arises. Although the Nepali people are the ultimate source of power and authority, the security sector reform should be the priority of political parties. In the fluid situation where parties squander the gains of the movement, temptation would be high for intervention by the army. Although the NA has not made any attempt as yet for usurping power independently of kings or other rulers, the situation now is different from the past. If the parties fail to deliver and attenuate their popularity, attempts would be made for taking over power, whether or not such grabbing of power may last long.

The Nepali bureaucracy, another agenda of reform, remains a mixture of the old and the new political cultures. Old culture is embedded in *chakari*, manipulation, hear-say, and the *Bhansun* system for either getting promotion or to be in lucrative places. Without developing contacts, paying obeisance to leaders of political parties and their brokers, no good assignment is possible. During the royal regime, such patronage routes were monopolized by the Palace secretaries and other persons connected to the establishment. So, in order to show their obeisance to them and to get favor, the interested persons used to show their presence. Such practice continues today in different forms along with the change of elites and contact persons and brokers. Political parties' functionaries from top to down are allegedly involved in such deals. Without developing routes to them and the mafia who virtually control politicians through their money power, no sincere bureaucrats or other ordinary persons would be rewarded. It has been admitted by police officials and other bureaucrats that they require to spend huge amount of money (bribery) for getting promoted or posted in good places. Sometimes, such deals go awry and the persons involved are caught. However, the persons drenched in corruption or in criminal activities are seldom penalized. Even when high power commissions give verdict for penalty of wrongdoers, most of them evade such punitive actions.

The bureaucracy in post-2006 Nepal, as other organs of government, has suffered from over-partisan spirit. All parties in coalition governments seem to favor their own members or supporters or regional expectants for appointment. Ministries headed by respective parties have their own sets of bureaucrats or political appointees for working as middle persons for striking various corrupt deals. It makes the government both corrupt and ineffective as it has to cater to the interests of various groups and individuals. The prime minister, who heads a government composed of heterogeneous parties and whose bureaucratic machinery is demoralized and is preoccupied with its own survival, can hardly become effective and respectful. Even when he tries to project his image by issuing *nirdeshan* (directive) to carrying out the decisions of the government speedily and efficiently, they go on deaf ears of his ministers and administrative staff. Moreover, the prime minister neither commands respect nor is feared. The crisis of governance therefore boils down to the gradual loss of respect and authority of political leaders, since they have not been able to free themselves from the old political and feudal culture. The system of *pajani* (reshuffling) continues in different garbs and the language the politicians use is not at variance with the culture found during the royal regime.

The foregoing narrative might be taken as disturbing trends of today's Nepal. It is very difficult for us as well to provide workable suggestions when the receptivity of the environment is low. Nevertheless, democracy has its own remedies that may create positive conditions as well. Democracy demands rationality and institutional norms and values. Democracy is not a *hukumi shashan* run by peremptory and preemptory command personified in an individual. It needs a system in which all institutions function on the basis of accepted norms and rules. Nepal's new rulers have learned the art of launching movements while in opposition, but lack the knowledge of developing institutions. As a result, all-round institutional decay and collapse are being observed. Unless parties' leaders who come to power by rotation realize the spirit of institutionalized bureaucracy, no efficient and dignified government and bureaucracy is possible.

Political parties cannot be seen in isolation. Parties are the essential features of modern democracy, even though party system varies from country to country, regime to regime. Twenty-eight political parties are in the CA despite the marked hierarchy of parties. The oldest party—the NC—has now become the second largest party followed by the CPN–UML and the Madhese and non-Madhese parties. But the composition, orientation, and style of functioning are not so much different from one another. In the given context, parties have to be taken as agents of change as well as the system builder and system maintainer. Failures of political parties both to preserve the gains and move ahead with the new agendas set by them before will prove detrimental to the progress of the country. The overall records so far shown by the parties in Nepal have dissipated high hopes pinned by the people on them. A former die-hard royalist and believer in constitutional monarchy and Nepal as a Hindu state has questioned the leaders of parties to prove him wrong that the transformation from monarchy to republic was essential for making democracy and nationalism strong.[19] Coming as they did in the context of parties' dismal failure, such remarks, however, do not convince the people at large that monarchy was indeed better system. Time alone determines the longevity of any regime and ruler. If one believes in modern democracy, secularism cannot be a wrong choice. Secularism alone fosters national unity because of a feeling of ownership of all people regardless of various dominant and nondominant religions existing within the country. How the Christians, Buddhists, Muslims, and other non-Hindu religious groups abstained from celebrating the Constitution Day on November 9, 1990, was an indication of their opposition to the incorporation of the "Hindu state" into the Constitution of the Kingdom of Nepal.

Trends of polarization on ideological or on any other grounds also defy the conventional thinking of ideological divide. The two largest communist parties of Nepal, for example, are poles apart from both "ideological" and strategic points of view. The CPN–UML considers itself as the real democratic party having all the prerequisites of a pluralist democracy, while the UCPN (Maoist) has joined the multiparty system but with the objective of establishing a one-party rule. As a senior CPN–UML leader has written: "UML believes in multiparty competitive system; the Maoist believes in one-party dictatorial system." UML accepts the existence of other communist parties in the country, while the Maoist believes in "one country, one communist party system."[20] According to the UML conclusion, the Maoist party is ultra-Left that carries the behavior of terrorism. The largest party—UCPN (Maoist)—is at a loss insofar as its ideological coherence is concerned. Its instability in thinking and drifting strategies has not helped the constitution-making process.

[19] Kamal Thapa, who differs from other politicians and adheres to constitutional monarchy and opposes secularism, has thrown down the gauntlet to the political leaders who, without thinking, abolished monarchy and declared Nepal secular. See his views on different aspects of the post-2006 politics in *Annapurna Post*, Kathmandu, October 1, 2010.

[20] Pradeep Nepal, "Bampanthi Ekata: Sapana ki Yatharthata" [Left Unity: Dream or Reality], *Annapurna Post*, ibid. See also Pradeep Gyawali, "Sambidhan Savama Bicharko Dwanda" [Conflict of Ideas in Constituent Assembly], *Kantipur*, October 13, 2010.

Other so-called Left parties work as satellite parties that neither join either of the two main parties—the UML and the Maoist—nor can they make themselves strong. Individual leaders, not being at ease with the two big parties, want to maintain separate identity expecting to reap some benefits in the high drama of coalition politics that also shows the importance of even the smallest party. Since it is the politics of number, the big parties that are denied absolute majority very often are tempted to court these smaller parties. This argument also applies to other non-Left parties which are also divided over personality issue. The RPP is now divided into three with different or similar nomenclatures despite their common background and orientation. The RPP–N has however tried to retain its pro-king identity, while the RPP and the RJP have opted republic maintaining it as a fait accompli. The NC, which held its 12ʰ national convention successfully, is yet to show how it will relate it to the emerging realities. Parties that comprised tried and tested leaders are incapable of running their parties according to new context and time. The election of party functionaries has shown a mixed result. Among the elected are those who have gone against the party's decision to accept republic and secularism. In the NC too, personalities matter more than ideology and background, pointing to the earlier trend that NC is also prone to fractious trends. The popularity it could demonstrate during the conference (2010) may dissipate if the leaders start picking up quarrels as they had done before, thus, leaving the field to other parties, although they too are not in proper shape.

Among the parties in today's Nepal, the three Tarai–Madhesh parties will not have the same aura and mobilizing issues as they had capitalized during the Madhesh movement. Short of issues and ideology, these parties will not have an easy sail in the future. These parties have confined more to the chrysalis of Madhesh region rather than becoming national. If certain national issues arise, they tend to be parochial. So it is yet to be seen how the current Madhese parties will survive and on what grounds.

On top of everything, sustainability of any party depends on ideological clarity and organizational bases. They have to ensure party homogeneity, although homogeneity in absolute sense is not possible in any vibrant democracy as dissidence is as much natural to a party as consensus. It is interesting to observe the functioning of the so-called real communist party like the UCPN (Maoist). This party is no less faction-ridden and conflict-prone than other parties. The restructuring of state agenda has also become the victim of interparty conflicts.

Common Agenda and End of Disparity Gap

Ending disparity in the country is an uphill task in the given political contex for mitigating poverty, social disparity, and enhancing political empowerment of people at large needs bold and concerted actions and policies. The fractured status of parties and division on parochial lines may frustrate any radical agenda to be brought about by a party. The post-2006 politics has, thus, failed to bring all the principal parties to certain common agendas needed for substantial changes to be made for ending all forms of exploitation. This is the flip side of development as changes made so far have not percolated to the grassroots level despite the numerical progress made for inclusive representation. Various commissions formed from time to time have had given good reports for land reforms, but no governments have ever made any attempt to implement them. Heaps of such reports prepared by the nonformal sectors have similar fate as if the money being pumped into studies is a sheer wastage.

Nevertheless, Nepal's march to progress needs to be examined from various perspectives. Progress made in the field of small farmer development, grameen bank, irrigation, diversification in agricultural activities, tourism, and increase in remittance economy making it as one of the sources of revenue in the country, and trends of investment in social sector are all positive indicators. Nevertheless, conflicting reports are in circulation in determining the actual percentage of people below poverty line. The government claims that 25.4 percent people continue to be under the poverty line. Increase in population contributed by more than 2 percent growth nationally as well as by international migration due to open border cannot give us the actual picture.

Nepal's overall development is marked by asymmetry with some sectors making progress and others becoming stagnant. Strikes, disturbances, insurgency, crises of governance, violence, and other anarchical activities carried out across the country have hard-hit on industrial output. Psychology of terror and the lack of appropriate response to it and rampant corruption all have fatal consequences for the economy. But Nepal has not reached a terminal stage economically. Although money allocated for projects remains partially unspent due to the political instability, the country has certain ingrained capabilities to sustain, though it cannot be called the indicators of growth.

Consensus on Foreign and Security Policies

The third chapter has adequately dealt with foreign policy and its relation to national security. Both are the two sides of the same coin as a sound foreign policy and diplomacy is the extended version of national policy. If political system is stable, political elites make a difference between individual interest and national interest and work toward forming minimum consensus on the characteristics on the positive aspect of nationalism, the country will be able to reap benefits from its strategic position between China and India. For formulating a sound foreign security policy, the ministries should be headed by persons who know the subject, situation, and context, and the prospective role Nepal needs to play in the changing regional and world political context.

The coordination between the ministry of foreign affairs and ministry of defense and home is a must with a view to avoid conflicting opinion and strategies coming from two ministries. Personnel recruited into the foreign ministry should also be trained in various fields concerning India, China, the US, the EU, other emerging powers, the UN, and regional organizations. Will China be reconciled to play the role of a regional power or is it likely to challenge the US to change the existing unipolar world into multipolar one? Its increasing stubborn attitude being shown to other Asian neighbors claiming territories or reacting sharply in threatening language show that China will soon spread its fangs for being

273

a world power. India, Nepal's closest neighbor, will be circumspect for challenging China, though its progress cannot be casually berated. As it depends on many variables and denouement of events, it is too early to prophesy about the future scenarios. However, trends seem to be developing toward tough competition among the major world players.

Nepal's representation in the UN and its active participation in the peace-keeping operations were both a symbol and substance for its independence and international status. Appreciated by all, including the permanent members of the Security Council, Nepali power elites felt that the country's independence and security was guaranteed by the UN. Although such insurance is not possible in today's power politics, the UN membership and Nepal's role within it were taken as rewarding. However, such bonhomie ended following the standoff between the UN secretary general and the Government of Nepal on the issue of extension of term of the UNMIN. Some political parties in government not only criticized the UNMIN for being partial on the issue of integration of Maoist combatants, but also the secretary general for supporting the UNMIN as well as for interfering in the internal affairs of Nepal.

Any sovereign nation has the right to express its opinion on any issue, but the manner in which the leaders of ruling parties (the NC and the UML) blamed the UNMIN and the secretary general did not show art of diplomacy. The prime minister was put on the wrong side when he himself had to retract from his previous view agreeing to extend the term of the UNMIN for a four-month period. Moreover, the chief of the army staff who also wanted to send back the UNMIN had to retract his words by going to the extent of applauding the role of the UN for peace-keeping missions in which the NA has been taking part actively. Surprisingly, the minister of foreign affairs did not come to the picture about these developments because the prime minister and minister of defense, both from the CPN–UML-raised their voice against the UN. Thus, lack of coordination and well-thought-out action plan often put the parties in government in an awkward situation.

Coming to bilateral front, Nepal's foreign policy is primarily India–China centric due to its physical proximity and interactions at various levels. But, Nepal–India relation is incomparable in the world due to Nepal's physical setting, landlocked condition, and common civilizational linkages, and people-to-people-level contacts through the open border. So, even the structural relations such as the 1950 Treaty of Peace and Friendship are dictated by formal and informal arrangements made by the two sides for continuity. Changes taking place across the world are also taken into account but the patterns of Nepal–India relations remain the same, notwithstanding occasional stresses and strains. How the growing Chinese presence and its assertive clout, which is also likely to ruffle Nepal's traditional feathers, will make a difference needs to be seen. As said in the preceding sections, if Nepal continues to be plagued by its inertia and casualness, whatever freedom of choice it has had been enjoying in foreign and security policies is likely to be curtailed further in the future. So, the country's own independence and sovereignty will be in peril if Nepal comes under the thumb of a particular country.

"China's overly assertive policies" as are evident in its relations with its Pacific Ocean neighbors may also produce heat in Nepal–China relations when the weak Nepali political leaders fail to design suitable foreign and security policies for mending fences with the neighbors. Tomorrow, if India, the US, the EU, and other countries threatened by the rising Chinese power put pressure on Nepal to be close to them, China may also try for bringing Nepal under its umbrella. Since Tibet is its soft belly, no anti-Tibet activities in overt and covert forms will be allowed by China. Giving a strong message to the Nepali president, the leader of the high-powered Chinese delegation said: "Your Excellency, anti-Chinese activities are on the increase in Nepal. They are directed against our internal integrity and sovereignty. We cannot tolerate them."[21] Presenting the possible Chinese moves across Asia, an Indian analyst has stated:

> China has shown itself adept at assertively promoting its national interests and playing classical balance of power geo-politics. But, in order to displace the US and assume the leadership in Asia, China must do more than pursue its own interests or contain potential rivals. Most fundamentally, what does China represent in terms of values and ideas?[22]

[21] As cited in *Nepal (Rashtriya Saptahik)*, Vol. 12, No. 8, October 3, 2010.
[22] See Brahma Chellaney, "New Asian Security Constellation," *Republica*, Kathmandu, October 3, 2010.

The unfolding geopolitical scenarios may not be favorable for Nepal given its stagnant economy, uncertain politics, and reckless conduct of state affairs by myopic leaders. Unless political direction is clear and stability assured, no new policies and their effective implementation are possible. Thus, raising the banner of *rashtrabad* (ultranationalism) that does not empower the people will be meaningless. Nor can the principle of noninterference be honored by the concerned countries if their own interests, in their perceptions, are threatened. What imperatives will Nepal have if the scenarios start developing toward confrontational course? Some of them are likely to be as follows:

- Deterioration of political and economic conditions of Nepal making it more dependent on India.
- Increasing trends of Chinese assertiveness putting pressures on Nepal to follow certain steps, provoking Indian response to them in more coercive manner.
- Compulsions for Nepal to be closer to West–India alliance in order to counter assertive Chinese power in the region.
- Chinese pressure on Nepal to practice relations based on parity, thus further diluting the traditional security and economic relations with India.
- Development of Chinese economic infrastructure near the Nepal–China border and its pressure on Nepal to have more intimate economic relations with China.
- More active involvement of Western powers, especially the US, in order to bolster Indian position in Nepal.
- Chinese efforts to cultivate Left parties for enhancing its position in Nepal and India's reciprocal action for strengthening its own political lobbies. It means the chances of greater polarization of forces along respective countries' lines. It was exemplified by India when it persuaded the Tarai Madhesh parties not to ensure the post of prime minister for the Maoist leader, Prachanda, until his party fully transformed into a civilian party. China did follow the suit by allegedly supporting the Maoist party by using a third person to provide NPR 500 million for Prachanda's victory. Surprisingly,

however, other political parties did not make hue and cry by whipping up anti-Chinese sentiment as the anti-Indian parties used to do before.

- Economic competition between China and India is likely to be intensified in the days to come, thus, both demanding more favorable treatment.

The alternative scenarios that matter for maintaining Nepal's balanced relations with neighbors are also significant. They are:

- Both India and Nepal will try to develop cooperative and coordinated policies without offending China. India's trade with China has already reached US$60 billion with all potentials of further development.
- China too cannot be unmindful of its soft bellies in Asia and the Indian Ocean areas. Its assertive postures that are likely to loom large will scare the Association of Southeast Asian Nations (ASEAN) countries, Japan, South Korea, Taiwan, and others. If it becomes more aggressive, the alternative alliance formations would follow. It will hamper Chinese ambition to become the next superpower, though the trajectory of such supremacy is still uncertain.
- China and India may continue their existing relations of cooperation and competition without resorting to force. Such policy would not distract them from their global outreach and engagement. India, more than China, suffers from internal vulnerabilities because of its diversities and openness. However, such diversities and openness themselves have helped reinforce India's democratic stability with progress, thus rejecting the arguments that authoritarian regime is better governed and developmental than chaotic democracies. If the India–China power equilibrium continues, Nepal's external threats might be low depending on the ability to derive benefits from such entente. But Nepal needs to concentrate on its internal security and development for catching up the changes underway in its neighborhood.

- India and Nepal may, in all probability, not disturb their traditional relations that encompass all aspects. Many controversies raised for abrogating the 1950 Treaty may also subside in order not to 'open Pandora's box.' If the two sides agree to review or even to abrogate it, they can do so amicably and in a spirit of cooperation and coordination. Such low-profile move on the part of Nepal may also not make India suspicious and retaliatory. Above all, Nepal's vital interest lies in making the country strong by accelerating development and by making people confident with a feeling of empowerment.

- Change in mindset on the sides of Indian and Nepali political elites including those of security sectors and bureaucracy alone can take Nepal–India relation to a new height. The Nepali politicians' perception suffering perennially from suspicion, fear, and perceptions that Indian attitude toward Nepal is imperial and hegemonic dictating its own terms to Nepal, needs to be changed. Even recent events might have demonstrated such dictations and "interferences" but they may not serve the bilateral interest. On the contrary, they give rise to anti-Indian sentiments. Ironically, Nepali politicians and security personnel seek Indian help for rescuing an individual or a party from problems. Thus, in my opinion, some "interventions" are sought and others are parts of coercive diplomacy that India used occasionally when it thinks that its vital interests will be in peril if the situation to be created by politicians or by external factors would go against it. Such mutual threat perceptions are basically heightened due to lack of cooperation and coordination. Only issues based on objective realties and comprehension of issues and problems together with possible repercussions can be resolved.

- Rethinking Nepal's foreign policy should be buttressed by internal development and cool and calculated strategies, both long term and short term. Nepal should never repeat the old game by trying to play off one neighbor against the other. Such policy is likely to be counterproductive for both the parties and the country. More openness and transparent efforts to be made for enhancing Nepal's relations with neighbors as well as with other countries that have been helping us for a long time will serve the country's interest.

- Misunderstanding that may crop up from time to time with the neighbors should be removed with sincerity and sobriety, especially through diplomatic channel. Rhetorical statements and adventurism should in no circumstances be used against any neighbor. Nepal–India relations have suffered setbacks from time to time when minor events take place. The UCPN (Maoist) misunderstanding with India in recent years was the fallout of Maoist's own lack of comprehension of the nature and limitations of Nepal's relations with India. The Maoist failure to win the confidence of its coalition partners and India while sacking the incumbent COAS strained the Maoist relations with India. Since India had become disillusioned with the Maoist impatience for imposing its own agendas after it came to power in 2009, India, taking a cue from other parties, decided to put a brake on the Maoist move. Yet India had not objected to the Maoists being in government after the CA election hoping that they would come in the democratic process. Now to restore such trust and confidence, both sides should mend their fences and restart the process of building bridges for better relations.
- Nepal's options are shrinking. What initiatives befitting the context and time will come are to be seen.

Understanding Nationalism

Nepalis generally understand nationalism in various ways. For the older generation leaders, antiforeign sentiment that sometimes drove the rulers to wars in name of patriotism was made out to be nationalism. Yes, for many countries of the developing world and countries under foreign rule for centuries, the war of national independence and sovereignty became the source of nationalism. India's independence movement or similar other movements across the world were therefore interpreted as nationalistic. This bore the meaning until these countries achieved independence but its spirit has changed, although the rulers in crisis often use it as the weapon for mobilization of people for regime survival. This is nothing new since the ancient time as the rulers were taught for pointing out distant enemies.

Nepal went to war with Tibet and China to the north and with the British to the south, taking patriotism as a mobilizing force. Its purpose was limited to satisfy the ego of rulers. It was called patriotic wars for the simple reason that those wars were fought in the name of Gorkha or Nepal. Territorial expansion and spread of the culture of ruling dynasty were the motivating factors for waging wars. Such adventurous course ended with the signing of Treaty of Sugauli in 1815–1816 following Nepal's surrender to the British by giving up claim over the territories won during the war.

Patriotism (*deshbhakti*) cannot be compared with *rashtrabad* (ultra-nationalism), although the use of the former was narrow in historical context. Love of the motherland is an internalized value embedded in each citizen, while *rashtrabad* or ultranationalism smacks of some sort xenophobia, which may not necessarily be positive for nation-state building. Nepali rulers in the post-1950 period have used *rashtrabad* loosely without any conceptual clarity. On the contrary, anti-Indian sentiment formed the core of Nepali nationalism. It was subsequently called "Mahendrabad" (Mahendraism) because, during the Mahendra period, Nepal–India relations witnessed some marked changes, but not of substantive nature, in their relations. However, what was being done in defining geopolitical reality was prompted by the presence of China in Tibet. Nepal's formal diplomatic relations with China and its use as a countervailing force to India subsequently were taken as the manifestation of Nepali nationalism. But it was not only King Mahendra but the first-ever elected prime minister, B. P. Koirala, at that time 90 years of age, who was also under geopolitical pressure after Sino–Indian relations deteriorated in the late 1950s and in the beginning of 1960.

Nevertheless, the real definition of nationalism was/is still elusive with parties, leaders, and other elites trying to examine through the prism of anti-Indian sentiment. Nationalism is an ingrained feeling toward the motherland. Since people become the core of the nation, their inclusive development (social, economic, and political) that makes them confident makes a nation strong. Nationalism "refers to the set of ideas and

sentiments which form the conceptual framework of national identity."
Territory, physical features, and their impacts on people's lives, culture,
language, ethnic mosaic, and international personality make an identity.
Since all these elements bind people together, their common feeling and
understanding of such togetherness makes a nation.

The operating principle of a nation is, therefore, people-centric.
Democracy that entails social justice, political freedoms, inclusiveness,
and empowerment becomes an integral part of nation. Anti-Indian sentiment may be taken as an expression of loyalty to the country during
crisis, but it does not provide us with the true spirit of nationalism.

Seen from this perspective, the Nepal–India relationship is the worst
sufferer. Politicians who spit fire against India when small things go
wrong do not understand that its remedy lies with the people. If a leader
carries the people with him, there is no point of being ultranationalist
or *rashtrabadi*. Alleviation of poverty, social justice in spirit, end of exploitation, empowerment of all the people contribute to positive nationalism. Thus, *rashtriyata* or nationality is a very important aspect of life.
Nationality is also a secular concept that inspires us to sacrifice our lives
for collective sentiment. When a Nepali returns from foreign countries
and starts seeing the peaks of the Himalayas, he feels that his country
is the best in the world for which he has surrendered his life.

How democracy and nationalism are intertwined can be observed
in the demands that all the people living within the boundaries of the
country should be treated equally. Modern democracy, which is common to all, has to be imbibed with the principle and practice of social
justice, freedom of expression, inclusiveness, empowerment, and culture
of accountability of both the rulers and the ruled. Democracy is nationalism with collective sentiments and collective mission of the good of
people. If a state becomes parochial by adhering to a particular religion
or language and culture, it naturally becomes prejudiced to a particular
group or religion thus violating the very foundation of democracy and
nationalism.[23]

[23] See Lok Raj Baral, "Ganatantra ra Rashtriyata" [Republic and Nationalism],
Kantipur, October 5, 2010.

This narrative tries to emphasize the points raised before that the true spirit of nationalism has not yet developed in Nepal. On the contrary, inherited formulation of parochial nationalism has continued to shape our minds even in the present time. The country's symbolic and actual strengths and status can alone command respect and avoid the falsification of the concept. As a mobilizing ideology, ultranationalism might be useful for instant reaction, but it becomes counterproductive for the vital interest of the country.

Governance and Future Nepal

Governance is a process for strengthening the role of the state and political system. Its attributes are: capacity to apply rules (coercive as well as persuasive power), legitimacy (constitutionally and by performance), sustainability based on a broad consensus, accountability, and vision. These attributes that are manifest in its delivery and regulative capacity make a government effective and functional. At a time when no one knows what would be the length or future of transition, security becomes an important part of governance. State security is characterized by the security provided by the state agencies—police, army, and bureaucracy under civilian authority—and by comprehensive security system that encompasses a variety of areas concerning the people. The gruesome murder of innocent school children and other general people for money and revenge has become a regular affair today in a country where, a decade ago, no Nepalis had ever thought of having to pass through such a dreadful situation. The governments formed in the post-2006 Nepal are invariably weak due to lack of cooperative attitudes of parties as well as of absence of a dominating leader whose role of clubbing together other leaders could have made a government strong. The fractured mandate received by the parties in the CA election has deprived every party of forming a government on its own and, hence. the enlarged of scope of interparty and intra-party conflicts.

Then the question arises: are the criteria identified for governance before attainable? Since objectives cannot be described in absolute sense, minimum level of performance is expected from any government. How the government works and how can it become legitimate and sustainable become the actual measuring rod. In the given context where politics is fluid and uncertain, our expectations of effective governance may not be possible. To the extent the Nepali politics is losing both the purpose and direction of change, no definite picture is yet clear. It does not mean that everything has collapsed by reaching the stage of a "failed state." Seen from the trajectory of growth, Nepal's economy is stagnant, but its resilience has by and large been maintained by other kinds of activities being carried out in nonindustrial, non-trade sectors. Diversification in agriculture, making villagers more receptive to innovations; employment opportunities being provided by semiprivate and private sectors, NGOs and INGOs; and remittances and tourism are positive sides of development. If politics is primarily responsible for abysmal economic growth, rampant corruption is no less a contributing factor for it. How helpless is the prime minister of the new Nepal can be observed by his own speeches. By way of addressing the civil servants in eastern Nepal, Prime Minister Madhav Kumar Nepal bemoaned: "How long you [civil servants] plunder the country? By way of looting, you are about to finish the country. Wherever we see, corruption is rampant."[24] Thus, instead of taking strong initiative to stem corruption or to enhance the quality of governance, the head of the government is confined to making speeches and giving directives which can hardly animate the governance.

Crisis of governance is manifested by "pervasive nepotism and corruption; misappropriation of state funds for personal or familial purposes; absence of transparency and accountability in public administration; lack of respect for the rule of law and ethical behaviour in public life."[25] So these features are pervasive in political parties, government, bureaucracy, security agencies, and educational institutions; thus, remedies are not in sight. Only a committed leadership supported by parties and civil society can take steps toward minimizing if not eradicating

[24] *Nagarik Daily*, Kathmandu, October 5, 2010.

[25] P. R. Chari, "The Crisis of Security and Governance in South Asia" in P. R. Chari, ed., *Security and Governance in South Asia* (Delhi: Manohar, 2001), p. 161.

corruption. The political nexus developed by black marketers, power brokers, and commission agents with the different organs of government has made corruption as an unbeatable monstrous. The increasing trends of criminalization of politics and politicization of crime have made the governmental system more problematic. Expensive elections, ostentatious lifestyle, and the new consumptive culture of people also encourage corruption.

End of corruption is not possible in the given conditions of Nepal. Nor does the present role of parties make us confident of any strong remedial measures for effective governance. Since both are intertwined, one cannot be extricated from the other. Thus, a dichotomous situation exists. Corruption of various forms and tentacles is eating up the vitals of the state. Unless the political elites follow minimum norms of governing a modern democratic state and provide effective governments, no improvement is possible. All such conditions boil down to political order on which democracy can be built. In absence of order, neither democracy nor forms of government is possible. Confronting plethora of problems simultaneously, Nepal, first, needs to stabilize the gains of the movement and then start rejuvenating the state.

A country of contrasts, Nepal has the potential of survival despite political turbulence it is passing through at the moment. For the first time in its history, both positive and dangerous developments are active at the same time. Positive because there has been tremendous public upsurge for political space with which all the social groups hitherto deprived and marginalized seek to share power and resources as other "privileged" groups. Their level of consciousness has increased along with the escalation of aspirations. From this perspective, Nepal's real integration process is on track. It will stay the course if political elites develop their own ability to understand this process. Admitting the resilience of the Nepali state, the International Crisis Group Report states:

> Development experts assume that the state is there to provide services and that if it fails to do so it will face a crisis of legitimacy. Nepal also tends to feature high on the lists of fragile or failing states. But the Nepalese state is more flexible than fragile. It endures—and has survived the conflict surprisingly unscathed, and unreformed. This is partly because its own raison d'être is not serving citizens so much as

servicing the needs of patronage networks and keeping budgets flowing and corruption going. The state is dysfunctional by demand. It is slow to reform because
elite incentives are invested in the status quo and public pressure is rarely acute.[26]

Paradoxically, the state has not reached the terminal point; neither
has it given us any promising picture for the future. Democracy is in
peril, so is the vitality of the state. Prolonged transition and polarized
and uncertain politics may be more alarming when foreign powers start
showing their active presence than ever before and when the political
and other elites become too weak to manage them. Political parties
that take positions for and against any country themselves would make
these powers active and interventionist as the recent developments have
demonstrated.

---

[26] International Crisis Group, *Nepal's Political Rites of Passage*, Asia Report
No. 194, September 29, 2010, p. 29.

BIBLIOGRAPHY

Adhikakri, Dhrubahari, "Ke Sena Bhumikabihin Janashakti Ho?" [Is the Army a Public Force without a Role?], *Bimarsha Weekly*, Kathmandu, November 10, 2000.

Adhikari, Indra, "Democratization of Nepalese Polity and The Role of Military, 1990–2007," PhD dissertation, School of International Studies, Jawaharlal Nehru University, New Delhi, 2010.

————, "Nepal: Trends of Militarization (1996–2005)," *Nepali Journal of Contemporary Studies*, (NCCS), Kathmandu, 8, 2, September: 2008, pp. 66–78.

————, "Women in Conflict: The Gender Perspective in Maoist Insurgency" in Lok Raj Baral, ed., *Nepal: Facets of Maoist Insurgency* (Delhi: Adroit Publishers, 2006), pp. 60–82.

Baral, Lok Raj, "Ganatantra ra Rashtriyata" [Republic and Nationalism], *Kantipur*, October 5, 2010.

————, "What Interference?" *Kathmandu Post*, November 11, 2009.

————, ed., *Nepal: New Frontiers of Restructuring of State* (New Delhi: Adroit Publishers, 2008).

————, ed., *Nepal: Facets of Maoist Insurgency* (Delhi: Adroit Publishers, 2006).

————, ed., *Non-Traditional Security: State, Society and Democracy in South Asia* (Delhi: Adroit Publishers, 2006).

————, *Rajtantraki Loktantra* [Monarchy or Democracy?] (Kathmandu: Bhrikuti Academic Publications, 2062 VS, 2005).

————, "The Unclear Road Map: Parties and the Political Process" in Lok Raj Baral, ed., *Political Parties and Parliament* (Delhi: Adroit Publishers, 2004).

————, "The Specter of Terror and Its Impacts on the Democratic Process in Nepal" in Sridhar K. Khatri and Gert W. Kueck, eds, *Terrorism in South Asia* (Delhi: Shipra Publications, 2003), pp. 223–236.

Baral, Lok Raj, ed., *Political Parties and Parliament* (Delhi: Adroit Publishers, 2003).

———, "Nepal in 2000: Discourse of Democratic Consolidation," *Asian Survey*, XLI, 1, January/February: 2001, pp. 138–142.

———, *The Regional Paradox: Essays in Nepali & South Asian Affairs* (Delhi: Adroit Publishers, 2000).

———, "Political Parties in South Asia" in V. A. Paipanandiker, ed., *Problems of Governance in South Asia* (New Delhi: Konark, 1999), pp. 158–198.

———, ed., *Looking to The Future: Indo-Nepal Relations in Perspective* (Delhi: Anmol Publications, 1996).

———, "The 1994 Nepal Elections: Emerging Trends in Party Politics," *Asian Survey*, XXXV, 5, May: 1995, pp. 426–440.

———, *Nepal: Problems of Governance* (New Delhi: Konark, 1993).

———, *Regional Migrations, Ethnicity and Security: The South Asian Case* (Delhi: Sterling, 1990).

———, *Nepals's Politics of Referendum: A Study of Groups, Personalities and Trends* (Delhi: Vikas Publishing House, 1983).

———, *Oppositional Politics in Nepal* (Delhi: Abhinav, 1977).

Baral, Lok Raj, Krishna Hacchethu, and Hari Sharma, *Local Leadership and Governance* (Delhi: Adroit Publishers, 2003).

———, *Leadership in Nepal* (Delhi: Adroit Publishers, 2001).

Bardhan, Pranab, *Awakening Giants, Feet of Clay: Assessing the Economic Rise of China and India* (Princeton: Princeton University Press, 2010), p. 192.

Baskota, Krishnahari, "Baideshik Lagani Akarshit Garne Upayaharu" [Means for Attracting Foreign Investment], *Nagarik Daily*, October 27, 2010.

Bauman, Zygmunt, *In Search of Politics* (Stanford: Stanford University, 1999).

Bendix, Reinhard, *Kings or People: Power and the Mandate to Rule* (Berkeley: University of California, 1978).

Bhandari, Krishna Murari, "Kangress Bhitra Kangress Khoi?" [Where Is Congress within Congress?], *Annapurna Post*, Kathmandu, September 15, 2010.

Bhasin, Avtar Singh, ed., *Nepal-India, Nepal-China Relations: Documents 1947– June 2005* (Delhi: Geetika Publishers, 2005).

———, ed., *Nepal's Relations with India and China: Documents 1947–1992*, Vol. 1 (Delhi: Siba Exim Pvt. Ltd, 1994).

Bhatt, Deepak Prakash, "Public Security Challenges and the Effective Mobilisation of Law-Enforcement Agencies" in Rajan Bhattarai and Rosy Cave, eds, *Changing Security Dynamics in Nepal* (Kathmandu: Nepal Institute for Policy Studies and Safeworld, London, n.d.), pp. 113–133.

Bhattachan, Krishna B., Dev Raj Dahal, Sheetal Rana, Jyoti Gyawali, Meen Bahadur Basnet, Kashi Ram Bhushal, and Ram Raj Pokhrel, eds, *NGO, Civil Society, and Government in Nepal* (Kathmandu: Central Department of Sociology/Anthropology, Tribhuvan University, 2001).

Bhattarai, Babu Ram, "Pragatisheel Rashtrabadko Antarbastu" [Internal element of Progressive nationalism], *Nagarik Daily*, Kathmandu, August 11, 2010.

———, "Aghosit Karyagat Ekata" [Undisclosed Working Relationship], *Kathmandu Post*, Kathmandu, June 9, 2001.

Bhurtel, Bhim Prasad, "Revisiting Economic Policy," *Kathmandu Post*, Kathmandu, April 17, 2010.

Bista, Dor Bahadur, "The Structure of Nepali Society" in Pashupati Shsumshere Rana and Kamal P. Malla, eds, *Nepal in Perspective* (Kathmandu: Centre for Economic Development and Administration, 1973), pp. 35–45.

Bohara, Alok, "Win-Win-Win: A Trilateral Agreement with India and China May Be the Only Way to Move Forward Together", *Nepali Times*, August 13, 2010.

Cameron, David, "A Stronger, Wider, Deeper Relationship," *The Hindu*, New Delhi, July 30, 2010.

CEDA, *Review of Development in Nepal's Foreign Affairs* (Kathmandu: CEDA, 1973–1983).

Chandhoke, Neera, *Beyond Secularism: The Rights of Religious Minorities* (New Delhi: Oxford University Press, 1999).

Chari, P. R., "The Crisis of Security and Governance in South Asia" in P. R. Chari, ed., *Security and Governance in South Asia* (Delhi: Manohar, 2001), pp. 159–178.

Chauhan, R. S., *Political Development in Nepal (Conflict between Tradition and Modernity)* (New Delhi: Associated Publishing House, 1971).

Chellaney, Brahma, "New Asian Security Constellation," *Republica*, Kathmandu, October 3, 2010.

———, *Asian Juggernaut: The Rise of China, India and Japan* (New Delhi: Harper Collins, 2006).

Choudhury, Shankar Roy, "Indo-Nepal Bhai Bhai," *Deccan Chronicle*, as reproduced by *Republica*, Kathmandu, March 24, 2010.

Citizenship Act, 1964 and the Constitution of the Kingdom of Nepal, 1990 (Kathmandu: HMG, Nepal).

Crouch, Colin, *Postdemocratie* (Berlin: Suhrkamp, Verlag, 2009).

Dahal, Dilli Ram, "Problems and Prospects of Relationship between Government Organizations and NGOs/INGOs in Nepal" in Krishna B. Bhattachan,

Dev Raj Dahal, Sheetal Rana, Jyoti Gyawali, Meen Bahadur Basnet, Kashi Ram Bhushal, and Ram Raj Pokhrel, eds, *NGO, Civil Society, and Government in Nepal* (Kathmandu: Central Department of Sociology/Anthropology, Tribhuvan University, 2001).

Department of Information, *Proclamations, Speeches and Messages* (Kathmandu: Department of Information, 1975).

Desai, Nitin, "When Two's Company?" *The Times of India,* January 4, 2010.

Diamond, Larry, *The Spirit of Democracy* (New York: Holt Paperbacks, 2008).

Dubey, Muchkund, "Some Reflections on India-Nepal Relations" in Lok Raj Baral, ed., *Looking to the Future: India-Nepal Relations in Perspective* (Delhi: Anmol Publications, 1996), pp. 47–57.

Eastwood, Jonathan R., "A Student's Introduction" in Liah Greenfeld, ed., *Nationalism and the Mind: Essays on the Modern Culture* (Noida: Brijbasi Art Press, Indian edn, 2007).

Engels, Jan Niklas/Gero Maass, "The New Promise of Happiness: Current State of Discussion on the Future of European Social Democracy," *International Politics and Society,* 4: 2010, pp. 40–60.

Friedman, Thomas, "Superbroke, Superfrugal, Superpower?" *Republica,* Kathmandu, September 6, 2010.

Fukuyama, Francis, *The End of History and the Last Man* (New York: Free Press, 1992).

Gabriel, A. Almond, "Comparative Political Systems," *Journal of Politics,* XVIII, 8: 1956, pp. 392–405.

Gaige, Frederick H., *Regionalism and National Unity in Nepal* (Kathmandu: Himal Books, 2009).

General Assembly Official Record (GAOR), *Session 26* (New York: UN General Assembly, December 7, 1970).

Ghosh, Jayati, "Thailand in Crisis," *The Asian Age,* Delhi, April 20, 2010.

Government of Nepal, Interim Constitution of Nepal 2007 (Kathmandu: Government of Nepal, 2007).

Gupta, Anirudha, *Politics in Nepal* (Bombay: Allied Publishers, 1964).

Gyawali, Pradeep, "Sambidhan Savama Bicharko Dwanda" [Conflict of Ideas in Constituent Assembly], *Kantipur,* October 13, 2010.

———, "Maobadi Bhitrako Bibad ra Tyaska Pravab" [Controversies within the Maoists and their Impacts], *Kantipur,* September 17, 2010.

Hachhethu, Krishna, *State Building in Nepal: Creating a Functional State* (Kathmandu: Enabling State Programme, 2009).

Hachhethu, Krishna, *Party Building in Nepal: Organization, Leadership and People: A Comparative Study of the Nepali Congress and the Communist Party of Nepal (Unified Marxist-Leninist)* (Kathmandu: Mandala Book Point, 2002).

Hall, John A. and G. John Ikenberry, *The State* (Delhi: Worldview, First Indian Reprint, 1997).

Hofer, A., *The Caste Hierarchy and the State in Nepal* (Innsbruck: Universitastsverglag, 1979).

Husain, Asad, *British India's Relations with the Kingdom of Nepal* (London: George Allen and Unwin, 1970).

Informal Sector Service Centre, INSEC Report of 2005 and 2007 (Kathmandu: Informal Sector Service Centre, 2005, 2007).

International Crisis Group Policy Report, *Nepal's Political Rites of Passage*, Asia Report No. 194 (Brussels: International Crisis Group, September 29, 2010.

————, *Nepal Future: In Whose Hands?* (Brussels: International Crisis Group, August 13, 2009).

————, *Nepal's New Political Landscape* (Brussels: International Crisis Group, July 3, 2008).

————, *Nepal's Troubled Tarai Region* (Brussels: International Crisis Group, July 9, 2007).

Jacques, Martin, *When China Rules the World: The Rise of the Middle Kingdom and the End of the Western World* (London: Penguin Books, 2009).

Jalal, Ayesha, *Democracy and Authoritarianism in South Asia* (Delhi: Cambridge University Press, 1995).

Jayal, Niraja Gopal, "Introduction: Situating Indian Democracy" in Niraja Gopal Jayal, ed., *Democracy in India* (New Delhi: Oxford University Press, 2001), pp. 1–45.

Jha, Prashant, "Plain Speaking," *Nepali Times*, May 7–13, 2010.

————, "Patronizing Behavior," *Nepali Times*, August 13–19, 2010.

Jha, Prem Shankar, *India & China: The Battle between Soft and Hard Power* (New Delhi: Penguin, 2010).

Joshi, Bhuwan L. and Leo E Rose, *Democratic Innovations in Nepal: A Study in Political Acculturation* (Berkeley: University of California Press, 1966).

Kaltwasser, Cristobal Rovira, "Moving Beyond the Washington Consensus: The Resurgence of the Left in Latin America," *International Politics and Society*, 3/2010, pp. 52–62.

Karobar Daily, "The Economic Policy Adopted by the Twelfth Conference of the NC," September 21, 2010.

Katuwal, Rukmangad, "Speech of the Outgoing COAS," *Rajdhani Daily*, Kathmandu, September 6, 2009.

Kishor, Chandra, "Taraima Surakchhya Chunauti" [Security Challenges in Tarai], *Kantipur*, Kathmandu, October 7, 2010.

Koirala, B. P., *Atmabritanta* (Kathmandu: Jagadamba Press, 2001).

———, "Rajtantra" [Monarchy], *Tarun Bulletin*, Varanasi, Nos 3–4, September 1971.

Koirala, M. P., *A Role in a Revolution* (Kathmandu: Jagadamba Prakashan, 2008).

Kumar, Dhruba, *Electoral Violence and Volatility in Nepal* (Kathmandu: Vajra Books, 2010).

———, "Nepal's Turbulent Quest for Peace and Stability," *Aakrosh*, Delhi, 12, 44, July: 2009.

———, "The Military Dimensions of Maoist Insurgency" in Lok Raj Baral, ed., *Nepal: Facets of Maoist Insurgency* (Delhi: Adroit Publishers, 2006), pp. 85–115.

Kurlantzick, Joshua, "A Global Decline iIn Political Freedom is Partly the Fault of the Middle Class," *Newsweek*, March 22, 2010.

Landon, Perceval, *Nepal* (London: Constable, 1928).

Laqueur, Walter, "Left, Right, and Beyond: The Changing Face of Terror" in James F. Hodge Jr and Gideon Rose, eds, *How Did This Happen? Terrorism and the New War* (New York: Public Affairs, 2001), pp. 81–82.

Lawoti, Mahendra, ed., *Contentious Politics and Democratization in Nepal* (New Delhi, SAGE Publications, 2007).

———, *Towards a Democratic Nepal: Inclusive Political Institutions for a Multicultural Society* (New Delhi: SAGE Publications, 2005).

Lawoti, Mahendra and Anup K. Pahari, eds, *The Maoist Insurgency in Nepal: Revolution In the Twenty-First Century* (New Delhi: Routledge, 2010).

Lijphart, Arend, *Thinking About Democracy: Power Sharing and Majority Rule in Theory and Practice* (London: Routledge, 2008), pp. 1–279.

Lipset, S. M., "Some Social Requisites for Democracy: Economic Development and Political Legitimacy," *American Political Science Review*, 53, 1: 1959, pp. 69–105.

Liu, Xuecheng, "China's Strategic Culture and its Political Dynamics" in V. P. Malik and Jorg Schultz, eds, *The Rise of China: Perspectives from Asia and Europe* (New Delhi: Pentagon Press, 2008), pp. 1–36.

Luitel, Anjana, Bishnu Raj Upreti, and Ashok Rai, "Militarization of the Youth: Hindering State-Building in Post-Conflict Nepal" in Anjana Luitel, Raj Upreti, Bishnu, and Ashok Rai, eds, *The Remake of a State: Post-Conflict*

Challenges and State Building in Nepal (Kathmandu: NCCR North-South and HNRSC, 2010).

Mahara, Krishna Bahadur, "Whether It Is True or Not Is Not an Important Matter, Even if It Is Correct, It Is a Plot," *Republica* and *Nagarik Daily*, September 4, 2010. Adio-taped conversation of Krishna Bahadur Mahara reportedly with one of the Chinese, September 13, 2010.

Mahat, Ram Sharan, *In Defence of Democracy: Dynamics and Fault Lines of Nepal's Political Economy* (Delhi: Adroit Publishers, 2005).

Mainali, Radhakrishna, "Bartaman Sarkar ra Maobadi Rajniti" [Present Government and Maoist Politics], *Annapurna Post*, Kathmandu, May 10, 2010.

Malla, Kamal P. "The Intellectual in Nepalese Society" in Pashupati Shsumshere Rana and Kamal P. Malla, eds, *Nepal in Perspective* (Kathmandu: Centre for Economic Development and administration, 1973), pp. 263–290.

Mandelbaum, Michael, *The Frugal Superpower: America's Global Leadership in a Cash-Strapped Era* (Baltimore: Johns Hopkins University, 2010).

Martin Chautari, *Policy Paper* (Kathmandu: Martin Chautari, No. 4, September 2010).

Mearsheimer, John J., *The Tragedy of Great Powers Politics* (New York: W. W. Norton, 2001).

Mihaly, Eugene Bramer, *Foreign Aid and Politics in Nepal: A Case Study* (London: Oxford University Press, 1965).

Ministry of Law, *Nepalko Antarim Sambhidhan 2063* (With Sixth Amendments), (Kathmandu: Ministry of Law, Justice and Management of Constitutional Assembly, 2007).

Mishra, Chaitanya, *Essays on the Sociology of Nepal* (Kathmandu: Fine Print Inc., 2007).

———, *Punjibad ra Nepal* [Capitalism and Nepal] (Kathmandu: Mulyankan, VS, 2062, 2005).

———, "New Predicaments of Humanitarian of Humanitarian Organizations" in Krishna B. Bhattachan, Dev Raj Dahal, Sheetal Rana, Jyoti Gyawali, Meen Bahadur Basnet, Kashi Ram Bhushal, and Ram Raj Pokhrel, eds, *NGO, Civil Society, and Government in Nepal* (Kathmandu: Central Department of Sociology/Anthropology, Tribhuvan University, 2001).

Mohanty, Manoranjan, "Towards a Creative Theory of Social Transformation" in Mohanty, ed., *People's Rights* (Delhi: SAGE Publications, 1998), pp. 9–26.

Muni, S. D., *India's Foreign Policy: The Democracy Dimension* (New Delhi: Cambridge University Press, 2009).

———, "Introduction" in S. D. Muni, ed., *Responding to Terrorism in South Asia* (Delhi: Manohar, 2006), pp. 11.

Muni, S. D., *Maoist Insurgency in Nepal: The Challenges and the Response* (Delhi: Rupa & Co., 2003).

———, *India and Nepal: A Changing Relationship* (New Delhi: Konark, 1972).

Naryan, Sriman, *India and Nepal: An Exercise in Open Diplomacy* (Bombay: Popular Prakashan, 1970).

Nayar, Baldev Raj, *The Geo-Politics of Globalization: The Consequences for Development* (New Delhi: Oxford University Press, 2005).

Nepal Gazette, Vol. 4, Magh 25 2011 VS, pp. 123–126.

Nepal Press Digest, 34, 18, Kathmandu, April 30, 1990.

Nepal, Pradeep, "Bampanthi Ekata: Sapana ki Yatharthata" [Left Unity: Dream or Reality)], *Annapurna Post*, Kathmandu, October 1, 2010.

Nepalese Army: A Force with History Ready for Tomorrow (Kathmandu, 2008), pp. 1–83.

Nepali, Chitra Ranjan, "Nepal ra Tibet ko Sambandha" [Nepal–Tibet Relations], *Pragati II*, 4, 10, 1990.

Nevitte, Neil, "Analysing Intercommoned Conflict: Theoretical Approaches and Comparative Cases" in Dhirendra Vajpeyi and Yogendra K. Malik, eds, *Religious and Ethnic Minority Politics in South Asia* (Delhi: Manohar, 1989), pp. 1–17.

Oommen, T. K., "Evolving Inclusive Societies through Constitutions: The Case of Nepal," An unpublished paper presented at a seminar on Social Inclusion Policies in South Asian States (Kathmandu: CNAS, June 25–27, 2009).

Pandey, Bhim Bahadur, *Tyash Bakhatko Nepal Part 2* [Then Nepal] (Kathmandu: TU, Centre for Nepal and Asian Studies, 1986–1987).

Pant, Harsh V. "China Rising" in Ira Pandey, ed., *IndiaChina: Neighbours: Strangers* (New Delhi: HarperCollins, 2009), pp. 94–103.

Patten, Chris, *What Next? Surviving the Twenty-First Century* (Victoria, Australia: Penguin Books, 2008).

Pfaff-Czarnecka, Joanna, "Debating the State of the Nation: Ethnicization of Politics in Nepal—A Position Paper" in Joanna Pfaff-Czarnecka, Rajasingham Senanayake, Ashish Nandy, and Edmund Terenc Gomez, eds, *Ethnic Futures: The State and Identity Politics in Asia* (Delhi, 1999), pp. 1–38.

Phadnis, Urmila, "Nepal: The Politics of Referendum," *Pacific Affairs*, 5, 3, Autumn: 1981, pp. 455–484.

Pinkney, Robert, *Democracy in the Third World* (New Delhi: Viva Books, second edn, 2008).

Pyakuryal, Bishwambher, "Political Economy of Inclusive Growth," *Kathmandu Post*, March 31, 2010.

Pyakuryal, Bishwambher, "Economic Diplomacy," *Republica*, Kathmandu, August 11, 2010.

Pyakurel, Uddhab, "Rashtriyatako Kasima 1950 Treaty [1950 Treaty in the Context of Nationalism], *Kantipur*, February 24, 2010.

Pyakurel, Uddhab, *Maosit Movement in Nepal: A Sociological Perspective* (Delhi: Adroit Publishers, 2007).

Ramakant, *Nepal, China and India* (New Delhi: Abhinav, 1976).

———, *Indo-Nepalese Relations, 1816 to 1877* (Delhi: S. Chand and Company, 1968).

Regmi, Mahesh Chandra, *Emperial Gorkha* (Delhi: Adroit Publishers, 1999).

———, *Imperial Gorkha: An Account of Gorkhali Rule in Kumaun (1791–1815)*, (Delhi: Adroit Publishers, 1999).

———, *Kings and Political Leaders of the Gorkhali Empire 1768–1814* (Patna, 1995).

———, *Land Tenure and Taxation in Nepal* (Kathmandu: Ratna Pustak Bhandar, 1978).

Remac Nepal, *Sushashan Barsha Pustak 2006* [Good Governance Book 2006] (Kathmandu: Remac Nepal, 2007).

Roka, Hari, "Bijuli Utpadanko Kichalo" [Wrangling over Hydropower Generation], *Kantipur*, September 27, 2010.

Rose, Leo E., *Nepal: Strategy for Survival* (Bombay: Oxford University Press, 1971).

Saptahik Weekly, G. P. Koirala's Interview, *Saptahik Weekly*, Kathmandu, June 19, 2001.

Schmidt, Burrowing Dan and Wolfgang J. Mommsens, "Imperialism" in *Marxism, Communism and Western Society: A Comparative Encyclopedia, 1973*, Vol. 4, p. 211.

Schwartz, Joseph M., "Left" in Joel Krieger, ed., *The Oxford Companion to Politics of the World* (New York: Oxford University Press, second edn, 2001), pp. 493–494.

Shah Deva, H. M. King Mahendra Bir Bikram, *Proclamations, Speeches and Messages* (Kathmandu: HMG, 1976).

Shah, Tula Narayan, "Pheri Madhesh Chukdai Chha" [Madhesh Losing Again] *Kantipur*, May 10, 2010.

Shaha, Rishikesh, *Modern Nepal: A Political History 1769–1955*, Vol. 1 (Delhi: Manohar, 1990).

———, *Modern Nepal*, Vol. II (Delhi: Manohar, 1990).

———, *Politics in Nepal 1980–1990* (Kathmandu: Ratna Pustak Bhandar, 1990).

Shah, Vivek Kumar, *Maile Dekheko Darbar:Sainik Sachibko Samsmaran* [The Palace I saw: Reminiscences of Military Secretary] (Kathmandu: 2067 [VS]. 2011).

Sharma, Ganesh Raj, ed., *M. P. Koirala: A Role in a Revolution* (Kathmandu: Jagadamba Prakashan, 2008).

Sharma, Jagadish, *Nepal: Struggle for Existence* (Kathmandu: Gorkhapatra Sansthan, 1986).

Sharma, Prayag Raj, "Nepali Culture and Society: Reflections on Some Historical Currents" in Kamal P. Malla, ed., *Nepal: Perspective on Continuity and Change* (Kathmandu: CNAS, 1989), pp. 65–77.

Shivanandan, A., "Integration vs. forced assimilation," *The Hindu*, New Delhi, September 14, 2006.

Shrestha, Nanda R., *In the Name of Development: A Reflection on Nepal* (Kathmandu: Educational Enterprise, 1999).

Sisson, Richard and Leo E. Rose, *War and Secession: Pakistan, India, and Creation of Bangladesh* (New Delhi: Vistar Publications, 1990).

Strayer, Joseph R., *Feudalism* as c mentioned in Walter C. Opello, JR, Stephen J. Rosow, *The Nation-State and Global Order* (Delhi: Viva Pvt Ltd, 2005).

Subrahmanyam, K. "Sub-Continental Security: Some Perceptions," *India's Foreign Review*, 18: 31, 15–30 September 1981.

"Text of Friendship between Great Britain and Nepal in Husain," in Asad Husain, *British India's Relations with the Kingdom of Nepal 1857–1947* (London: George Allen and Unwin, 1970), pp. 391–392.

"Text of Understanding Signed by the Royal Nepalese Ambassador (Y. N. Khanl) and Y. D. Gundevia, Foreign Secretary to the Government of India" in S. D. Munni, *India and Nepal: A Changing Relationship* (New Delhi: Konark, 1992).

"Text of UNMIN Representative Karin Landgreen's Report to the UN Security Council Presented on September 7, 2007" as published in *Kathmandu Post*, Kathmandu, September 9, 2010.

"Texts of the Letter Accompanying the 1950 Treaty and for Agreement Signed in New Delhi on January 30, 1965 in S. D. Munni, *India and Nepal: A Changing Relationship* (New Delhi: Konark, 192).

Thapa, Bishwa Bandhu, "Pradhanmantriya Pratispardha" [Prime Ministerial Competition], *Annapurna Post*, Kathmandu, September 28, 2010.

Thapa, Gagan, "Maobad ki Loktantrabad" [Maoism or Democracy], *Kantipur*, December 7, 2010.

Thapar, Romila, "The Vamsvali From Chamba: Reflections of a Historical Tradition," The Mahesh Chandra Lecture, Social Science Baha, Kathmandu, October 14, 2009.

Thapliyal, Sangeeta, The Mutual Security: The Case of India-Nepal (New Delhi: Lancer, 1998).

"The Treaty of 'Peace and Friendship' Between the Government of India and the Government of Nepal, July 31, 1950" in A. S. Bhasin, ed, Nepal's Relation with India and China 1947–1992 (Delhi: Siba Exim Pvt. Lmt. 1994), pp. 38–40.

Tiwari, Bishwa Nath, "Impact of Remittance from India on Nepalese Economy," Paper presented in seminar on the 60th year of the 1950 Treaty of Peace and Friendship (Kathmandu: NCCS, September 12, 2010).

UNDP, Nepal Human Development Report 2009 (Kathmandu: UNDP, 2009).

Upadhyaya, Bishwanath, Interview, Kantipur, October 2, 2000.

"US Department of State, 2003: 3" cited in Dhruba Kumar, "Emergency, Militarization and the Question of Democratic Recovery" in Lok Raj Baral, ed., Nepal: Quest for Participatory Democracy (Delhi: Adroit Publishers, 2006), pp. 160–182.

Varshney, Ashutosh, "Checks and Balances: An Analysis of the Strengths and Weaknesses of China and India as Competitors," India Today, August 9, 2010.

Wagle, Geja Sharma, "Failed State Syndrome," The Kathmandu Post, August 4, 2010.

Walter C. Opello, J.R. and Stephen J. Rosow, The Nation-State and Global Order (Delhi: second edn, Indian edn, 2005).

Weiner, Myron, "The Political Demography of Nepal," Asian Survey, 13 (6): 1973, pp. 617–630.

Whelpton, John, History of Nepal (Noida: Cambridge University Press, Indian edn, 2005).

Zedong, Mao, Selected Military Writings of Mao Tse-tung (Peking: Peking Foreign Language Press, 1967).

Newspapers

Annapurna Post, October 1, 2010.
Himal Khabar Patrika (Kathmandu), March 29–April 13.

Indian Express, May 7, 2009.

Kalpana (Kathmandu), November 29, 1959. *Himal Khabar Patrika*, March 14–28, 2005.

Kathmandu Post, November 1, 2009.
Kantipur, October 31, 2010.
Kantipur, September 29, 2010.
Karobar Daily, September 24, 2010.
Mulyankan Montly, June–July, 2010.

Nagarik Daily, October 5, 2010.
Nepal Press Digest, 34, 29, July 16, 1990.
Nepal Press Digest, 39, 16, April 17, 1995.
Nepal Press Digest, 44, 40, October 2, 2000.

Nepal (Rashtriya Saptahik), 12, 8, October 3, 2010.
Republica, August 5, 2009.
Republica, September 25, 2010.
Republica (Kathmandu), August 1, 2010.
Republica (Kathmandu), September 4, 2010.
Rising Nepal, February 12, 1983.
Rising Nepal, December 9, 1983.

The Hindu (Delhi), March 22, 2010.
The Hindu (Delhi), September 5, 2009.

The Times of India (New Delhi), August 2, 2010.
The Times of India, August 19, 2010.
The Times of India (New Delhi) September 7, 2010.
The Kathmandu Post, August 5, 2009.
The Kathmandu Post, August 24, 2009.
The Rising Nepal, June 29, 1969.
The Statesman, November 28, 1959.
The Statesman, September 9, 1970.
The Tribune (Chandigarh), April 6, 1971.
Kathmandu Post, June 4, 2001.

Himalayan Times and *Rajdhani Dailies*, September 6, 2009.

Annapurna Post, September 6, 2009.

Rajdhani Daily, September 6, 2009.

Mulyankan Monthly, June–July, 2010.

The Times of India, "Racing The Dragon," *The Times of India*, August 19, 2010.

Hari Roka, "Bijuli Utpadanko Kichalo" [Wrangling over Hydropower Generation], *Kantipur*, September 27, 2010.

Web site

www.election.gov.np

INDEX

ABOUT THE AUTHOR

Lok Raj Baral is Professor and Executive Chairman of Nepal Centre for Contemporary Studies (NCCS), Kathmandu, Nepal. He has served as Professor and Chairman of the Department of Political Science at Tribhuvan University during 1976–1989. He was also the President of the Nepal Political Science Association, Nepal Council of World Affairs, and Society for Constitutional and Parliamentary Exercises (SCOPE).

Professor Baral was a member of the delegation to the United Nations General Assembly in 1990 and International Research Committee member of the Regional Centre for Strategic Studies (RCSS), and also served as Nepal's ambassador to India in 1996–1997. He was Visiting Professor at the University of Illinois at Urbana-Champaign, USA, and Fellow at CHR Michelsen Institute, Bergen, Norway.

His previous publications include *Nepal: Quest for Participatory Democracy* (2006); *Elections and Governance in Nepal* (2005); *Nepal: Political Parties and Parliament* (2004); *The Regional Paradox: Essays in Nepali and South Asian Affairs* (2000); *Nepal: Problems of Governance* (1993); *Regional Migrations, Ethnicity and Security* (1990); and *The Politics of Balanced Interdependence* (1988).